P9-DCX-514

THE EDGE OF THE IMAGE

Marianne Moore, William Carlos Williams,
and Some Other Poets

THE EDGE OF THE IMAGE

MARIANNE MOORE

WILLIAM CARLOS WILLIAMS

---

and Some Other Poets

A. KINGSLEY WEATHERHEAD

❧ ❧

UNIVERSITY OF WASHINGTON PRESS

Seattle and London

Copyright © 1967 by the University of Washington Press
Library of Congress Catalog Card Number 67–21198
Printed in the United States of America

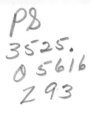

For my father and mother

ACKNOWLEDGMENTS

EXCERPTS FROM "Tom Fool at Jamaica," "The Arctic Ox (or Goat)," "Saint Nicholas," and "Leonardo Da Vinci's" are from *A Marianne Moore Reader* by Marianne Moore, copyright © 1959 by Marianne Moore. The poems originally appeared in *The New Yorker*. Reprinted by permission of The Viking Press, Inc.

The excerpt from "Bitch and Friend" is from *A Marianne Moore Reader* by Marianne Moore, copyright © 1954 by Marianne Moore. Reprinted by permission of The Viking Press, Inc.

The excerpt from "In the Public Garden" is from *A Marianne Moore Reader* by Marianne Moore, copyright © 1959 by Marianne Moore. The poem originally appeared in the *Ladies Home Journal*. Reprinted by permission of The Viking Press, Inc.

Excerpts from "The Jerboa," "Camellia Sabina," "The Frigate Pelican," "The Fish," "In the Days of Prismatic Colour," "England," "When I Buy Pictures," "A Grave," "New York," "People's Surroundings," "An Octopus," "Sea Unicorns and Land Unicorns," "The Monkey Puzzle," "To a Steam Roller," "An

Egyptian Pulled Glass Bottle in the Shape of a Fish," and "Silence" reprinted by permission of The Macmillan Company and Faber and Faber Ltd. from *Collected Poems* by Marianne Moore. Copyright © 1935 by Marianne Moore, renewed 1963 by Marianne Moore and T. S. Eliot.

Excerpts from "What are Years?" "He 'Digesteth Harde Yron,'" "Spenser's Ireland," "The Pangolin," and "The Paper Nautilus" reprinted by permission of The Macmillan Company and Faber and Faber Ltd. from *Collected Poems* by Marianne Moore. Copyright © 1941 by Marianne Moore.

The excerpt from "In Distrust of Merits" reprinted by permission of The Macmillan Company and Faber and Faber Ltd. from *Collected Poems* by Marianne Moore. Copyright © 1944 by Marianne Moore.

Excerpts from "The Steeple-Jack," "The Icosasphere," "His Shield," and "Voracities and Verities Sometimes are Interacting" reprinted by permission of The Macmillan Company and Faber and Faber Ltd. from *Collected Poems* by Marianne Moore. Copyright © 1951 by Marianne Moore.

Excerpts from "After Apple-Picking" and "Birches" from *Complete Poems of Robert Frost*. Copyright © 1916, 1930, 1939 by Holt, Rinehart and Winston, Inc. Copyright © 1944, 1958 by Robert Frost. Copyright © 1967 by Lesley Frost Ballantine. Reprinted by permission of Holt, Rinehart and Winston, Inc. and Jonathan Cape Ltd.

Excerpts from *Here and Now* by Denise Levertov, copyright © 1957, *Kora in Hell* by William Carlos Williams, copyright © 1964, *Howl and Other Poems* by Allen Ginsberg, copyright © 1959, and *Kaddish: Poems 1957–60* by Allen Ginsberg, copyright © 1961, reprinted by permission of City Lights Books.

"Oread" by H. D., is from *Selected Poems of H. D.*, published by Grove Press, Inc., copyright © 1957 by Norman Holmes Pearson.

Excerpts from "Atlantis" by Hart Crane is from *The Com-*

plete *Poems and Selected Letters and Prose of Hart Crane.* By permission of Liveright, Publisher, New York. Copyright © 1966 by Liveright Publishing Corp.

Excerpts from the "Prologue to Kora in Hell" are from *Selected Essays of William Carlos Williams.* Copyright © 1931 by William Carlos Williams. Reprinted by permission of New Directions Pubishing Corporation.

Excerpts from "About Marriage" and "Our Bodies" from Denise Levertov, *O Taste and See,* copyright © 1962, 1963 by Denise Levertov Goodman. Reprinted by permission of the publisher, New Directions Publishing Corporation.

Excerpts from "The Dead Butterfly," "At the Edge," "A Straw Swan Under the Christmas Tree," and "Art" from Denise Levertov, *With Eyes at the Back of Our Heads,* copyright © 1958, 1959, by Denise Levertov Goodman. Reprinted by permission of the publisher, New Directions Publishing Corporation.

Excerpts from "A Sequence," "Come into Animal Presence," "Corazon," "The Weave," "Canticle," "The Rose," "Sierra," "Clouds," and "Lonely Man" from Denise Levertov, *The Jacob's Ladder,* copyright © 1958, 1959, 1960, 1961 by Denise Levertov Goodman. Reprinted by permission of the publishers, New Directions Publishing Corporation, and Jonathan Cape Ltd.

Excerpt from "Thou Shalt Not Kill" from Kenneth Rexroth, *In Defense of the Earth,* copyright © 1956 by New Directions. Reprinted by permission of the publishers, New Directions Publishing Corporation, and Hutchinson Publishing Group Ltd.

Excerpt from "Canto LI" from Ezra Pound, *Cantos,* copyright © 1937 by Ezra Pound. Reprinted by permission of the publishers, New Directions Publishing Corporation, and Faber and Faber Ltd.

"Prelude to Winter" and excerpts from "Two Pendants: for the Ears" and "Choral: The Pink Church" from William Carlos Williams, *Collected Later Poems,* copyright © 1944, 1950 by

William Carlos Williams. Reprinted by permission of the publishers, New Directions Publishing Corporation, and MacGibbon and Kee Ltd.

"Proletarian Portrait" and "The Red Wheelbarrow" and excerpts from "Good Night," "Spring and All," "Poem," "Tract," "To Waken an Old Lady," "Queen-Ann's-Lace," "Spouts," "The Widow's Lament in Springtime," and "Brilliant Sad Sun" from William Carlos Williams, *Collected Earlier Poems,* copyright © 1938, 1951 by William Carlos Williams. Reprinted by permission of the publishers, New Directions Publishing Corporation, and MacGibbon and Kee Ltd.

Excerpts from *Paterson* by William Carlos Williams, copyright © 1946 (Book I), 1948 (Books II and III), 1951 (Book IV), 1958 (Book V) by William Carlos Williams, reprinted by permission of the publishers, New Directions Publishing Corporation, and MacGibbon and Kee Ltd.

Excerpts from "The Orchestra," "To a Dog," "The Yellow Flower," "The Mental Hospital Garden," "The Desert Music," "Asphodel, That Greeny Flower," "Shadows II," and "Come On!" from William Carlos Williams, *Pictures from Brueghel and Other Poems,* copyright © 1949 and 1954 by William Carlos Williams. Reprinted by permission of the publishers, New Directions Publishing Corporation, and MacGibbon and Kee, Ltd.

Excerpts from *Homage to Clio* by W. H. Auden reprinted by permission of Random House and Faber and Faber Ltd.

Excerpts from *Poems 1938–1949* by Robert Lowell reprinted by permission of Faber and Faber Ltd.

I am grateful to the Office of Scientific and Scholarly Research of the University of Oregon for the gift of a summer and for other miscellaneous support; to Carolyn Callahan, Alan Gribben, and Mary Jensen for their help with the manuscript; to Robert McCollough and his staff in the University of Oregon

Library for preparing bibliographies; to my wife, Ingrid, and to my colleagues William Cadbury, William Strange, and Christof Wegelin for reading and criticizing parts or the whole of the book, for the faults in which they are, of course, blameless.

A. K. WEATHERHEAD

Eugene, Oregon
June, 1967

CONTENTS

THE EDGE OF THE IMAGE

Marianne Moore, William Carlos Williams,
and Some Other Poets

INTRODUCTION

THIS ESSAY is mostly about William Carlos Williams and Marianne Moore. I have brought these two together because some features of their work are similar and because at the same time their differences within broad similarities serve to illuminate each other reciprocally. The most important of their common features is that they represent objects and scenes clearly and preserve the hard contours of these representations against the kind of blurring and softening that they suffer in other kinds of poetry. The separate chapters on these poets are an effort to tease out the essential principles which in each have determined the nature of the poetry. There is a certain amount of cross reference, comparison, and contrast, but these I have not pressed unduly; adopting a practice which seems attractive to the poets themselves, I have let the two studies stand in juxtaposition to reveal by themselves what they will of both poets.

Then, just as the characteristics of these two are mutually revealing, so the work of some of the so-called "beat" poets throws light on techniques and procedures of Williams and to a lesser extent of Miss Moore; in the last chapter, therefore, I consider a few of these poets who have recently come down-stage in their street clothes proclaiming that poetry is an open field, that the world is holy, and that Williams is their prophet. But these again are not treated exclusively by comparison with Williams or Miss Moore or one another.

I

In their reflections of the real world, Williams and Miss Moore operate according to the faculty that Coleridge distinguished as the fancy. This fact seems of fundamental significance to their work, and thus I have devoted to the subject a chapter which, in order to make the distinction clear, includes discussions of poets and poems of both fancy and the opposite faculty, imagination.

One wants, naturally, to say many things about the poems of these two people in addition to describing the manner of their clear representation of the world. There is the matter of the over-all form of the poems, with which this feature is involved and which is discussed partly in the chapters devoted to the two poets and partly in the last chapter. And then, beside the tendency to protect the image, there is the matter of the phrase and the varying degrees to which it is permitted to develop free from the controls of rhythm. But the clarity of the imagery seems central and primary in their work. And thinking of this, I have titled the essay *The Edge of the Image*. Williams supplies the actual term in a remark about Miss Moore: he describes her as treating words with acid to remove the smudges; she uses a word in such a way "that it will remain scrupulously itself, clean perfect, unnicked beside other words in parade. There must be edges." [1]

A caveat about the perceptions and interpretations in the following pages is perhaps due. Looking at certain of the poems

---

[1] "Marianne Moore" (1948), *Selected Essays of William Carlos Williams* (New York: Random House, 1954), pp. 128–29. Hereafter *SE*.

of Miss Moore and Williams and even more those of their disciples, I have not intended to conceal here and there the blank misgivings of a creature moving about in worlds not realized. A few years ago Kenneth Rexroth said, "I certainly don't have any friends who ever question but that Bill [Williams] is the greatest living American poet";[2] and I had better confess, I suppose, at the outset that "with that bright believing band I have no claim to be." It seems to me possible that sometimes our sophomores or Eliot's perfect audience of those who can only just read is better prepared, by being less "prepared," to experience certain of the most recent poetic productions. There is always, for the rest of us, the Formal Literary Education controlling our responses, as if Matthew Arnold with granite sideburns looked down on us from Mount Rushmore to make us remember the higher seriousness. Who, after all, briefed as to the regular and regulated haunts of Apollo, versed in the hierarchy of classics (not to mention required Anglo-Saxon), did not look askance when first exposed to "The Red Wheelbarrow" or wince a little at some of the later efflorescences of those who have grown up in Williams' shadow? One needs also, perhaps, to be wholly American. William Empson reports that English critics do not feel that Williams is a poet at all, and says, "He has renounced all the pleasures of the English language, so that he is completely American; and he only says the dullest things, so he has won the terrible fight to become completely democratic as well." [3] Then, speaking of an interpretation of one of his own poems by a *Times Literary Supplement* reviewer who had, apparently wrongly, gone deep into symbolism, Robert Creeley says that

[2] Kenneth Rexroth, "The World Is Full of Strangers," *New Directions* 16 (Norfolk, Conn., 1957), p. 195.

[3] William Empson, quoted from "Two More Cultures," *New Statesman and Nation*, LXVII (Jan. 24, 1964), 130. Compare G. S. Fraser (in "Auden: The Composite Giant," *Shenandoah*, XV [Summer, 1964], 55): "Almost nobody in England can *hear* . . . the late William Carlos Williams. . . ."

. . . the two cultures are separated really by the terms of a whole spiritual environment. I mean, when one lives in the States, even so recently as, say, my own childhood, the terms of that environment are most usually ones that demand an immediate recognition of facts and substantial data in that environment. Now this is what Williams meant, I think, when he said, "No ideas but in things." It's the old characteristic that has become so associated with American pragmatism.[4]

Such instances of the difference in outlook and of mutual misunderstanding abound, and it is worth my drawing attention to them against the possibility of a native critic declaring some of the interpretations in the following pages to be quite wrong, or even one of the poets, settling a pillow by his head, saying, "That is not what I meant at all." Further, although the poetic principles of the poets studied have been derived from the poetry itself, who knows how much one's expectations—these in turn controlled by previous literary experience—may have entered into what is intended to be an empirical effort and pure product? At best, one is an academic—a member of the company who would not know poetry, Allen Ginsberg tells us, if it came up in broad daylight with a species of sexual assault that one's education, again, precludes naming.

The Atlantic makes a difference. In 1889 Tennyson, who according to George Saintsbury had set the style for English poetry of the second half of the nineteenth century, published "Crossing the Bar," which contained, according to the same authority, the lines which were the very essence of his style:

> But such a tide as moving seems asleep,
> Too full for sound and foam,
> When that which drew from out the boundless deep
> Turns again home.

[4] "Robert Creeley in Conversation with Charles Tomlinson," *the Review*, No. 10 (January, 1964), pp. 25–26.

Within about thirty years, William Carlos Williams published *Spring and All*, of which Number XXI is now known as "The Red Wheelbarrow":

> so much depends
> upon
>
> a red wheel
> barrow
>
> glazed with rain
> water
>
> beside the white
> chickens.[5]

Between the two poets there is, first, the big difference in situation: one thinks of Tennyson as the official poet, the laureate—Max Beerbohm's frock-coated rhapsodist animating, at her command, Victoria's imperial emotions; one thinks of Williams as a busy practicing physician, jotting down poems between office visits and urinalyses. And of course there is the even larger difference of the calendar, which we must mention again in a moment. But then, too, there is the difference in place: Williams' poem comes out of the environment which, Creeley says, demands the recognition of its facts and substantial data. Also, while in England Tennyson was "mouthing out his hollow oes and aes," in what was to become Williams' America, Walt Whitman, born the same year as Tennyson, was yawping his barbaric new world utterances, listing the items of his world in order to make them his.[6]

It is not the causes, however, but the fact of the differences between these poems that I wish to dwell on for a moment, and in particular the difference in the handling of the images,

[5] William Carlos Williams, *The Collected Earlier Poems* (Norfolk, Conn.: New Directions, 1951), p. 277. Hereafter *CEP*.

[6] See Roy Harvey Pearce, *The Continuity of American Poetry* (Princeton, N.J.: Princeton University Press, 1961), p. 166.

in which matter Tennyson's practice will serve as a foil for present purposes. The description of the sea is hardly a description, hardly an image: the poet is not directing our attention to it as a *thing*; he is not concerned to present it in its full objectivity, to show us how it looks or feels or smells or sounds. He is merely *using* it in order to get at something else: he wants to make those famous full vowel sounds (on which account he used to make fun of himself)—"full," "sound," "foam"—because he loves words for the sake of their lovely sounds; and, much more important, he wants to suggest by means of the sea the idea of vastness and mystery. In the other poem the opposite is true: Williams is presenting objects to us with concern for their *thinginess*, not using them. He is not concerned with the pleasure of the actual words. He wants us to see clearly what the things look like in their own sharp contours. If the images also have an ulterior purpose—since the familiar rule "no ideas but in things" does not mean no ideas—it is negligible against that in Tennyson.

These different ways of dealing with the outside world, however, do speak also to the different periods from which the poems come; the thirty-odd years that separate them, though from here they seem a relatively brief period, had, after all, contained the war that had ushered in the modern world. Tennyson, with his imagery of sea, bar, ship, and pilot, has his eye on something beyond all these: the fact that he does not know how ships use pilots is irrelevant. Just as a traditional painting groups its minor details in such a way as to point beyond themselves and lead the eye by perspective to the single important subject of the canvas, so Tennyson is looking beyond the concrete details designated. Williams, on the other hand, though he has grouped his images with the "beside," has created something more similar to the flat canvases of Picasso where objects are not subordinated one to the other. It is possible to go a step further in drawing down into these poems the acceptances of their respective *zeitgeists* and observe that Tennyson is interested in essence, Williams in existences.

A significant and growing body of American poetry reveals and is even dominated by a concern and a respect for the things in the world of which its images are reflections. It is faithful to the contours of reality; it *presents* its objects as Williams does in "The Red Wheelbarrow" rather than merely designating them for *use* as Tennyson does. To such images we respond with our senses.

Middleton Murry, quoting a passage from *Hamlet,* says, "The image is made to rise not before the vision but the imagination. . . . What has happened is not what seemed at first—that the spiritual has been brought down to the physical—but the physical has been taken up to the spiritual." Murry is engaged in extolling the value of "concreteness," but in so doing he is anxious not to sanction what he calls "the old misreading of *ut pictura poesis*" by which poets "imagined that they could become plastic by imitating what they (mistakenly) believed to be the process of the plastic artist, the laborious transcription of all the detail seen by the eye. . . ."[7] Wallace Stevens, somewhat similarly, claimed that we must all see and deal with the sensible world through the imagination; and it is significant that in his own poetry the occurrence of a hard concrete image with unblurred edges, a mere representation of a thing, is most infrequent: the "dresser of deal, / Lacking the three glass knobs" in "The Emperor of Ice-Cream," is "a very rare instance of 'haecceity' ";[8] as Stevens says in another poem, "one desires / so much more than that." But the imagery in modern American poetry with which we are concerned is hard and concrete, and it is produced by the practice Murry decries—the transcription of visual detail, though not necessarily laborious transcription and

[7] Middleton Murry, *The Problem of Style* (Oxford: Oxford University Press, 1922), pp. 88 and ff.

[8] George McFadden, "Probings for an Integration: Color Symbolism in Wallace Stevens," *Modern Philology,* LVIII (February, 1961), 189.

not necessarily *all* the detail. And it appeals primarily not to the imagination but to the inward eye or other inward senses: it exists first of all to be sensed.

Speaking of Miss Moore and Williams, Kenneth Burke says they share an important quality which Williams calls "by the trade name of 'objectivist'"; "in objectivism," says Burke, "though an object may be chosen for treatment because of its symbolic or subjective reference, once it has been chosen it is to be studied in its own right." [9] An object can only give the appearance of being "studied in its own right" when the study given it is apparently irrelevant to the total structure. Many of the images and individual parts of poems considered below will appear, on first sight at least, to be irrelevant, and some have been so labeled in criticism. Burke's generality is good and useful even though there are obviously variations among the ways in which images are treated by these two poets—variations within one poem, and needless to say wider ones certainly in their respective collected works. There is variety too in the degree to which "symbolic or subjective reference" is manifest: on occasion, out of profound respect for objectivity, the poet has deliberately moved so far away from the reference that gave cause for the image that the reference is totally obscured and the poem may appear to be, may indeed *be* only a bland description. At other times, images presented in the fullness of their detail, either alone or reacting with one another, deliver up meaning.

In the following, often-quoted passage Miss Moore wants us first of all to see the object for itself, and our initial response is sensory:

> . . . the smaller,
> Camellia Sabina
> with amanita-white petals; there are several of her
>
> pale pinwheels, and pale

---

[9] Kenneth Burke, *A Grammar of Motives* (New York: Prentice-Hall, 1954), p. 486.

stripe that looks as if on a mushroom the
sliver from a beet-root carved into a rose were laid.[10]

It seems at first as if Miss Moore cared nothing more than that
we should see this flower. And yet as the flower has its role in
the poem, so too the method of description has its own meaning:
the curious care, the roundabout approach which employs other
plants—amanita, mushroom, beetroot, and rose—speaks to the
artificial means by which the camellia is nurtured.

Williams, on the other hand, in writing the following has
little to give other than a visual impression:

> A big young bareheaded woman
> in an apron
>
> Her hair slicked back standing
> on the street
>
> One stockinged foot toeing
> the sidewalk
>
> Her shoe in her hand. Looking
> intently into it
>
> She pulls out the paper insole
> to find the nail
>
> That has been hurting her.
> (CEP, p. 101)

This is much more nearly a mere picture, as its title "Proletarian
Portrait" suggests. It is a sight that means something to the poet,
and some of that meaning must leak through to any other
human who shares the sight, even vicariously. But, as we shall
see in discussing "The Red Wheelbarrow" below, the ability to
communicate what a simple object or scene means to the poet
may not lie in a stark presentation of that scene like the one
above.

[10] Marianne Moore, *Collected Poems* (New York: Macmillan, 1959), p.
22. Hereafter *CP*.

II

There exists, by now, no small body of poetry that presents scenes and objects that have much less natural potential for bearing meaning than the above examples. Long ago in the *Times Literary Supplement,* some of Eliot's early work was complained of as follows:

> Among other reminiscences which pass through the rhapso-dist's mind and which he thinks the public should know about, are "dust in crevices, smells of chestnuts in the streets, and female smells in shuttered rooms, and cigarettes in cor-ridors, and cocktail smells in bars."
>
> The fact that these things occurred to the mind of Mr. Eliot is surely of the very smallest importance to any one—even to himself. They certainly have no relation to "poetry" and we only give an example because some of the pieces, he states, have appeared in a periodical which claims that word as its title.

Let that austere reviewer consider, if he still may, what curious assemblages of items today's reader is so frequently invited to entertain in his mind: shoes, sealing wax, cabbages—not ships or kings—and a thousand other specimens of those small, tough, prosaic, resistant, material things from which literature had been habitually wont to release the mind.

The practice of presenting an object apparently for itself and imagery primarily for the senses appears in the American poetry of this century from Ezra Pound at the beginning to whomever one may pick as its most recent exponent—at least to Jack Spicer, who writes, "I would like to make poems out of real objects. The lemon to be a lemon that the reader could cut or squeeze or taste—a real lemon like a newspaper in a collage is a real newspaper. . . . The poem is a collage of the real." [11]

[11] Jack Spicer, "Letter to Lorca," included in "Statements on Poetics," *The New American Poetry: 1945–1960,* ed. Donald M. Allen (New York: Grove Press, 1960), p. 413.

The practice is not, of course, an exclusive one with any poet: Miss Moore and Williams, chief exemplars, may on occasion use their imagery with as little respect for its proper contours as that habitually paid by Tennyson.

Pound, the great advocate of the image in our time, provides many fine instances of the respect imagery shows for the real object it refers to. In Canto LI, he seems to be entirely given over to the fine texture of the matter he is describing:

> Blue dun; number 2 in most rivers
> for dark days, when it is cold
> A starling's wing will give you the colour
> or duck widgeon, if you take feather from under the wing
> Let the body be of blue fox fur, or a water rat's
> or grey squirrel's. Take this with a portion of mohair
> and a cock's hackle for legs.
> 12th of March to 2nd of April
> Hen pheasant's feather does for a fly,
> green tail, the wings flat on the body
> Dark fur from a hare's ear for a body
> a green shaded partridge feather
>   grizzled yellow cock's hackle
> green wax; harl from a peacock's tail
> bright lower body; about the size of pin
> the head should be. can be fished from seven a.m.
> till eleven; at which time the brown marsh fly comes on.
> As long as the brown continues, no fish will take Granham[12]

The poet is momentarily absorbed in the exact lineaments of the trout flies; he is presenting them to the reader, in and for themselves. During the reader's pursuance of these lines, the imagery is only *incidentally* an instance of the theme it is purveying—that increase should be obtained not by resorting to such perversions as usury but by applying art to nature, the method approved by Aristotle and cited by Dante. This fact is at the very back of the reader's mind because the imagery is not

[12] *The Cantos of Ezra Pound* (London: Faber and Faber, 1954), p. 262.

merely an example of it; it is not exclusively being used. Many other such instances, long and short, appear in the *Cantos*: imagery is dwelt upon, and the *dinglichkeit* of objects existing in their own right is celebrated.

On the other hand, there is a great deal of imagery in Pound which we do not see or otherwise sense but respond to with the imagination, somewhat in the way suggested by Middleton Murry. In his review of the first thirty cantos, Williams praises the quality we are considering:

> We have, examining the work, successes—great ones—the first molds—clear cut, never turgid, not following the heated trivial—staying cold, 'classical' but swift with a movement of thought.
>
> It stands out from almost all other verse by a faceted quality that is not muzzy, painty, wet. It is a dry, clean use of words. Yet look at the words. They are themselves not dead. They have not been violated by 'thinking.' They have been used willingly by thought.[13]

Very often with Pound, however, the imagery points to actions and objects that are unfamiliar to experience; it is not *our* world that he characteristically retails. His recurring images are not common or garden objects as they most often are in Williams: they are of girls in gold or ivory sandals; of the whiteness of stripped almonds; fragments of marble, chrysoprase, and amber; muslin; fingers moving over lyres; wine jars; lighted torches; olive leaves; and hyaline forms materializing in water—one could lead a reasonably rich life and never see any of these. The image to which we respond with the senses need not be more carefully detailed than the image that appeals otherwise; but clearly, to such images of Pound's as these, because they are unfamiliar, we most often respond with imagination and not with our senses alone. Williams, in his poetry, tells, by strong contrast, of sparrows, a wheelbarrow, local fruit trees, and the

---

[13] Williams, "Excerpts from a Critical Sketch: A Draft of XXX Cantos by Ezra Pound," *SE*, p. 111.

piece of broken glass among the cinders. Miss Moore occupies a middle ground in this matter: her animals and flora are often exotic and unfamiliar; and even when they are not they are almost always seen at a scientific and hygienic distance, not close to hand like the meadow mouse Theodore Roethke brought in from the fields or the geranium he watered with "dead beer." [14]

Furthermore, Pound's deliberate intention in his choice of words is, often enough, not simply to delineate an object accurately but to designate it in such a manner as will release the reader's imagination. This effect is manifested ubiquitously, especially in his early work; despite the lessons of the Chinese ideogram, he is not in fact, in a great deal of his verse, a very concrete poet. He admired the Chinese manner of definition which put together concrete objects—

>red   cherry
>iron rust   flamingo—

above the western manner of receding into abstraction—"red, color, vibration, mode of being." [15] But his own practice did not exclude such recedings away from objectivity. Thus, for instance, in his "Homage to Sextus Propertius," he writes, "their Punic faces dyed in the Gorgon's lake," where "Punic" supplants the simple "red" for the reason Pound explains in a letter to A. R. Orage: "Punic (*Punicus*) used for dark red, purple red by Ovid and Horace as well as Propertius. Audience familiar with Tyrrian for purple in English. To say nothing of augmented effect on imagination by using Punic (whether in translation or not) instead of 'red.' " [16]

Then to Pound, nothing is original, but only something old

[14] Theodore Roethke, *The Far Field* (Garden City, N.Y.: Doubleday, 1964), pp. 60, 63.

[15] Ernest Fenollosa, *The Chinese Written Character as a Medium for Poetry*, ed. Ezra Pound (New York: Kasper and Horton, n.d.), p. 76. Mentioned by Pound in a letter to George Santayana, *The Letters of Ezra Pound 1907–1941*, ed. D. D. Paige (New York: Harcourt, Brace and Company, 1950), p. 333.

[16] Pound, *Letters*, p. 149.

made new; and consonant with this notion his perception of reality is made often in terms of culture and hence indirectly. For Williams, on the other hand, poetry is original by definition; and nothing, as a matter of conscience, refracts the light that comes from his immediate world to his eye. Nor, even when he is dealing with the more familiar, local, and contemporary images, does Pound really immerse himself in the *dinglichkeit* of the world, as one feels Miss Moore and Williams do. There are passages like the one about trout flies where Pound describes familiar things, but he does not withdraw from before them so that they stand out in thick relief in the mind's eye: Pound has nothing to match Miss Moore's cat carrying the mouse—"the mouse's limp tail hanging like a shoelace from its mouth"—or that other cat with eyelashes a "small tuft of fronds / or katydid-legs above each eye." Such visual images fill the whole screen of our attention; with Pound's imagery, one half of that screen is always taken up by Pound talking, and the object he is talking about lies always in his huge shadow. There is no self-effacement in him before objects or people, in life or in art.

It might seem natural that the poets of the imagist movement, with its emphasis on definition and the concrete, should be interested in producing images with the quality under discussion. This, however, is clearly not a feature necessary to imagism. Pound called for "direct treatment of the 'thing' . . ." but that "thing" is not necessarily a part of the outside world: ". . . the 'thing' whether subjective or objective," he goes on. Later he says, "Don't be descriptive" and instructs the poet not to try to imitate the painter.[17] He considered that H.D.'s "Oread" embodied imagist ideals:

> Whirl up, sea—
> whirl your pointed pines,
> splash your great pines
> on our rocks,

[17] *Literary Essays of Ezra Pound*, ed. T. S. Eliot (London: Faber and Faber, 1954), pp. 3, 6.

hurl your green over us,
cover us with your pools of fir.[18]

This poem is successful; if we were talking about communication, we should have to say that it is more successful than many stark and single presentations of images which bear the hope of the poet that by mere simplicity they will convey to others the simple impact their originals made upon him. All the same, a treatment in metaphorical terms is obviously not a *direct* treatment: H.D.'s sea does not simply invite inspection as in itself it really is. It is a good deal closer to objectivity than Tennyson's, but the image as she presents it is deliberately confused with that of pine trees. Miss Moore and Williams are more direct. Their treatment of the image is more like one suggested in Jean-Paul Sartre's *What Is Literature?*

> For the artist, the color, the bouquet, the tinkling of the spoon on the saucer, are *things*, in the highest degree. He stops at the quality of the sound or the form. He returns to it constantly and is enchanted with it. It is this color-object that he is going to transfer to his canvas, and the only modification he will make it undergo is that he will transform it into an *imaginary* object. He is therefore as far as he can be from considering colors and signs as a *language*.[19]

This, admittedly, is the description of a painter and not a poet; but Sartre adds later that though "the writer deals with significations . . . a distinction must be made. The empire of signs is prose; poetry is on the side of painting, sculpture and music." And indeed, much of the work of Miss Moore and Williams and of other poets today is closely related to the work of painters and produces comparable effects, and their attitude to objects approaches in its purity the one described here by Sartre. H.D.'s poems, on the other hand, are evocative: she is evoking a feeling

---

[18] *Collected Poems of H.D.* (New York: Boni and Liveright, 1925), p. 81.
[19] Jean-Paul Sartre, *What Is Literature?* trans. Bernard Frechtman (New York: Philosophical Library, 1949), pp. 8–9, 11.

by describing the sea in terms of the pine; and the imagery is one stage further removed from the real than the imagery of representation pure and simple would be. As Charles Tomlinson says, "Art exists at a remove / Evocation, at two."

The imagist program, then, does not necessarily call for images with their edges unnicked; and the practices of Miss Moore, who has disclaimed the influence of this movement, and Williams, who has repudiated it, though in various ways they apparently follow the precepts of T. E. Hulme, should not be thought of as strictly related either to his teaching or Pound's hectoring. Nor should we look to T. S. Eliot's treatment of the image for comparison. In his preface to Marianne Moore's *Selected Poems,* Eliot says that although our attention tends to be directed merely to the carefully detailed objects within the poems, the poems have emotional value and "the detail has always its service to perform to the whole." [20] The functions of the details in Marianne Moore vis-à-vis the whole poems of which they are parts are various, as will be seen in the examples of her work cited below. But there is a hint here, in the implied connection between emotion and detail in his comment, that Eliot has found in the poems what his own treatment of imagery would predispose him to look for. Whereas Burke observes that the details are paraded out of interest in or respect for the object which is "to be studied in its own right," Eliot finds that the details are related to the whole poem, which has emotional value. The remark is vague; but it looks rather as if he is discovering in Miss Moore's treatment of her images an affinity with his own. In Eliot's characteristic practice, the image is not developed as if it were of interest in itself; it is not presented but used. The term Eliot made famous, the objective correlative, describes the role of his imagery, which functions in the poem as the formula for particular emotions. The way in which Miss Moore uses imagery, however, is otherwise: although strong emotion is unquestionably present in the poems, curbed or con-

[20] Marianne Moore, *Selected Poems* (New York: Macmillan, 1935), p. x.

trolled or, in a sense, being avoided, the imagery is not a correlative for it—not in the manner that Eliot's "ancient women / Gathering fuel in vacant lots" may be, or a snatch of speech like "Marie, hold on tight."

Donald Davie distinguishes Pound's treatment of imagery from Eliot's use of it as an objective correlative, aligning Eliot, in this analysis, with the symbolists; and it is on Pound's side of the division that Miss Moore and Williams must be classified. Their use of imagery is most often similar to what Davie calls a "cardinal case of 'the image,' for Gourmont as for Pound":

> [it is] the carefully exact image the biologist constructs of the organisms he studies—an image created by nothing more recondite than scrupulously close and disciplined observation of the object as his senses apprehend it. It is not clear whether this is ever in T. S. Eliot's mind when he uses the word "image"; it is difficult to see how it can be, for "image," as Eliot used the word, seems to comprise also what he has called "the objective correlative." And according to Eliot, the artist, in constructing his objective correlative out of phenomena offered to his senses, is not at all interested in these phenomena for themselves, in their objectivity, but only to the extent that they may *stand in for* the subjective phenomena (such as states of mind or of feeling) which can thus be objectified through them.[21]

The imagery in Miss Moore, Williams, and Pound does not characteristically come, as it does in Eliot, as the product of the search for something in the outward world to correspond to the feelings.

On account of his concept of the image as a "scrupulously close and disciplined observation of the object" Rémy de Gourmont is to be linked with Pound and surely, by the same criterion, with Miss Moore and Williams. But in other contexts Gourmont's position is different from that of the last two at

[21] Donald Davie, *Ezra Pound: Poet as Sculptor* (New York: Oxford University Press, 1964), pp. 73–74.

least. In *Le Problème du Style*, which is a reply to the prescriptions on style of Antoine Albalat, he finds among Albalat's shortcomings his recommendation of Homer as the supreme model for imitation in writing.[22] Gourmont finds fault with this advice, because the Homeric style reflects a primitive manner of seeing life. There are no metaphors in Homer: he offers one fact and then another, linking them as a simple simile; he does not confuse his impressions and blend his images. As an example of a modern writer whose method contrasts Homer's, Gourmont cites Flaubert in a passage where images *have* been blended: " 'The elephants . . . the rams of their breast-plates like the prows of warships, were cleaving their cohorts; they flowed back together in great waves.' " [23]

As we shall see below, there are metaphors in the poetry of Miss Moore and Williams; but in neither of them do the metaphors provide the sudden compelling flash of identity that we experience in the metaphors of Shakespeare, or William Butler Yeats, or Robert Lowell, among others; they give the impression, rather, of being carefully thought through. This aspect of imagery will be further considered in the next chapter. We may notice in passing, however, that on being told, for example, that the glacier in Miss Moore's "An Octopus" is "an octopus of ice," we feel not so much the rightness of the comparison as the curiousness of the mind that proposed it. Nor does this poet submit her comparisons with any bravura: she is scrupulous about their limitations, as we see in the same poem in the word "misleadingly" when she says that the glacier "hovers forward . . . misleadingly like lace." Williams, who makes more structural use of metaphor than Miss Moore, frequently first submits the object of which the figure is to be made without its metaphorical meaning; then, quite often, the poem works out its metaphorical

<hr>

[22] See Glenn S. Burne, *Rémy de Gourmont: His Ideas and Influence in England and America* (Carbondale, Ill.: Southern Illinois University Press, 1963), pp. 102–3.

[23] Quoted in *ibid.*

meanings in public, as it were. The familiar usage of metaphors, however, is not the most remarkable method by which these poets proceed; characteristically their verse tends to present images in juxtaposition. They proceed by what Philip Wheelwright calls the diaphor, "the sheer presentation of diverse particulars in a newly designed arrangement" [24] from which new meanings emerge. In this respect their method is closer to Homer than to Flaubert, though Gourmont dismisses Homer's practice as that of a primitive view of the world. It will have already occurred to the reader that, in the proliferation of detail that seems to go beyond relevance, the imagery of these modern poets is rather like that of the Homeric simile, with its elaboration of detail.

The kinship with Homer is deeper, however: a Greek clarity radiates through this poetry, which springs from its finitude. Both poets see things clearly by the light of the ordinary sun. " 'Infinite,' to a Greek, meant vague, obscure, unintelligible, offensive, ugly; 'finite' meant bright, precise, mathematical, admirable, brilliant, beautiful." [25] The second series of epithets (begging the question about admirability and beauty) fits the general impressions one carries in mind of the poetry of Miss Moore and Williams. "The Greeks liked smoothness," says Miss Moore, "distrusting what was back / of what could not be clearly seen" (*CP*, p. 83). Williams is perhaps less brilliant than Miss Moore; but he is not a whit less finite. His techniques have reminded critics of the classic aesthetic and of Edith Hamilton's epitome of it:

> Clarity and simplicity of statement . . . were the Greek poets' watchwords. . . . The Greeks were realists, but not as we use the word. They saw the beauty of common things and were content with it. . . . The things men live with, noted as men

[24] Philip Wheelwright, *Metaphor and Reality* (Bloomington: Indiana University Press, 1962), p. 81.
[25] Douglas N. Morgan, *Love: Plato, the Bible and Freud* (Englewood Cliffs, N.J.: Prentice-Hall, 1964), p. 16.

of reason note them, not slurred over or evaded, not idealized away from actuality, and then perceived as beautiful—that is the way Greek poets saw the world.[26]

Such poetic characteristics are what T. E. Hulme called for in the beginning of the century. In "Romanticism and Classicism," the best known chapter of his *Speculations,* he opts for classicism. "I want to maintain that after a hundred years of romanticism, we are in for a classical revival. . . ." Classicism makes for reserve:

> . . . even in the most imaginative flights there is always a holding back, a reservation. . . . In the classical attitude you never seem to swing right along to the infinite nothing. If you say an extravagant thing which does exceed the limits inside which you know man to be fastened, yet there is always conveyed in some way at the end an impression of yourself standing outside it, and not quite believing it, or consciously putting it forward as a flourish.

A classical poem is "all dry and hard"—not lachrymose, that is; without "emotions that are grouped round the word infinite." It is down to earth, lit by ordinary daylight and not "the light that never was on land or sea." Then: classicism, unlike romanticism, is able "to admit the existence of beauty without the infinite being in some way or another dragged in"; it finds beauty, in fact, in "small, dry things." And, "the great aim is accurate, precise and definite description." [27]

It is incredible to think that either Miss Moore or Williams should have *obeyed* the *rules* that Hulme drew up, which must have had about as much direct effect upon them as the weather

[26] Quoted by Robert Beum, "The Baby Glove of a Pharaoh," *Perspective,* VI (Autumn-Winter, 1953), 221, and by Linda W. Wagner, *The Poems of William Carlos Williams: A Critical Study* (Middletown, Conn.: Wesleyan University Press, 1964), pp. 17–18. On Williams' classical concept of invention, see Ralph Nash, "The Use of Prose in 'Paterson,'" *Perspective,* VI (Autumn-Winter, 1953), 199.

[27] T. E. Hulme, *Speculations,* ed. Herbert Read (New York: Harcourt, Brace and Company, 1924), pp. 120–32 *passim.*

forecast upon the wind that bloweth where it listeth. But in her control of emotion, in her reduction of an infinite subject to finite terms, and in his celebration of hard dry things, we do find Hulme's principles implemented with a rather striking fidelity.

Associated with classicism, and a "necessary weapon" for the "cheerful, dry and sophisticated" verse which Hulme said we were going to get, is the technique of the fancy. But this with all its implications requires a separate chapter.

꿏 CHAPTER II ᝐ

IMAGINATION AND FANCY

A DISCUSSION of the two kinds of treatment accorded to imagery by fancy and imagination respectively as Coleridge distinguished them will reveal certain characteristics of poetry written in the mode of fancy and hence certain characteristics of the work of Marianne Moore and William Carlos Williams. The question as to whether there actually are two separate faculties in the creative mind which produce the two techniques need not detain us; the techniques may be spoken of as if they were the products of fancy or imagination, even if the separate existence of these faculties, like the distinction between form and content, is only a useful fiction.

I

For Coleridge the imagination is superior to the fancy; indeed it is the supreme faculty in the making of poetry. He says it "dissolves, diffuses, dissipates, in order to recreate. . . . It struggles to idealize and to unify. It is essentially *vital*, even as all objects (*as* objects) are essentially fixed and dead." [1] In the

---

[1] Samuel Taylor Coleridge, *Biographia Literaria*, ed. J. Shawcross (Oxford: The Clarendon Press, 1907), I, 202.

two lines which Coleridge quotes from "Venus and Adonis"—
"Look! how a bright star shooteth from the sky, / So glides he
in the night from Venus' eye—" [2] Adonis and the shooting star
are brought together by the influence of the imagination, which
Coleridge calls "esemplastic"—from εἰς ἓν πλάττειν, to shape into
one.[3] Coleridge adumbrates the fusion that occurs: "How many
images and feelings are here brought together without effort
and without discord, in the beauty of Adonis, the rapidity of
his flight, the yearning, yet hopelessness, of the enamored gazer,
while a shadowy ideal character is thrown over the whole!" [4]
I. A. Richards elaborates as follows:

> . . . the more the image is followed up, the more links of
> relevance between the units are discovered. . . . Here Shake-
> speare is realizing . . . Adonis' flight as it was to Venus, and
> the sense of loss, of increased darkness, that invades her. The
> separable meanings of each word, *Look!* (our surprise at the
> meteor, hers at his flight), *star* (a light-giver, an influence, a
> remote and uncontrollable thing), *shooteth* (the sudden, ir-
> remediable, portentous fall or death of what had been a guide,
> a destiny), *the sky* (the source of light and now of ruin),
> *glides* (not rapidity only, but fatal ease too), *in the night* (the
> darkness of the scene and of Venus' world now)—all these
> separable meanings are here brought into one.[5]

An unlimited number of qualities that are not explicitly adduced are brought into play to enrich the idea of Adonis' flight.
But we observe from both Coleridge's and Richards' elaborations
of the metaphor first that the qualities evoked (though Coleridge speaks of "images") are mostly abstract ideas, not sensuous
features; as Wordsworth says about the resemblance coined by

---

[2] *Ibid.,* II, 18.
[3] *Ibid.,* I, 107.
[4] "Shakespeare: A Poet Generally," *Complete Works of Samuel Taylor
Coleridge,* ed. W. G. T. Shedd (New York: Harper and Brothers, 1860),
IV, 48.
[5] I. A. Richards, *Coleridge on Imagination* (London: Kegan Paul, Trench,
Trubner and Co., 1950), p. 83.

the imagination, it depends "less upon outline of form and feature, than upon expression and effect; less upon casual and outstanding, than upon inherent and internal, properties." [6] We observe also that as the star thus surrenders to the imaginative process of dissolution and diffusion it is itself lost as a clearcut visual image with a discrete identity—a loss which is discussed below.

The role of the imagination in the large structure of a work is to modify each part, shaping it so that it contributes to the controlling idea of the whole: imagination has the power, Coleridge says, "by a sort of fusion to force many into one." [7] This activity is similar to that of the mind of the neurotic or psychotic who interprets each event of reality in such a way as to contribute to a ruling obsession; thus Lear attributes Edgar's misery to filial ingratitude and asks, "What! have his daughters brought him to this pass?" [8] The distinction between fancy and imagination, Coleridge suggests, is "no less grounded in nature" than that between delirium and mania. Lear in this passage is a maniac. But the mind of Luther, who was not a maniac, must be thought of as working similarly when he saw the devil—an incident discussed by Coleridge in *The Friend*.[9] Out of the various configurations on the wall, his mind molded and shaped the image of the devil; and on coming to himself but before the rational powers of his mind had reasserted themselves, Luther threw the inkstand at it.

The imagination effects the molding and shaping of individual images. Fancy, on the other hand, works by the association of sensuous particularity: images are merely brought together "by some one point or more of likeness." No shaping occurs as it does with imagination: fancy, says Coleridge, "has

[6] "Preface to the Edition of 1815," *The Poetical Works of William Wordsworth*, ed. Ernest de Selincourt (London: The Clarendon Press, 1944), II, 441.

[7] Coleridge, *Works*, IV, 48.

[8] Quoted in Coleridge, *Biographia Literaria*, I, 162.

[9] Coleridge, *Works*, II, 134–36.

no other counters to play with, but fixities and definites." [10]
The images in the following lines, which Coleridge cites, do
not, we understand, dissolve and fuse together but remain discrete:

> Full gently now she takes him by the hand,
> A lily prisoned in a jail of snow,
> Or ivory in an alabaster band:
> So white a friend engirts so white a foe! [11]

One cannot pursue here an endless series of similarities as one
may between Adonis and the star. In the "jail of snow," for
instance, the snow's whiteness and its softness may be attributed to Venus' hand, but its coldness, which is possibly
the reader's first response to "snow," obviously may not. Nor
are we trafficking in ideas: the images are not diffused; they
retain their integrity and remain objects of the world.

Coleridge thought that poetry must do more to fulfill its
office than merely showing images of the everyday world. It
must, by the efficacy of the imagination working upon such
images, render up the universal realities behind them. William
Carlos Williams, on the other hand, in an essay of which we
have already seen one part, denigrates as "the smears of mystery"
the kind of vague product Coleridge looks for. Speaking of
Marianne Moore's presentation of the apple in her poem
"Marriage," he says, "One is not made to feel that as an apple
it has anything particularly to do with poetry or that as such it
needs special treatment; one goes on. Because of this, the
direct object does seem unaffected. It seems as free from the
smears of mystery, as pliant, as 'natural' as Venus on the
wave." [12] Under the influence of the imagination, on the other
hand, the images of the world we know when we are getting
on with our practical lives are dissolved or blurred for the

---

[10] Coleridge, *Biographia Literaria*, I, 202.
[11] Coleridge, *Works*, IV, 48.
[12] *Selected Essays of William Carlos Williams* (New York: Random
House, 1954), p. 125. Hereafter SE.

sake of the idea and the feeling to which they are subordinate.

It is the slighting of the *dinglichkeit* of the image to which I wish to draw attention. With the imagination working upon it, the texture of the object, the actual sensuous appearance or sound or texture of the thing, is apt to be unimportant and hence to lose both brilliancy and integrity: Wordsworth says that the imagination "recoils from everything but the plastic, the pliant and the indefinite." [13] The integrity of the image is lost as the image is exploited for the feeling and idea that it can be made to contribute to the whole work. The star in "Venus and Adonis" has no importance in itself, only that its starriness can be exploited and grafted on to Adonis and his flight. Throughout a great deal of poetry, images are used in just this way: they are used, in fact, rather than presented. In Coleridge's own masterpiece, "The Ancient Mariner," the images are subordinate to the narrative, which in turn is subordinate to the ideas. And hardly anywhere in this poem, though all the various particulars are recognizable, is there any sharp evocation of that actual chaos of impressions that would strike the senses of a man in a ship under canvas. The fact that Coleridge had never been to sea did not restrain him from choosing this narrative as a vehicle; for the nautical sensations are all subordinate to the feeling and the idea. In the lines "Merrily did we drop / Below the kirk," which is an observation from the point of view of someone ashore and not aboard a ship, and in most of the lines thereafter, the poem is almost devoid of starkness in the sights and sounds incident to actual seafaring. When, on the other hand, images are purveyed by fancy, however little description is accorded them, they at least stand more chance of being experienced in themselves, because the attention of the reader is not withdrawn into idea and feeling and he is not led to blend one image with another. Poetry of the fancy is dehumanized, in Ortega y Gasset's sense, and differs from that of the imagination as twentieth-century art

[13] Wordsworth, *Poetical Works*, II, 441.

differs from nineteenth. The latter, according to Ortega, rendered life and was felt; the former is artistic and is looked at, not looked through.[14] We are reminded, in passing, of a remark by Wyndham Lewis about himself and T. E. Hulme: ". . . both he and I preferred to the fluxions in stone of an Auguste Rodin (following photographically the lines of nature) the more concentrated abstractions-from-nature of the Egyptians." [15]

II

Before we proceed to apply Coleridge's distinction to specimens of modern American poetry, T. E. Hulme must claim our attention, since he raided Coleridge and brought some of his terms into the twentieth century to use, like the Elgin marbles, for his own purposes; and certain of his precepts and predilections will throw light on the practices of Miss Moore and Williams, either because these poets implement them or because they noticeably fail to. In "Romanticism and Classicism," as we have seen, Hulme opts for classicism. And fancy is to be "the particular weapon of this new classical spirit, when it works in verse." He goes on to speak of "the superiority of fancy," by the operation of which we shall get the new metaphors that can make plain speech precise; it will abet classical restraint and have no truck with the infinite.

In these respects Hulme's fancy may appear to be like Coleridge's, but other essays introduce inconsistencies. Murray Krieger points out that in his essay on Bergson, Hulme expects the poet to give us not merely the familiar world but "the rare world beyond, which he somehow intuits"; and the faculty with which he does so, says Krieger, is not far removed from the Coleridgean imagination: "Surely we may doubt the power of fancy to operate at these profound levels. Hence, we

[14] José Ortega y Gasset, *The Dehumanization of Art and Other Writings on Art and Culture* (Garden City, N.Y.: Anchor Books, 1956), pp. 18–30.
[15] Wyndham Lewis, *Blasting and Bombadiering* (London: Eyre and Spottiswoode, 1937), p. 110.

cannot accept Hulme's plea for a poetry of fancy and his condemnation of a poetry of imagination as his final or his only word." [16] In spite of his support for "small dry things," the "smears of mystery" are apparently not outlawed. Hulme's notion of fancy, says Stanley Coffman, "appears to be imagination with its egotism deflated, its emotion held in check by reason, and, one suspects, its attitude tempered by a sense of humor." [17]

In addition to his muddying up of the concept of fancy, Hulme objected to its *play:* "When the analogy has not enough connection with the thing described to be quite parallel with it, where it overlays the thing described and there is a certain excess, there you have the play of fancy—that I grant is inferior to imagination." [18] But of course the play of fancy, at least as Coleridge conceived of this faculty, is one of its unavoidable products. There is always "excess"; if, as Coleridge says, commenting upon the fanciful passage in *Venus and Adonis,* fancy brings things together "by some one point or more of likeness," then the *other* points—those of unlikeness—are bound to constitute a "certain excess." One cannot see clearly just what Hulme wants in this part of his essay. Whatever it may be, with the fancy as with cake, consumption and retention are incompatible.

In this kind of instance Hulme is disappointing: calling for small dry things he seems to be supporting the rights of the image and to be anticipating the shape of things to come; but in his unwillingness to countenance any free development of the description of the object in excess of the purpose to which it is to be put he queers his pitch, or ours at any rate. His unwilling-

[16] Murray Krieger, *The New Apologists for Poetry* (Bloomington: Indiana University Press, 1963), p. 34.

[17] Stanley Coffman, *Imagism: A Chapter for the History of Modern Poetry* (Norman: University of Oklahoma Press, 1951), pp. 66–67.

[18] T. E. Hulme, *Speculations,* ed. Herbert Read (New York: Harcourt, Brace and Company, 1924), pp. 137–38.

ness is consistent, however, with his dislike of irrelevant details in paintings. Of the work of Roger Fry and his friends, he says,

> These pictures are filled by contours which . . . one can only describe as meaningless. They are full of detail which is entirely accidental in character, and only justified by the fact that these accidents did actually occur in the particular piece of nature which was being painted. One feels a repugnance to such accidents—and desires painting where nothing is accidental, where all the contours are closely knit together into definite structural shapes." [19]

What Hulme wants from fanciful details is analogy: "Never, never, never a simple statement. It has no effect. Always must have analogies. . . ." [20]

In the poems of Marianne Moore, even though in many of them the assembled details display a judgment as iron filings display a magnetic field, the play of the fancy is still manifest. In William Carlos Williams, who, for a great part of his career, seems to have been in perpetual revolt against any literary device or mental process which compromised the actuality of the actual, there is even more. And we shall find in both these poets that where there are analogies there are parts of the fanciful image that are not all used up. And we shall find in both of them a predilection for the kind of fanciful painting for which Hulme felt repugnance.

III

Coleridge illustrates the fancy's power of association and the imagination's power of dissolution by a metaphor and a simile respectively from "Venus and Adonis." Modern American poetry, however, frequently disposes of half of the simile

[19] "Modern Art III: The London Group," *Further Speculations by T. E. Hulme*, ed. Sam Hynes (Minneapolis: University of Minnesota Press, 1955), pp. 129–30.
[20] *Ibid.*, p. 87. Quoted in Coffman, *Imagism*, p. 53.

or metaphor: the image which heretofore had amplified or enriched meaning now carries it entirely. Thus, in transporting the Coleridgean terms into a study of modern poetry, one must appeal to the principles rather than the examples. In the following pages, where poems of Robert Lowell and Marianne Moore are used to reveal the different products of imagination and fancy, since the tenor of the simile or metaphor is often only implied, we must study the relationship between vehicle and vehicle to see which faculty is at work.

Often in modern poetry the contribution of images brought into the poem by fancy is subtle and indirect; the patterns they form do not immediately come into focus, and they appear to exist primarily in their own right for their own sake. This important characteristic of images of the fancy is observed by Kenneth Burke in the passage quoted above. His remark that objects may be chosen because of symbolic reference should draw our attention to the fact that the fancy as well as the imagination may handle symbols. The extent to which the poet is devoted to the detail of an image, however, does not depend on whether the image is a symbol. A symbol has, certainly, an underlying abstract meaning, just as the image of the imagination has an ulterior motive; but the symbol need not have multitudinous features in common with the abstraction it stands for. The extent to which the reader is encouraged to dwell on detail is variable both among symbols and among literal images. In images of fancy the attention is arrested on the image and does not drift into the idea; the object tends to keep its sharp edges unblurred and to remain inviolate in the mind. At the same time the fancy does not present images merely arbitrarily, and their contribution to other parts of the poem is not nil: the fanciful images that Coleridge quotes from "Venus and Adonis" are associated at least through their common whiteness; in modern poems, we shall sometimes find meaning emerging from the patterned arrangement of fancifully associated images.

The body of contemporary poetry that best illustrates imagination as Coleridge outlines it is *Lord Weary's Castle* by Robert Lowell. The poems in this volume, more noticeably than in his others, subordinate the actual substantial nature of the image to the ideas and feelings it can be made to evoke. Lowell's tendency here is to seek out images important for their contribution rather than for themselves. This use of imagery may, I think, account for the difficulty of some of Lowell's poems: with much of the poetry of this century we have been accustomed to dwelling on the imagery for its literal sensuous detail; with *Lord Weary's Castle* we find that such literalness is not the point and may even be misleading. In the most important poem in this volume, "The Quaker Graveyard in Nantucket," the images of the Atlantic, though they are descriptive, are not a series of independent pictorial entities, associated by sensible features. Primarily they exist to supply an idea: they are used in the way of the imagination—dissolved, diffused, and dissipated—to recreate what amounts, I suppose, to the feeling of God—the omnipotent, terrible God of the Old Testament. To this end they fuse together and are fused also with the images of Poseidon; we respond to them not so much with the inward senses and cool analysis but with the feelings. The images of wind are similarly acted upon by the imagination to produce an evocation not of the thing itself but of the idea of human striving. And the fruitlessness of human striving is the strongest impression the poem leaves. This fine poem must be read without undue attention to the literal detail of the imagery, which is subordinate to ideas.

The same is true of "The Death of the Sheriff," [21] which may be submitted to a closer study of the work of the imagination—here operating at white heat. The most important image in this poem is that of the wheeling constellation of the Great Bear. To avoid worse awkwardness, the image may be said, awkwardly enough, to symbolize the relentless and inscrutable order by which God works out His purposes. This order overrides the human will, outflanks human strategies, and shapes human ends; but, like the constellation, it is beautiful. We do not have an explicit simile like the one Coleridge works over in Shakespeare's poem. But an exploration of the possibilities of the image would find it to be saturated with features that could be perfectly well attributed to the divine order; any hymn book would, as a matter of fact, supply a host of "links of relevance." It is an image, like the shooting star in Shakespeare, coined by the imagination.

I wish to consider, however, the structural function of the image and not its relation to what it symbolizes: the image dominates the structure, drawing incidents and other images into itself like a vortex. The constellation is referred or alluded to throughout the poem by all its names: Great Bear, Dipper, Wain, and Plough. The image interpenetrates the incidents in Part I and concludes Part II and the whole poem. We have here an elaboration of the situation in *King Lear:* by the line quoted in Coleridge, Shakespeare indicates that mania has subjected all the king's experiences to the one idea—filial ingratitude. Lowell, returning again and again to the image, shows us a mind in the grip of imagination actually going through the operation which subjects experience to the obsessive idea. And finally to this idea of God's order the poet is hostile.

Before studying the image more closely it is necessary to say a word about the poem, which is a lyric expression of feelings about atonement. One may expand the literal meaning of the epigraph of Part I, *Noli Me Tangere,* and read, "Do not question My inscrutable order." And predominantly, in this part of the poem, which the image of that order pervades, the poet does not question it: the homicidal sheriff has been committed, but there was some justification—"The State had reasons"; then the sheriff has received as guest the Angel of Death and has atoned for his deeds. However, one question is introduced:

> . . . Who'll atone
> For the unsearchable quicksilver heart
> Where spiders stare their eyes out at their own
> Spitting and knotted likeness?

Deeds may be atoned by deeds, but what of the heart's evil, the evil rooted in mankind, of which the sheriff partakes, certainly, but of which he is also a victim?

By the end of the poem, to look forward, the poet, having severely questioned God and His order, has concluded that human evil is indeed God's and that Lucifer has been framed:

> . . . It is God's curse,
> God's, that has purpled Lucifer with fear
> And burning. God has willed. . . .

Both evil and the pain or death by which it is atoned are part of the great order of God that the poet had formerly held as beautiful. In Part II of the poem, inspired by whisky and willing to attack evil at its source, the poet hubristically attacks God in the form of Poseidon, the injured divine figure whose anger must be paid for. Poseidon, as a figure of God, is the owner and author of the order of which the sheriff is victim; in the second part that order is seen as a treacherous beauty by which man is trapped. Two images are used in this part to embody the idea of treacherous beauty: the *Parmachenie Belle,* the alluring trout fly with its murderous hook, and Helen of Troy, whose beauty brought about the wholesale slaughter of the Trojan War. These images are coinages of the imagination: they are not related by the fancy, which associates concrete features, like the white snow and the white hand of Venus; they are related, to each other and to whatever else is beautiful but fatal, by their common contribution to the idea. Similarly, the identity between the poet and Aeneas is the work of the imagination, not the fancy: there are no concrete resemblances, but both are angry at having lost their kinsmen on account of beautiful cheats, respectively Helen and God; and both are prepared to attack the objects of their anger. To render its beauty harmless, the poet files away the barb of the trout fly; his attack on God, however, is frustrate, like Aeneas' on Helen: the divine order of the stars and Helen will each appear again. But both Aeneas and the poet may besmirch the beauty of their objects of hate: Helen's fabulous beauty is marred with the bestial word in the line, "White Helen on her hams by Vesta's shrine . . ."; and in the following, the image of the constellations is rendered as a spurious beauty:

> . . . the mourners' cars
> Wheel with the whited sepulchres of stars
> To light the worldly dead-march of the sun.

From the idea of God's great order, to the image of the constellations, to a fishing fly, and to Helen of Troy: the items are wildly disparate; and the links connecting them are tenuous—between the last two, for instance, the overt, dramatic link is "I try the barb upon a pencilled line / Of Vergil." But we must think of the poet's faculty of imagination sweeping over his experience and committing to its crucible whatever in whole or in part can be dissolved and diffused into an evocation of the ideas and feelings to be expressed. And we need to follow the poet in apprehending the meaning of his images rather than their sensuous effects. If the poem be read with the expectations proper to a poem of the fancy and similarity between manifest concrete details be sought, it will be hard to see the relationship of the story of Aeneas to that of the sheriff; for the former is relevant only as far as it lends itself to be imaginatively fused with other incidents and images to convey the poet's developing hostility toward the divine order, which makes apparently arbitrary dispositions of men's lives.

In the image which stands for divine order, that of the wheeling constellation, the power of the Coleridgean imagination to "force many into one" may be seen most clearly at work. By an act of that imagination, the poet recognizes that all things are controlled by this order, just as Lear, by an act of mania, "recognizes" that all pain is caused by unfiliality. In the divine order human activity is subsumed; and accordingly with the image that represents order the other imagery is fused. We have the situation of Luther's devil once again: the configurations on the wall are lost as separate entities as they fuse together to create the imagined picture. Thus, the image of the undertaker who has come to collect the sheriff's body is drawn into the vortex of the controlling image. First

> The undertaker who collects antiques
> Will let his motor idle at the door
> And set his pine-box on the parlour floor.

Then

> . . . the light
> Wanderers [the stars] show a man with a white cane
> Who comes to take the coffin in his wain,
> The thirsty Dipper on the arc of night.

The Wain and the Dipper are alternative titles for the same constellation. The man—in his stellar apotheosis he ceases to be the definitive undertaker—carries a white cane because he is part of the divine order, which, in turn, being inscrutable may be considered as blind from the human point of view. Hence the following, which contains allusion to the constellation as the Bear:

> Night draws us closer in its bearskin wrap
> And our loved sightless smother feels the tap
> Of the blind stars descending to the west. . . .

We must notice also in Part I the other human good work which is absorbed into God's will: "To lay the Devil in this pit our hands / Are draining like a windmill." This is the second appearance of the image of the windmill. In the first,

. . . red-flannelled madmen look through bars
At windmills thrashing snowflakes by an arm
Of the Atlantic. . . .

The madmen are behind bars atoning; and what they see of
the universe is the image of God's relentless order (the order
has presumably occasioned both their incarceration and the
weakness of the brain which necessitated it), the circular motion of windmills, matching that of the stars. But in the second
windmill image, "we" are performing the circular motion, our
hands are draining the pit, with the Dipper presumably, which
is designed to lay the Devil. Our work of atonement blends with
God's order.

In Part II the activities of the mourners in their cars, in the
image of the sheriff's funeral cited above, are also blended into
God's order. This is recalled in the words "wheel" and "dig-
ging," the latter alluding to the Plough, another name for the
constellation. But in this part, the poet is in rebellion against
the divine order and is making his own human (and Pelagian)
attack on the source of evil; thus his activities are not of the kind
to be absorbed into the order, and the images describing them
are not connected with the wheeling stars but are the action
of the file and the intended aberrant sword stroke.

This poem is obscure if we respond to it at a level less deep
and less vague than that of feeling and idea. Its way of working through feeling may be summarized by observing how the
sexual activity is retailed. Unless I misread the poem, the
mutual, romantic kissing in Part I degenerates in Part II to
unloving and nonmutual coitus. But it would be easy to misread, for there are the merest skeletal dramatic signs: "We
park"; "We kiss"; "our hands." Also, what is less than overtly
dramatic—the shift from the plural pronoun in Part I to the
singular in Part II, when the activity becomes unilateral; and
finally, "I am chilled." The rest of the story is told in terms of
successive emotional experiences which fill in what cannot be

called a picture: the sense of charm in the "full sky of the stars"; the rising of passion in "My bile / Rises"; the loathing and the sensation of committing a hostile act in the threat against Helen; the powerlessness, in "It is God's curse . . ."; and the final depression.

IV

To revert for a moment to the *Parmachenie Belle*—it is impossible to imagine a poet of the fancy passing over by a mere reference, as Lowell does, one of the prettiest objects fabricated by the human hand, with its scarlet and white wings and hackle, its yellow body, and gold ribs. We have seen, by way of contrast, Ezra Pound's detailed presentation of the trout fly in Canto LI and might adduce the fanciful treatment of the fly in "Spenser's Ireland." But another poem of Marianne Moore's will better illustrate the operation of the fancy, in which images are concretely presented and associated "by some one point or more of likeness."

The images in "Saint Nicholas" [22] are apparently presented for their own sake, in Miss Moore's characteristic manner; and yet the details contribute in their subtle way to the total meaning of the poem. The images are linked, tenuously enough, to the extent that they are images of possible Christmas gifts she would accept or decline. At first sight this is the only reason for gathering such disparate objects into a poem. Might she have, first, a chameleon; if not this, a dress or suit of *qiviut* ("the underwool of the arctic ox"—a material to which Miss Moore, ubiquitously interested in fabric of all kinds, has devoted a poem) and a taslon shirt, but not one with collar points that button down; not a trip to Greenland or to the moon, though if the moon should come down and spread some marvel on her floor that she could wear she would ask nothing more; or finally might she have a picture postcard of the St. Hubert

[22] Marianne Moore, *O To Be a Dragon* (New York: Viking Press, 1959), pp. 25–26.

of Hans von Marees. Why, one wonders, should she want something from such a motley collection?

Each image is filled out with circumstantial details and gives the impression of a stubbornly unique item from the solid world that the poet has described for its own sake. Among these details are further connecting links: the shirt, for instance, which could be worn "either in daylight or at night," has this adaptability in common with the chameleon; the moonlight, as we have seen, has the quality of a fabric. The last stanza is full of fanciful associations with what has gone before:

> form erect—in velvet, tense with restraint—
> hand hanging down: the horse, free.
> Not the original, of course. Give me
> a postcard of the scene—huntsman and divinity—
> hunt-mad Hubert startled into a saint
> by a stag with a Figure entined.
> But why tell you what you must have divined?
> Saint Nicholas, O Santa Claus,
> would it not be the most
> prized gift that ever was!

The form "tense with restraint" is associated with the chameleon's tail, in the first stanza, "that curls like a watch spring." The suggestion in the detail "the horse, free" that Hubert is not free is also associated with the chameleon; for the chameleon, with vertical stripes on its body to show that it has been behind bars, has been changed by captivity. The chameleon is thus associated also with the poet's repudiation of conventional notions of freedom, such as the trips to Greenland or the moon (the value of unfreedom is one of Marianne Moore's favorite motifs: in "Spenser's Ireland" she says, "you're not free / until you've been made captive by / supreme belief"). The huntsman becoming saint is a chameleon-type change. The "prized gift" of the last line is associated with the chameleon's back, which is beaded "as if it were platinum." Then the stag wearing

Christ is linked with the clothes the poet has asked for. I uncertainly link the request for merely a reproduction of the picture, which is characteristic of a modesty that runs through all Miss Moore's work, with the taslon shirt—not real cotton, but imitation and good enough. Finally, because the stag's points have caught the Figure, by association, the poet does not want the kind of shirt with button-down collar points.

These items and their details which seemed at first so arbitrarily mustered are, with the last stanza, seen as having a structural function; if the imagination creates an internal organizing principle like a backbone, the fancy here may be thought of as providing an external one—an exoskeleton. Assisted by the pun in "divined," these items add up to the poet's request for the gift of spiritual conversion. But the poet contrives to be emotionally uninvolved by reducing the subject of the poem to terms which she can handle analytically; she addresses not God but Santa Claus, and she renders inward renewal as the assumption of a new skin or new clothes. At this low emotional voltage she works with fanciful likenesses and is in complete intellectual control.

The difference in kind between fancy and imagination as seen in these two poems is worth elaborating. Both poems contain images which seem at first sight to be entirely unrelated to each other, but both poems rely upon links of relevance between these images. In Lowell's poem images are fused together by virtue of the idea: it is not literal, concrete features described in the poem that link the trout fly with Helen, for example, but the idea of each as a beautiful cheat. And with this idea presiding, a long series of similar evocations might be drawn up. On the other hand, the image of St. Hubert in the final stanza of Miss Moore's poem cannot be said to draw other images into itself: there is nothing of the dissolution and re-creation of which Coleridge speaks and which Lowell's poem manifests. Between the chameleon and St. Hubert the extent of similarity is confined to certain concrete details which are adduced in the poem: the tense back and the change wrought by captivity. The reader does not need to explore in the penumbra of idea for the discovery of relevance.

V

In these two examples we have been concerned largely with the effects upon the imagery of the two different faculties. It is now worth looking briefly at a broader consideration: the questions as to the degree to which the operation of fancy and imagination may be expected to yield up truth, and the kind of truth it will be. Coleridge supposed that the imagination would purvey universal realities; and, although the presence of these in a poem would, by their very nature, be hard either to establish or to deny, it is worth while considering the less sublime kind of truth (or untruth) that is served up by the imagination or by procedures that use its strategies. To Luther, if his experience be a fair analogy of the working of the imagination in poetry, it was, one may say, a *kind* of reality that was manifested; but in Lear, the imagination run wild led to delusion. The faculty of the imagination, which "dissolves, diffuses . . . and struggles to idealize" and which selects from the phenomenal world only such aspects as it can use for the overwhelming idea, is clearly vulnerable to delusion like Lear's or at least to sentimentality. In "The Ancient Mariner" one might claim that what is manifested is a reality, an otherwise ineffable truth about, say, the regeneration by descent to the depths of being; but in other poems the faculty that procured reality for Coleridge, or at least a faculty operating in the same way, may serve up the merely sentimental:

> What became of Jim Oppenheim?
> Lola Ridge alone in an
> Icy furnished room? Orrick Johns,
> Hopping into the surf on his
> One leg? Elinor Wylie
> Who leaped like Kierkegaard?

Sarah Teasdale, where is she?
Timor mortis conturbat me.[23]

These lines are a part of a poem that names a number of
poets who fell on evil days in despondency or madness or worse
and finally concludes with the information that the reader—a
son of a bitch in a Brooks Brothers suit and presumably a symbol of the bourgeoisie—murdered Dylan Thomas. But the
conclusion is as specious as Lear's: just as the phenomena Lear
surveyed need not in fact have led to the conclusion that all
human misery is attributable to ungrateful daughters, so here
the fates of the poets named can be laid at the door of the
bourgeoisie only by a kind of sentimental preoccupation. If
the people listed in this poem had been presented discretely,
each in his own right as it were, as might be the case in a
poem dominated by the faculty of the fancy, the various circumstances and causes of their adversities would have precluded them from being merely lumped together and used for
the single idea.[24]

The admiration Coleridge shows for the imagination with
its ability to furnish forth the truth seems anachronistic to us,
who have less faith in the ability of any human faculty to
arrive at truth and who see on all hands what miserable harvests
are gathered when such an ability is assumed. And much of
our twentieth-century poetry is not forcibly directed toward a
single truth but represents a whole situation, a situation presented without rigid tendentious selection. Such poetry, if it
contain elements that give rise to one theme, make one point,

[23] Kenneth Rexroth, "Thou Shalt Not Kill, A Memorial for Dylan
Thomas," *In Defense of the Earth* (Norfolk, Conn.: New Directions, 1956),
p. 54.
[24] That William Dunbar's *Lament for the Makaris* escapes such censure,
although it too gathers a list of names for use and pays no more attention
to particularity than the other poem, is due to the greater control of the
imagination exercised by Dunbar. Indeed that control is so great that one
may say the imagination is not at work at all, but only logic. See J. V. Cun-
ningham, *Tradition and Poetic Structure* (Denver, Colo.: A. Swallow,
1960), pp. 50–53.

or reveal one attitude, contains also those that give rise to opposing ones; it is "a poetry which does not leave out what is
apparently hostile to its dominant tone." [25] Such a poetry is
what Robert Penn Warren has called impure, and I. A. Richards
the poetry of synthesis; John Crowe Ransom has compared it
with a democratic state which has a state policy but does not
deny its constituents their autonomous rights.

With less confidence in the ability of poetry to purvey the
universal reality, we look for its explorative propensity. And
this surely is greater in poetry of the fancy than in that of the
imagination. Unlike the imagination, which works toward
meaning and despoils its images accordingly, fancy assembles
the "fixities and definites"; the meaning to be seen among them
is derived rather than imposed and leaves beyond itself the
possibility of other meanings. In this sense I think one can talk
of poetry as being exploratory.

Discovery as a product of poetry is a concept that may give
rise to perplexity or even impatience. "How can a poem discover anything?" it is reasonable to ask, or "What can it dis-

---

[25] Cleanth Brooks, "Irony as a Principle of Structure," *Literary Opinion
in America,* ed. Morton Dauwen Zabel (New York: Harper, 1951), p. 732.
Elsewhere, speaking of this kind of poetry, Brooks says, "the insistence on
the element of conflict between attitudes will also throw more light upon
Coleridge's account of the imagination as the synthesizing faculty of the
mind" (*The Well Wrought Urn* [New York: Harcourt, Brace and Company,
1947], pp. 257–58), and quotes in a footnote the famous passage about the
imagination's power, which "reveals itself in the balance or reconcilement
of opposite or discordant qualities." Although these words of Coleridge or
Brooks's quotation of them have often been invoked to describe modern
poetry, is it not really the fancy rather than the imagination that presides
over a poetry which contains opposing elements and irrelevancies? In the
examples of poetry discussed above does not Marianne Moore's treatment
of imagery meet Brooks's requirements for the poet better than Robert
Lowell's—his image of the trout fly, for instance? The poet, Brooks says,
"must establish the details, must abide by the details, and through his
realization of the details attain to whatever general meaning he can attain.
The meaning must issue from the particulars; it must not seem to be arbitrarily forced upon the particulars" ("Irony as a Principle of Structure,"
p. 729 [italics mine]). In Rexroth's poem, of course, nothing like this occurs.

cover?" Hulme speaks to the subject in a section titled "A Poem" in "Notes on Language and Style": he used to think, he says, that the poet "tried to find new images to express what he felt" and built these up into poems. But now he sees this to be wrong;

> . . . the very act of trying to find a form to fit the separate phrases into, itself leads to the creation of new images hitherto not felt by the poet. In a sense the poetry writes itself. This creation by happy chance is analogous to the accidental stroke of the brush which creates a new beauty not previously consciously thought of by the artist.

Then he says, "*Creative* effort means *new* images. . . . The accidental discovery of effect, not conscious intellectual endeavour for it." [26] Here Hulme apparently welcomes minor accidents, whereas in the passage quoted above, details that were not knit into the structure were repugnant.

The discovery vouchsafed by the happy accident is one of effect: successful artistic achievement in a poem, come upon in part by chance. Other poets have acknowledged this kind of good luck: in the same vein, surely, is the comment by Robert Lowell (even granting a generous courtesy toward his critics) upon the commentaries on "Skunk Hour," that "much that never occurred to me has been granted me. What I didn't intend often seems now at least as valid as what I did." [27]

There are, however, other kinds of discovery that may be justifiably claimed for poetry. We need to think, for one thing, of form as a means of discovery in the sense in which R. P. Blackmur speaks of this matter: ". . . the chaos of private experience cannot be known or understood until it is projected and ordered in a form external to the consciousness that enter-

---

[26] Hulme, *Further Speculations*, p. 95.

[27] From "The Poet and His Critics. III: A Symposium on Robert Lowell's 'Skunk Hour,'" ed. Anthony Ostroff, *New World Writing XXI* (New York, 1962), pp. 131–59. "Skunk Hour" is published in Lowell's *Life Studies*; it is not like the poems in *Lord Weary's Castle*.

tained it in flux." [28] At the same time, a structural form that closely confines the material cannot but be a limitation to the free play of images and ideas (there may indeed be all kinds of dividends, including discoveries, to be got from the tension between such free play and the form, but that is another matter). Where such free play exists, I believe we may speak of the discovery of relationships in poetry—a discovery less mechanical than that from the errant brush in Hulme or that to which Dryden refers when he admits that in seeking rhymes he came upon ideas, but less mysterious than the discovery which Coleridge claims as the product of the imagination.

Without knowing just what it discovers, I believe Elizabeth Bishop's "The Man-Moth" ("Newspaper misprint for 'mammoth,'" the note tells us) is one example of a poem that is a pure exercise in fanciful association; it gives the impression that the poet has left the work open to whatever discoveries the images or their patterns may produce. For sake of brevity I quote only the third of its six stanzas:

Up the façades,
his shadow dragging like a photographer's cloth behind him,
he climbs fearfully, thinking that this time he will manage
to push his small head through that round clean opening
and be forced through, as from a tube, in black scrolls on the light.
(Man, standing below him, has no such illusions.)
But what the Man-Moth fears most he must do, although
he fails, of course, and falls back scared but quite unhurt.[29]

The imagery is related throughout, but it does not force us forward to a meaning. There are, for example, images of what

[28] R. P. Blackmur, *Form and Value in Modern Poetry* (Garden City, N.Y.: Anchor Books, 1957), p. 262. W. H. Auden says that "the form develops and shapes the poet's imagination so that he says things which he did not know he was capable of saying" ("Alexander Pope," *Essays in Criticism*, I [July, 1951], 217–18. Quoted by John G. Blair, *The Poetic Art of W. H. Auden* [Princeton, N.J.: Princeton University Press, 1965], p. 147).

[29] Elizabeth Bishop, *North and South* (Boston: Houghton Mifflin, 1946), p. 13.

one may catalogue as optical tricks: moonlight and shadows, the "photographer's cloth" and the "black scrolls" (a film, presumably) in the stanza quoted, then later the pupil of an eye which fails to contract in light and the magnification of the eye with its "haired horizon"—the kind of view one receives when one's own eye is reflected from the surface of a lens one is peering into.

Such images as these in loose association supply the short natural history of the man-moth. The poem has no meaning; it is pure fancy and exploration. Robert Lowell has spoken of it as follows:

> . . . a whole new world is gotten out and you don't know what will come after any one line. It's exploring. And it's as original as Kafka. She's gotten a world, not just a way of writing. She seldom writes a poem that doesn't have that exploratory quality; yet it's very firm, it's not like beat poetry, it's all controlled.[30]

We shall see something of this kind of exploration in the work of Miss Moore and Williams. Miss Moore likens poetry to science and quotes Jacob Bronowski as saying that "science is the process of discovering." "Do the poet and scientist not work analogously?" she asks. "Both are willing to waste effort."[31] One ought not to look for discoveries with the demonstrable results that science produces; the fancy, however, going from one thing to another, may discover relationships as science does but as the imagination, which selects its imagery in favor of an overwhelming purpose, may not. There is, of course, in the former procedure a waste of effort; in the latter with its selection there is an economy.

The concept of poetry as a process of discovery seems more manifestly apt for the method of William Carlos Williams than

[30] Robert Lowell, "The Art of Poetry III: Robert Lowell," *Paris Review*, XXV (Winter, 1961), 69.

[31] "Interview with Donald Hall," *A Marianne Moore Reader* (New York: Viking Press, 1965), p. 273.

for Miss Moore, in part because he performs the full operation of poetry within the poems themselves: as will appear, nine tenths of his iceberg is above water. Miss Moore's work varies in this matter: some poems, like "An Octopus," seem deliberately exploratory; others seem more predetermined. Robert Frost's pejorative remark that "everything is planned" in her verse is unjust; but in any given poem of hers (or, I suppose anybody else's) it might be hard to distinguish whether the poet were discovering a theme by a new relationship of images or were presenting by such means a theme previously realized. At least it would be very difficult to know at what stages in the act of poetic composition—between the germs at the very spring of inspiration and the correction of proof—discoveries are made.[32] A poem may more strongly *seem* to be making discoveries when those discoveries are latent than when they are explicitly brought forth. In "An Octopus" and also in Williams' "The Desert Music," both of which are discussed below, it does seem, however, that fancy, not forging ahead to a selective end but puttering about as it were among the images, is a mode conducive to discovery.

Williams makes a fairly firm connection between the fancy and discovery in the important passage in *Paterson IV* where the discovery of radium is being celebrated:

> A dissonance
> in the valence of Uranium
> led to the discovery.

He wants to emphasize the point and repeats:

> Dissonance
> (if you are interested)
> leads to discovery.[33]

[32] Auden once made a minor discovery of the kind discussed above by *not* correcting proofs, keeping the printer's error "ports" for his own "poets" in the passage that appears now as "And the ports have names for the sea."

[33] William Carlos Williams, *Paterson* (Norfolk, Conn.: New Directions, 1963), p. 207.

But dissonance, as Roy Harvey Pearce has pointed out, is not only the means of discovery for Madame Curie: it is the method of the poem *Paterson* "put down in a single word." [34] The poem does not proceed by the harmonious blending of elements presided over by the imagination, but their fanciful assemblage; they come together in "antagonistic cooperation," a process Williams opposes to that of love: "Love, the sledge that smashes the atom? No, No! antagonistic cooperation is the key. . . ." And thus the poem may itself be regarded as a means of discovery like Madame Curie's scientific procedures.

VI

The poems of Miss Moore and Robert Lowell examined above suggest that a useful distinction may be made between the two kinds of images by employing Coleridge's terms. It must be remarked that, as in "Venus and Adonis," so in a modern poem fancy and imagination may both be at work. If "Saint Nicholas" is a poem predominantly of the fancy, the image of the moon descending to the poet's "dark floor" is nevertheless a coinage of the imagination. It does not pose as an item fancifully associated with others on the list; it lends itself to the idea of the descent of spiritual grace. And multitudinous similarities between the image and the idea may be drawn out. The image has about it a sense of the numinous, and the reader's attention is not strongly pre-empted by its objective phenomenality.

Despite occasional anomalies, however, one may place certain poets according to which faculty they use predominantly. Just as Coleridge speaks of Milton and Cowley as possessing respectively "highly imaginative" and "very fanciful" minds, one may speak of Miss Moore and William Carlos Williams as poets of the fancy and of Robert Lowell—the Lowell of *Lord Weary's Castle*—as one of the imagination. W. D. Snod-

---

[34] Roy Harvey Pearce, *The Continuity of American Poetry* (Princeton, N.J.: Princeton University Press, 1961), p. 128.

Lowell's most significant disciple, is also a poet of the
ation; so, at least, he shows himself in "Heart's Needle,"
which is shot through with images of agriculture and snow, the
Korean War, the jaw and its teeth, among other things, which
scarcely command the senses but are related by idea and feeling to the poem's subject—the loss, by divorce, of a daughter.[35]

Finally, in connection with fancy and imagination we must
speak of Wallace Stevens; because in significant ways he is
similar to Williams and because in prose and poetry he wrote
so much on the subject of imagination, he may not be left out
of the discussion. But what critic has not wished—once, at least,
in his most degraded moment—that Stevens were a little less *sui
generis,* so that he could be placed somewhere in relation to
other poets in a more or less familiar spectrum? Stevens does not
submit, however; the "squirming facts" of his poetry repeatedly
"exceed the squamous mind" of the critic: and not surprisingly
we shall fail to fit him neatly into either of the categories under
discussion.

His subject is the imagination and its power of giving form
and order to phenomena. In "Anecdote of the Jar," for instance,
the jar orders the wilderness; in "Sea Surface Full of Clouds,"
the poet's own faculty, *"mon enfant, mon bijou, mon âme,"* repeatedly reorders the elements of the scene; in "Idea of Order
at Key West," the song orders the sea; later, *Notes Toward a
Supreme Fiction, An Ordinary Evening in New Haven,* and
other longish poems discursively ponder the theme. As Marius
Bewley has shown, "The Man Whose Pharynx Was Bad," like
Coleridge's "Dejection Ode," is occasioned by the failure of
the imagination.[36]

But these are poems *about* the "shaping spirit of Imagina-

---

[35] It is interesting to see how strenuously these two poets of the imagination are condemned by Le Roi Jones and Gilbert Sorrentino in *Yugen*
(No. 7 [1961], pp. 4–5, 5–7), a journal which honored Williams and
gave hospitality to his devotees.

[36] Marius Bewley, "The Poetry of Wallace Stevens," *Partisan Review,*
XVI (September, 1949), 895–915.

tion"; in considering the method of the poetry as opposed to the subject it ubiquitously celebrates, we may begin by observing that Stevens does not present his images in their fullness in the manner that Burke observed in Miss Moore and Williams. There are, as already mentioned, few places in the whole canon where an object is brought impressively before us by an image. On the contrary, the imagery characteristically defies our sensory abilities: how is one to *see*, for instance, a "greenest sun"? Even images that are not flagrantly impossible to visualize are often so vague as to preclude any precise sensation of their shape: ". . . a calm darkens among waterlights" suggests the increase of an area of water which, being out of the wind, has no ripples and therefore reflects no light; but it only suggests this picture vaguely. Whatever activity the poet visualized when he wrote "you come dripping in your hair from sleep," a line Frank Kermode attests to be among the loveliest in literature, is not described by that line; we get no sensory impression of what it is the lady is about. How often, in Stevens' imagery, is it the sound of the words designating the object or scene rather than the physical lineaments of the latter that impresses us:

> Let purple Phoebus lie in umber harvest,
> Let Phoebus slumber and die in autumn umber,
>
> Phoebus is dead, ephebe.[37]

It seems that images in Stevens are despoiled of their *dinglichkeit*. Are they, then, rather used for their ideas? That the color of "morning summer" on the deck, in "Sea Surface Full of Clouds," should make one think of "rosy chocolate" and "gilt umbrellas" is not due to the kind of similarity in physical properties with which fancy has been seen to work earlier in this chapter. The chocolate and the umbrellas are related inasmuch as when they are rosy and gilt respectively they conjure up feelings and ideas of happiness. In later sections other kinds of

---

[37] *Notes Toward a Supreme Fiction, The Collected Poems of Wallace Stevens* (New York: Alfred A. Knopf, 1954), p. 381.

chocolate and umbrellas conjure up other feelings and ideas: in Section II, a sense of evil, for example; in Section III, a sense of fragility and uncertainty, and so on.[38]

Over and over again in his poetry, because his images have no "edges" and because he is not interested in their physical properties, Stevens seems to be using them, to be blending them together for the sake of ideas. He seems to do so. But before we decide that he is a poet of the imagination and not of the fancy, we must observe that fancy does not always extensively display the lineaments of the "fixities and definites" that constitute its imagery and also that, as we shall see later in Miss Moore's work, fancy can assemble objects which have very little physical similarity. Furthermore, if the images of chocolate and umbrellas are coined by imagination, we should expect to find a host of "links of relevance"; and we do not. And the idea or feeling delivered up by their conjunction is the slightest and makes only the smallest impression.

Then: what idea or feeling does the poem *in toto* convey? We have seen in Lowell how the imagination gathers widely and is able to encompass disparate imagery and dissolve it and mold it into idea. But "Sea Surface" resists the kind of interpretation to which the poems in *Lord Weary's Castle* submit. Of the images, R. P. Blackmur says, "it would be very difficult to attach special importance to any one of them." Then later, "Directly they do nothing but rouse the small sensations and smaller feelings of atmosphere and tone. The poem itself, what it means, is somewhere in the background; we know it through the tone." [39] The "know" of the last clause is a begged question; clearly the poem goes nowhere, argues nothing out: finally, after all the playful modulation, the imagery does not add up to a grand meaning. To a minimal extent individual

[38] These are described by Joseph N. Riddel, " 'Disguised Pronunciamento': Wallace Stevens' 'Sea Surface Full of Clouds,' " *Texas University Studies in English*, XXXVII (1958), 177–86.

[39] Blackmur, *Form and Value in Modern Poetry*, pp. 192, 194.

images point to a mood in a flux of moods, but cumulatively they point to nothing.

The inconclusiveness of the poem is characteristic of Stevens. What we miss in his work, however liberated we may be from Aristotle's precepts, are features that would fit nicely into the categories of beginning, middle, and end. He is likely to offer instead a beginning, which may be a dramatic situation or a proposition, followed by a questioning or a commentary upon it, one or more new starts, more questions, sometimes a gallimaufry of odd items, observations, or aphorisms, and then an *ad hoc* conclusion, pulled suddenly from the hat: "That's it" or an image which we accept as conclusive because it flatters our senses. A whole poem may be a series of rough drafts in search of an expression which comes, apparently arbitrarily, in the last line. How often the progress of the so-called argument of a poem is muddied by questions or compromised by passages beginning "perhaps," "say," or "it may be"; though at the end of the poem, seduced by the imagery of blossoming shrubs, we may feel content that we have arrived somewhere. Even in "Sunday Morning," which has survived the survey course to be popular partly because there is a discernible argument, the points in that argument as it proceeds by question and answer are made by lines which have lyrical rather than logical beauty.

In Stevens, the idea of the poem—the idea toward the expression of which the imagination might have shaped the imagery—is most frequently beyond our discernment. But if he does not deploy his imagery in this way to give broad illumination to his idea but rather throws flashes of light upon it haphazardly from one angle or another, it is because, in the end, he wants to prevent it from being clearly revealed. "Poetry," says Stevens, "must resist the intelligence almost successfully," and he has been successful in making it do so. The extraordinary degree of difference in the interpretations of single passages of his work or single poems is a familiar feature of the

, and it speaks to this fact about the poet. There are, of course, conflicting opinions throughout the great wealth of interpretive criticism of modern poetry in general; but unlike the Stevens criticism, they do not seem to preclude the possibility that broad agreement can be reached. The various opinions about a Stevens poem suggest that the people expressing them have completely different things they want to say about the lines they are describing. Often there simply is not just one single right meaning to be abstracted from a poem.

One can easily imagine that the man whose nine-to-five life was given over to the statistical accommodation of "squirming facts" in the insurance world would demand, in the evenings and on week ends, some utterly different disposition of them from his poetry. During the day he was one of the millions, epitomized as the soldier in the epilogue to *Notes Toward a Supreme Fiction,* who labor for their sustenance in the common struggle; in the evening, in that other room, he was the Arabian (of Number III of the first part of the same poem) with his magic, from which he wanted a poem that would give him entry into a kind of knowledge of the world different from the kind he was obliged to use during the day, a kind of knowledge according to which A might be both A and not A. One can imagine this: what is empirically clear is that again and again the employment of "irrational distortions" in a poem has preserved it from the mordant grip of a single meaning.

This policy would seem consonant with the ideas of the world that permeate the poetry; the basic premise about Stevens' world is that it is the product of the imagination playing upon a fundamental reality: the imagination constantly creates from the chaos of raw material. But what is also basic to his world is the fact that the fictive thing created must be ephemeral; as "Sunday Morning" expresses better than any other single poem, the old established myths must be broken down to make way for new ones. Stevens works between the two extremes of the formless, uncreated world and the finished, hardened form, "the jungle and the monumental hero." [40] Thus, if we ask of "Anecdote of the Jar" whether the jar be a good or a bad agent, we must find that it is each in turn: good when it orders chaos, as the poetic imagination does; but bad when it stands pat and dominates: latterly it is "tall and of a port in air" and takes "dominion everywhere." Though he had originally installed it, the poet comes to disapprove of it. His disapprobation is marked in the second half of the poem by rhyme, which Stevens frequently introduces into otherwise nonrhyming lines to ridicule wrong attitudes or behavior.[41] The fictive thing must be evanescent, not solid and built to last forever like the First Methodist Church. Similarly, in "Bantams in Pine Woods," the inchling who rebels against the dominating creative power of the imagination is given a hearing.

This concept of Stevens' requirements for his world may be thought of as a concept that governs the poetry also; to some degree at least the words on the page are the raw material out of which our imagination creates the poem. The poem may or may not come; if it does, then our imagination is at work following a trail indefinitely blazed by the poet with unmarked cul-de-sacs opening upon it. Poor as we are, like "Cinderella fulfilling herself beneath the roof," we make our poems, which, as we have seen, may be varying constructions upon Stevens' data; and we may ask, as Stevens asks of the angel in *Notes Toward a Supreme Fiction*, "Is it he or is it I that experience this?" We must think of ourselves, then, as poets, an idea both Stevens and Coleridge would allow: "You feel him to be a poet," says Coleridge of Shakespeare, "inasmuch as for a time he has made you one—an active creative being." (It is amusing that Henry Green, the second most eminent business man of letters, speaks,

---

[40] Howard Nemerov, "The Poetry of Wallace Stevens," *Sewanee Review,* LXV (January–March, 1957), 12.

[41] For a good, brief commentary both on this poem and on fancy and imagination in Stevens with conclusions that differ somewhat from mine, see Patricia Merivale, "Wallace Stevens' 'Jar': The Absurd Detritus of Romantic Myth," *College English,* XXVI (April, 1965), 527–32.

though no doubt a little whimsically, of his novels as the audience before which the reader lives his own life.)

The fictive thing we discover, however, must be ephemeral,
not lasting.

> We do not prove the existence of the poem.
> It is something seen and known in lesser poems.
> It is the huge, high harmony that sounds
> A little and a little, suddenly,
> By means of a separate sense. It is and it
> Is not and, therefore, is. . . .[42]

The last sentence is at the heart of the matter: "It is and it / Is
not and, therefore, is." It is a kind of "moment in and out of
time" that Stevens is after or, what is probably the same, the
moment when "the burden of the mystery . . . is lightened."
For the capture of this moment, Stevens breaks up the solid
meaning of a poem; it is the moment when "the marble
statues / Are like newspapers blown by the wind" or when we
"behold / The academies like structures in a mist." But whereas
for Eliot the moment in and out of time is "unattended" and
comes from nature as a gratuitous gift, for Stevens the moment
is the poet's own creation. It is a creation he happens upon, a
"flick of feeling" discovered in a fanciful relationship, not a
calculated one; but still it is not given. Thus, while for Eliot
the poetic task is to assimilate these given moments into form,
for Stevens the task is to generate the moment by creating the
conditions—the medium—into which it may be born. And he
does so throughout the poetry by all those disturbances which
dissolve the idea just at its point of crystallization.

When, therefore, we come back to our question as to which
faculty Stevens uses in his poetry, we must settle for the fancy.
It is fancy with no respect for the haecceity of things; indeed
it has no respect for "things as they are," which are changed by
the blue guitar of the art process. Fancy works, as it will appear

[42] *Collected Poems of Wallace Stevens*, p. 440.

also to work in Miss Moore and in a slightly different way in Williams, to prevent the poem from coming to the fulsome feeling or the overwhelming statement. Its irrational modulations are the golden apples that Stevens bowls off the course, confident that in pursuit of them the reader will lose the race.

Part of our difficulty is that Stevens talks so much about the Coleridgean imagination; and part of the trouble is that so frequently he presents his miscellaneous fanciful anecdotes, incidents, and even single images as if they were the product of the imagination and crystallized a stage in or a conclusion to the argument. An anecdote about Professor Eucalyptus or the introduction of an hidalgo or a rabbi looks as if it should fit a central theme, whereas in fact it is merely peripherally associated and throws upon the whole a partial broken light. In addition, in images and abstractions he uses words connoting music as if the poem were a realized harmony of parts blended by the imagination, when in fact what harmony there is, remote from the document itself, awaits our own momentary construction. Stevens himself does not force us to that end point in idea at which poetry of the imagination characteristically arrives; he works toward, perhaps, but not quite to it. It is always ahead. "Until . . . I call you by name," he says; and then he immediately does; but it is a name writ in water: ". . . my green, my fluent mundo."

CHAPTER III

MARIANNE MOORE

ONE MAY SPEAK of Marianne Moore's poetic practice very generally as follows: feeling is expressed by concrete images; these are very carefully perceived, and to the extent that the poem pays attention to them, elaborating them for their own sakes with the play of fancy, the feeling is restrained; to the extent that the opposite occurs, in the limited number of instances where Miss Moore uses an image in the mode of the imagination, feeling is unrestrained. One may make a parallel statement about moral judgment, which is precise when the fancy is at work and attention is being paid to the precise lineaments of the concrete world, but in the opposite situation may be sentimental or otherwise false. First let us consider the clear perception upon which feeling and truth must be firmly based; second, the variety of ways in which feeling is restrained by fanciful associations.

The act of perception upon which so much depends is predominantly a visual one. It is necessary, however, to distinguish between two kinds of vision: the bird's-eye view presents a general panorama and fails to recognize discrete particulars;

the close-up, accurate study recognizes the particulars and does not subordinate them to a general picture. Often the two kinds of perception may be observed to be at work in the same poem, each contributing its own images. And, briefly, the images purveyed by the general view give rise to false conclusions and express sentimental feelings, while those that are the product of the accurate detailed study give rise to careful moral judgments and express, with some reticence, discriminated feelings. Sometimes, as a variation, two different attitudes toward a single visual scene, one of them analogous to the general view, the other to the close-up, counterpoint one another. When there are two views or attitudes present in a poem, the cruder one is generally dismissed, most often implicitly, in favor of the accurate one; or the former is corrected by the latter.

The two kinds of vision may be easily recognized in "The Steeple-Jack," where an important contrast is formed between the images provided by the bird's-eye view of the town—the view enjoyed by the steeple-jack aloft—in the first part of the poem and those that come from a close study in the second. In the first four stanzas of the shortest version of the poem,[1] the emphasis on sight is apparent: there are "eight stranded whales / to look at"; "You can see a twenty-five- / pound lobster"; and the storm is visible: ". . . it is a privilege to see so / much confusion." But the view in this part of the poem provides less a description of a town than a description of a sentimental picture of one: water is "etched / with waves," gulls sail around the lighthouse, the sea is too richly tinted.

The storm destroys the romantic picture exactly as it does in Hawthorne's "Sights from a Steeple." In the fifth stanza, with the lines "A steeple-jack in red, has let / a rope down as a spider spins a thread;" the point of view changes, and the general

[1] Marianne Moore, *Collected Poems* (New York: Macmillan, 1959), pp. 13–14. Hereafter *CP*. In *Selected Poems* (New York: Macmillan, 1935) the poem has twelve stanzas. Hereafter *SP*. It was revised in 1961 and appears with thirteen stanzas in *A Marianne Moore Reader* (New York: Viking Press, 1965), pp. 3–5.

view gives way to the close study. The act of seeing is now different; the words describing it are not now "You see," but "One sees," "one" being the pronoun the poet frequently uses for personal observations. The items now perceived are parts of the real everyday world, the schoolhouse, the post office, the fish- and hen-houses; they are not necessarily picturesque, but simply objects seen by a viewer with, literally and figuratively, her feet on the ground.

One important image purveyed by the accurate view is the sign set up by the steeple-jack. Its message is given some prominence in the poem, appearing as the first word of a stanza: the sign

in red

and white says

Danger. . . .

We are warned not only of the physical danger but of the danger of sentimentally concluding that the town is merely the picturesque place that has been presented in the images mediated through the vision of the steeple-jack, which have occupied us up to this point. There follow the realistic details; and we deduce, among other things, that the livelihood of the town, depending as it does on the unpredictable sea, is more precarious than the birds-eye view had suggested:[2] the storm which had been a glorious sight had had other implications. All the same, the final stanza begins, "It scarcely could be dangerous to be living / in a town like this" and concludes by describing the steeple-jack gilding the star which "stands for hope." The point is that when the danger has been fairly faced, as it has here by the acknowledgment of the realistic situation, it has been contained. The realistic view has neutralized the sentimental

---

[2] Louise Bogan, "Reading Contemporary Poetry," *College English*, XIV (February, 1953), 258. See also Marie Borroff, "Dramatic Structure in the Poetry of Marianne Moore," *The Literary Review*, II (Autumn, 1958), 112–23.

one; and from ground level looking up one may safely
tain hope—a hope based on solid foundations, as the
based on the steeple of the church.

The statement the poem makes is not, surely, only pertinent
to the local situation. In many places throughout the poetry of
Marianne Moore, a careful study of realistic particulars forms
a protection against the danger of sentimentality and inaccurate
judgment or the evils associated with these, moral obtuseness
and arrogance, which the general view is apt to incur. The
arrogant man in "A Grave," for instance, who took the view
from Miss Moore and her mother, is condemned for his attempt
to "stand in the middle of a thing," the sea (*CP*, p. 56). The
sea is a large vague abstraction; and one may be sentimental
about it, but poetry is incompetent to deal with it accurately
as a whole and had better not approach it except by way of
clear, discrete particulars. Aware of this, the poet assumes toward the sea a respect which is quite contrary to the intruder's
brashness. Her vision is directed to particular, finite phenomena
at the periphery or on the surface: there are the famous fir
trees which "stand in a procession, each with an emerald
turkey-foot at the top" or the wrinkles at the surface which
"progress among themselves in a phalanx—beautiful under net-
works of foam." The same instinct controls her in her approach
to New York in the poem so titled: ". . . one must stand outside and laugh," she says, "since to go in is to be lost" (*CP*,
p. 60).

The extent of the poet's contempt for people or things which
disregard details is sometimes amusing. The steamroller, for
instance, in a poem quoted below, is an object of it; so are the
culprits of crimes committed over a disputed legacy in "The
Icosasphere." These are charged, of all things, with a failure in
"integration" and are compared unfavorably with birds, which
" 'weave little bits of string and moths and feathers and thistle-
down / in parabolic concentric curves' " (*CP*, p. 142), and with
the inventors of the icosasphere who have so learned to manage

details that sheets of steel can be rounded to a ball with maximum economy.

The principle, implicit throughout Marianne Moore's work, that attention must be paid to details and that truth and feeling must be based on the perception of them is clearly embodied in "The Paper Nautilus." There are the minutely perceived details

> the intensively
> watched eggs coming from
> the shell free it when they are freed,—
> leaving its wasp-nest flaws
> of white on white, and close-
>
> laid Ionic chiton-folds
> like the lines in the mane of
> a Parthenon horse,
> round which the arms had
> wound themselves. . . .
>
> (CP, pp. 122–23)

These "intensively watched" details give rise to the conclusion that

> . . . love
> is the only fortress
> strong enough to trust to.

But this is not ceremoniously submitted as a universal truth in quotable form: one is not supposed to carry it away like, say, a couplet of Pope's. On the contrary, it is a very particular truth firmly attached to the percepts which gave rise to it:

> . . . the arms had
> wound themselves as if they knew love
> is the only fortress. . . .

The scrutinized details that produce the moral judgment also express personal feelings. The paper nautilus is in a sense the poet herself, who, working indeed with paper, constructs a form, a part of herself, in which to foster and deliver her ideas. These "coming from / the shell free it when they are freed" and leave evidence of the love and care that had encompassed them. In such a way the poem expresses with extreme reticence the complex of personal feelings, conflicting senses of freedom and deprivation, that attend the poetic act.[3]

No images from the bird's-eye view are presented in "The Paper Nautilus." But in contrast to the poet herself, persons like the intruder in "A Grave," who would be likely, out of arrogance or sentimentality, to use the general view are referred to; and we learn that for them the activities of the paper nautilus are irrelevant:

> For authorities whose hopes
> are shaped by mercenaries?
>   Writers entrapped by
>   teatime fame and by
> commuters' comforts? Not for these
>   the paper nautilus
>   constructs her thin glass shell.

The bird's-eye view, most frequently associated with sentimentality or arrogance, need not be so and is not always incapable of appreciating particulars. In "Tom Fool at Jamaica"[4] Signor Capossela has a point of vantage—"Up in the cupola comparing speeds" (of race horses). But he keeps his head: " 'It's tough,' he said; 'but I get 'em; and why shouldn't I? / I'm relaxed, I'm confident, and I don't bet.' " He doesn't bet: there is no overriding consideration which might compromise the accuracy of his perception of the details. The fact is important in a poem whose message is, Do not let any system—any *general* view

---

[3] Kenneth Burke says of this poem that "the themes of bondage and freedom . . . are fiercely and flashingly merged" (*A Grammar of Motives* [New York: Prentice-Hall, 1954], p. 502).

[4] Marianne Moore, *Like a Bulwark* (New York: Viking Press, 1957), pp. 12–13.

of things, one may legitimately gloss—compromise fidelity to particular truths:

> Be infallible at your peril, for your system will fail,
> and select as a model the schoolboy in Spain
>   who at the age of six, portrayed a mule and jockey
>   who had pulled up for a snail.

The notes supply the drawing of the mule and jockey checked for the sake of the small particularity!

In poems where two kinds of approach to a scene or situation are posited, vision need not, of course, be literal; although it is interesting that it so frequently is. In "England," the poet's remark, "To have misapprehended the matter is to have confessed / that one has not looked far enough" (CP, p. 54), speaks of a discrimination fairly familiar in her work. The extravaganza in "He 'Digesteth Harde Yron'" are a matter of general visibility, whereas their meaning, which is solicitude and which is derived only from scrutiny, is not:

> Six hundred ostrich-brains served
>   at one banquet, the ostrich-plume-tipped tent
> and desert spear, jewel-
> gorgeous ugly egg-shell
>   goblets, eight pairs of ostriches
> in harness, dramatize a meaning always missed
> by the externalist.

> The power of the visible
> is the invisible. . . .
>   (CP, p. 104)

We may observe in passing how often Marianne Moore tries to press the claims of the inward and the invisible against those of the outward and generally visible. "In Distrust of Merits" is just such an attempt, distrusting appearance, apparent merits even, and condemning the failure of the inward self: "I in-

wardly did nothing. / O Iscariotlike crime!" (*CP*, p. 137).
"The Mind Is an Enchanting Thing" (*CP*, pp. 133–34) is another piece of advocacy for the "something" that, in Miss
Moore's words, is "more important than outward rightness." [5]
In this poem it is a variable quality, like iridescence, which can
accommodate inconsistency "like Tom Fool's / left white hind
foot—an unconformity," in "Tom Fool at Jamaica"; and it is
unlimited by immutable outward systems: it is "not a Herod's
oath [the outward cause of the beheading of John] that cannot
change."

One of the most interesting and complex poems in which
the meaning resides in the relationship between the two kinds
of literal vision is "An Octopus." The poem is complex partly
because its subject is complex. Its subject is truth and how one
may approach it; and as a part of this subject the poem is concerned to show how the general view is attended by happiness
while the more penetrating one—the one which will attain to
truth—precludes it. The poem has two parts between which
the division is indicated. The first part presents, not exclusively,
an unfallen world, perceptible by those who look at it with a
bird's-eye view. The second part, again not exclusively, presents
the truth as it may be approached and discerned by fallen
mortals. These two themes occur also in the two poems which
respectively precede and follow "An Octopus" in the *Collected
Poems* and which, as Kenneth Burke has pointed out,[6] are associated with it. In "Marriage," Eden appears in "all its lavish-
ness," while in "Sea Unicorns and Land Unicorns" truth is
imaged as a unicorn with "chain lightning" about its horn,
" 'impossible to take alive', / tamed only by a lady inoffensive
like itself. . . ." In "An Octopus," truth is imaged by the glacier, with "the lightning flashing at its base"; and the discipline

[5] Author's Note quoted in *Modern Poetry: American and British*, ed.
Kimon Friar and J. M. Brinnin (New York: Appleton-Century-Crofts,
1951), p. 523.

[6] Burke, *A Grammar of Motives*, p. 496 note.

required in approaching it—largely a matter of being inoffensive
—is detailed:

> It is self-evident
> that it is frightful to have everything afraid of one;
> that one must do as one is told
> and eat rice, prunes, dates, raisins, hardtack, and tomatoes
> if one would 'conquer the main peak of Mount Tacoma,
> this fossil flower concise without a shiver. . . .'
>
> (CP, p. 83)

The terms one must accept in order to climb are, of course, a
metaphor for the self-discipline of clear perception and "relentless accuracy" that the poet accepts prior to the discovery and
utterance of truth in her poetry. The vision of the truth at the
end of the poem—a vision not brashly arrogated but earned by
the discipline—is a harsh one: the glacier

> . . . receives one under winds that 'tear the snow to bits
> and hurl it like a sandblast
> shearing off twigs and loose bark from the trees'.
> . . . .
> . . . the hard mountain 'planed by ice and polished by the wind'—
> the white volcano with no weather side;
> the lightning flashing at its base. . . .

   The first part of the poem presents on the whole a happy
general view punctuated occasionally by uncomfortable glances
into the real nature of things. It dwells mostly not upon the
glacier itself nor the measures that must be taken to approach
it but upon flora and fauna which may be observed in the surrounding park. There was, in fact, a ready-made hint for the
poet that she should present this as a prelapsarian world, for the
park around Mount Tacoma has the name "Paradise" and de-
serves it. Some of the perceptions in this romantic part of the
poem are reminiscent of the tamed nature of eighteenth-century
pastoral: ". . . the polite needles of the larches" are " 'hung to
filter, not to intercept the sunlight' "; or there are "dumps of

gold and silver ore enclosing The Goat's Mirror— / that lady-fingerlike depression in the shape of the left human foot. . . ."

The anthropomorphic distortion of real nature is extended to the descriptions of the animals: "the exacting porcupine," the rat pausing "to smell the heather," " 'thoughtful beavers / making drains which seem the work of careful men with shovels,' " the water ouzel "with 'its passion for rapids,' " and the marmot, a victim of " 'a struggle between curiosity and caution.' " Among these creatures are the guides, presented as parts of the happy animal kingdom, who have withdrawn to this paradise from the complex world of hotels and are therefore safe in sloughing off their protective covering as animals sometimes do:

> those who 'have lived in hotels
> but who now live in camps—who prefer to';
> the mountain guide evolving from the trapper,
> 'in two pairs of trousers, the outer one older,
> wearing slowly away from the feet to the knees'. . . .

Enjoyment of this paradise depends upon ignorance and therefore upon the imperfection of vision. Some of the creatures here are so placed that they have a vantage point from which to view this world; and for the sake of their felicity it is as important that they should *not* see clearly as that S. Capossela, judging winners from his cupola, should. He is concerned to find truth; his felicity is not under consideration. Similarly, the poet may arrive at truth by her fallen approach; but the animals' happiness is contingent upon their avoiding it. The passage "He / sees deep and is glad" from "What are Years?" might seem at first sight to offer an opposite theory. But seeing deep here transpires, paradoxically, to be the prerogative of one who recognizes limitations. The poet's concern with the animals' felicity in "An Octopus" reminds one of her admitted tendency upon encountering animals "to wonder if they are happy."

In connection with her descriptions of the goat and the eagles in the park, the poet toys with the word "fall": to experience the sensation of a fall would be to experience *the* Fall. But the vision of these animals is vague enough to preclude them from knowledge: on its pedestal the goat has its eye "fixed on the waterfall which never seems to fall." The eagles are perched on places from which humans would fall, but they see nothing:

> 'They make a nice appearance, don't they',
> happy seeing nothing?
> Perched on treacherous lava and pumice—
> those unadjusted chimney-pots and cleavers
> which stipulate 'names and addresses of persons to notify
> in case of disaster'. . . .

The distinction made earlier between the two parts of "An Octopus" as the products respectively of the romantic view and the realistic is only a relative one. The glacier, for instance, notwithstanding the horrendous description at the end of the poem, is referred to earlier in the second part as the "fossil flower"; while in the first part, the word "misleadingly" in the following description of the glacier gives due warning that it may not be such a docile object as it looks from a distance and as the images from human fabrication suggest:

> dots of cyclamen-red and maroon on its clearly defined pseudo-podia
> made of glass that will bend—a much needed invention. . . .
> . . . .
> it hovers forward 'spider fashion
> on its arms' misleadingly like lace. . . .

Some of the difficulty of the poem is due to its lack of recognizable structural form. As we shall see below, many of Marianne Moore's poems have form—form gained from rhymes, rhythms, and patterned arrangements of lines. But she avoids form that results from the organization of parts—a process in which details are selected, shaped, and ordered to contribute and conform to the whole, such as the faculty of the imagination, the "shaping spirit," would follow. To subordinate particulars to a general picture is contrary to her characteristic practice;

and, as will appear, it is equally uncharacteristic in Williams. When she does subordinate details, she does so to provide a foil for the kind of perception which appreciates them. For subordinating particulars for the sake of conformity, she pours contempt upon the steamroller, to which details are only interesting to the extent that they can be applied to something else:

The illustration
is nothing to you without the application.
   You lack half wit. You crush all the particles down
      into close conformity, and then walk back and forth
      on them.

Sparkling chips of rock
are crushed down to the level of the parent block.
(CP, p. 90)

Her way in "An Octopus" is to present and appreciate the details as they appear—she is not making a map, but engaging in what Ezra Pound called a "periplum," a voyage of discovery which gives, not a bird's-eye view but a series of images linked by the act of voyaging: "Not as land looks on a map," says Pound, "but as sea bord seen by men sailing." There is, of course, a degree of recognizable order in the broad difference between the two parts of the poem. But a too exact structural control would defeat the poet's aim, which is to accommodate fragments which may perhaps give " 'piercing glances into the life of things.' " [7] Then "An Octopus" may also be properly thought of as a poem in which discoveries are made by means of the fanciful relationships that are established: that is, one may conceive that in the act of composition, in the act of relating its fanciful items, truths that the poet had not initially intended to demonstrate became manifest in the poem. It is possible to suppose that, as she read about the gay living the fauna and flora in Paradise Park enjoyed despite the proximity of the hor-

[7] Cf. Mildred Hartsock, "Marianne Moore: 'A Salvo of Barks,' " *Bucknell Review*, XI (December, 1962), 31–32.

rendous glacier, she experienced one of the truths the poem now conveys, that one may live in innocence and felicity by confining attention to immediate particular realities and avoiding the vast abstractions—an existence which is not less a paradise for being a fool's paradise. Or it is possible to imagine that, in the assortment of facts about Mount Tacoma assembled by fancy, the disciplines the mountain imposes upon its climbers flashed into recognition as analogous to the terms which the search for moral truth imposes upon a poet. If one may speak guardedly of discovery in this way, one may recognize it as a product of fancy.

The phrase above about piercing glances comes from the poem "When I Buy Pictures." Throughout the poetry, images are often presented as pictures, sometimes with the employment of the terms of painting; and often the pictures are sentimental. One example is the first view of the town in "The Steeple-Jack"; another is the goat in "An Octopus," which, watching the panorama with a romantic gaze, is itself deliberately presented as an *objet d'art* on a pedestal "in stag-at-bay position" as sentimental as one of Landseer's creations:

black feet, eyes, nose, and horns, engraved on dazzling ice-fields,
the ermine body on the crystal peak;
the sun kindling its shoulders to maximum heat like acetylene,
    dyeing them white—
upon this antique pedestal. . . .

But in the poem concerned with buying pictures, or pretending to own them rather, the poet appears to dislike the kind of picture which is too strongly bent upon making a point. She says,

Too stern an intellectual emphasis upon this quality or that detracts
    from one's enjoyment.
It must not wish to disarm anything; nor may the approved triumph
    easily be honoured—
that which is great because something else is small.

(CP, p. 55)

One assumes she would prefer Brueghel or such paintings of Dürer as provide the eye with opportunity for play among phenomena. She quotes Goya, having recovered from his paralysis, as follows: "In order to occupy an imagination mortified by the contemplation of my sufferings and recover, partially at all events, the expenses incurred by illness, I fell to painting a set of pictures in which I have given observation a place usually denied it in works made to order, in which little scope is left for fancy and invention." Miss Moore comments as follows:

> Fancy and invention—not made to order—perfectly describe the work; the *Burial of the Sardine*, say: a careening throng in which one can identify a bear's mask and paws, a black monster wearing a horned hood, a huge turquoise quadracorne, a goblin mouth on a sepia fish-tailed banner, and twin dancers in filmy gowns with pink satin bows in their hair. Pieter Brueghel, the Elder, an observer as careful and as populous as Goya, "crossed the Alps and travelled the length of Italy, returning in 1555 to paint as though Michelangelo had never existed," so powerful was predilective intention.[8]

In her own poetic practice she avoids the strong approach to a central theme, by way of the imagination for instance, preferring to dwell appreciatively among her images. A picture should be " 'lit with piercing glances into the life of things' "; but a glance is not a gaze or the rapacious look of the arrogant man in "A Grave."

II

By dwelling upon the imagery for its own sake or by proliferating images linked by fanciful association Marianne Moore achieves the control of feelings, that justly celebrated restraint and classic decency which is perhaps the most superb feature of her work. "Tom Fool at Jamaica," which as we have seen is a

---

[8] *A Marianne Moore Reader*, p. 179. A note attributes the quotation about Brueghel to Fritz Grossmann, *The Paintings of Brueghel* (New York: Phaidon Press, 1955).

poem about restraint, will serve to illustrate: after the image of
the jockey and the mule exercising restraint, the poem proceeds
to show among other things how the poet is checked in full
career and achieves restraint when she is in danger of senti-
mentalizing over Tom Fool, the race horse. Aware that her
enthusiasm is carrying her away into "a rhapsody," a sentimental
appraisal not based upon strict perception, she breaks off her discourse about the horse and side-steps into a new series of images
of jazz musicians:

> like centaurs' legs in tune, as when kettle-
>   drums compete;
>   nose rigid and suede nostril spread, a light left
>   hand on the rein, till
>   well—this is a rhapsody
>
>   Of course, speaking of champions, there was Fats Waller
> with the feather touch, giraffe eyes, and that
>   hand alighting in
> Ain't Misbehavin'! Ozzie Smith and Eubie Blake. . . .

The image of Fats Waller is linked to that of the horse by the
fact that both are champions, by the simile of kettledrums, and
perhaps (the picture in the issue of the *New York Times* referred to in the notes does not show the hands) by the fact that
a "hand alighting" with grouped fingers is a little like a race
horse at that point in its stride when the hooves appear bunched
together. It is not important to trace the exact track of the association; the point is that the poet, facing the danger of unrestrained feeling, proliferates images that are only fancifully
related to the object to which the strong feeling is attached.[9]

The practice of displaying fanciful images in order to achieve
restraint over feeling is observed frequently in Miss Moore's
poetry. It appears to a small extent in "The Paper Nautilus,"
where the perception of "wasp-nest flaws / of white on white"

[9] A different interpretation of "well—this is a rhapsody" appears in Marie
Borroff, " 'Tom Fool at Jamaica' by Marianne Moore: Meaning and Structure," *College English*, XVII (May, 1956), 466–69.

leads, via the image in "Ionic," to the imagery of "the mane of / a Parthenon horse." But the begetting of fresh images is checked at this point, and the moral statement comes forth. A similar kind of control of feeling is operating in "Leonardo da Vinci's," where the poet seems to be amused at her own trick and tells us that really it is not impossible to trace the links between her associations! The end of the poem playfully associates his pet lion with St. Jerome, who "left us the Vulgate"; and by this means, the poet masks her strong admiration for the saint, the "pacific," "passionate," and "great" man, and for his legacy. In the following lines we see her leading away from the matter containing the emotional content by fancifully linking St. Jerome and his Vulgate, the great spiritual nourishment, with the fact that the Nile rises in the sign of the zodiac Leo to fertilize the crops and the fact that fountains frequently discharge their water through the mouths of lions. Thus the production of the Vulgate may also be allowed to be a leonine quality.

> . . . That in *Leo*,
> the Nile's rise grew food checking famine,
>   made lion's-mouth fountains appropriate,
>
> if not universally,
>   at least not obscure.[10]

In these last two lines the poet seems to be casting an amused, oblique glance at her own technique of fanciful associations. But she can do even better!

> . . . Blaze on, picture,
> saint, beast; and Lion Haile Selassie, with household
>   lions as symbol of sovereignty.

The picture itself is also leonine because its painter is Leonardo; and we must not forget the Emperor of Abyssinia, who is the Lion of Judah. If there is amusement in this, it is only one side of a strategy that, like the wit of John Donne who

[10] Marianne Moore, *O To Be a Dragon* (New York: Viking Press, 1959), p. 31.

prayed to God in puns and conceits, can be put to the most serious use.

With some of her poems one feels that Miss Moore is more content to conceal the message of the poem than to run the risk of being carried away by her feelings and overstating it. She is reminiscent of her own frigate pelican, not only because in her use of quotations she takes "on the wing, from industrious crude-winged species / the fish they have caught," but because, with admirable *sprezzatura,*

> the unconfiding frigate-bird hides
> in the height and in the majestic
> display of his art. . . .
>
> (CP, pp. 31–32)

In one fairly recent poem she virtually admits to the policy of concealment. The poet's concern "In the Public Garden" (*Dragon,* pp. 20–21) is the plight of refugees. But this is not the official concern of the poem, and the subject of the refugees is introduced overtly only as one item in a catalogue of casually associated images and ideas. At the end of the poem, expressing the intention "to wish poetry well" (in the first version, "to wish real poetry well" [11]), the poet is glad that poetry may legitimately have a personal component—"glad that the Muses have a home and swans—"; and in the last two lines, she is "happy that Art, admired in general, / is always actually personal." She is glad that she has been able, even in a public poem officially about a public garden, to deliver herself with great reticence of her private feelings.

In "The Steeple-Jack," meaning lay in the relationship between two kinds of vision; the meaning of "In the Public Garden" lies in the relationship between two attitudes to a scene and situation. Corresponding to the general view is a public description of spring at Cambridge and the presentation of memories associated with it; corresponding to the accurate,

[11] *Ladies' Home Journal* (January, 1959), p. 88.

close-up study is the poet's own, nearly private response to the scene. The poem first presents the features of spring and certain memories. But then the poet turns from these items to the train of private thoughts they arouse in her. It is as if, at the sight of spring and all it brings forth, she turns inward, like Moschus in his "Lament for Bion" and so many subsequent elegists, to the private sorrow at the thought of what the season cannot bring—freedom and opportunity for the refugees in the trans-shipment camp.

The poem begins,

> Boston has a festival—
> compositely for all—
> and nearby, cupolas of learning
> (crimson, blue, and gold) that
> have made education individual.

The poet then recalls the remark of a taxi driver: " 'They / make some fine young men at Harvard.' " She recalls the gilding of the weathervane on Faneuil Hall "by / a -leafer and -jack," that is a gold-leafer and a steeple-jack. And she notes some features of spring.

In the second part of the poem (the division is not indicated on the page) the poet enters King's Chapel

> to hear them sing: "My work be praise while
> others go and come. No more a stranger
> or a guest but like a child
> at home."

A chapel or a festival, she proceeds, means gifts, among which are

> black sturgeon-eggs—a camel
> from Hamadan, Iran;
> a jewel. . . .

Other gifts are silence and freedom—" 'freedom to toil' / with

a feel for the tool." Then immediately follows the situation of
the refugees:

> Those in the trans-shipment camp must have
> a skill. With hope of freedom hanging
>   by a thread—some gather medicinal
>
> herbs which they can sell.
> Ineligible if they ail.

In "The Steeple-Jack," once again, the vision in the first part
of the poem is corrected by that in the second: when looked
at realistically the town is not merely the pretty picture we
had first been shown. So here, the sweetness of the imagery
of spring turns sour when we see how it is related to the central
subject. The sweetness is deliberately overdone: spring is "a
more than usual / bouquet of what is vernal"; from its description, nothing must be omitted:

> . . . O yes, and snowdrops
>   in the snow, that smell like
>   violets. . . .

The attitude is gently blasé—spring and all that! The tone is
slightly reminiscent of Milton's description of the vernal garden
where there was "enormous bliss." And the comparison is not
completely wayward, since, as we have seen, hints of the prelapsarian world among general views elsewhere in Miss Moore's
poetry are subjected to delicate ridicule. The images in the
first part of the poem are not, as they initially seem, merely a
collation that presents itself to a free-wheeling mind. They are
all related, more or less ironically and by one point or another,
to the central subject, the plight of the refugees. And the
poet's tact in concealing feeling may be judged in part by observing the sentimentality of the following comments in which
the relationship is expressed. There is a public garden and a
festival "for all"; but neither is open to the refugees. There is
the greater privilege—the private university for learning skills

individually; but the refugees, though they also may be "fine young men," unless they already have a skill, have no access even to general freedom, let alone a university. Faneuil Hall is known as the "Cradle of Liberty"; the situation of the "-leafer and -jack" may have been precarious, but so is that of those whose *hope of freedom* is "hanging by a thread." (The gilding of the weathervane may possibly be directly associated here with hope, as it is in "The Steeple-Jack.") Spring produces lavishly its herbaceous benefits, and "A chapel or a festival / / means giving"; among the refugees, on the other hand, herbs are gathered to be sold.

The tenuousness of these relationships is, of course, calculated to conceal the poet's feelings. At the point where she enters King's Chapel, the feeling attached to the plight of the refugees and to her own hope for them finds direct utterance. In the lines quoted above, the words "stranger," "child," and "home" are strongly emotive. But once again in the presence of the danger of sentimentality the poet resorts to the protection of a fanciful series of images—the "black sturgeon-eggs" and others, which, with the internal rhyme, lead away quickly from the emotion aroused in the words named. It would have been quite foreign to Miss Moore's good manners to allow personal sentiment to dominate a poem which was read at the Boston Arts Festival in 1958.

III

The poems all show the poet resorting for the control of strong feeling and of sentimentality to the elaboration of sensory details and the kind of association that fancy produces. The presence, therefore, of the carefully delineated object may make us suspect the presence of strong feeling; and herein lies, I think, an answer to the question about the poem "Silence," which is asked in the Lit. for Teachers text: "Why does Miss Moore develop the image of the cat?"

Self-reliant like the cat—
that takes its prey to privacy,
the mouse's limp tail hanging like a shoelace from its mouth. . . .

(*CP*, p. 95)

At least one answer is that the development of an image indicates the poet's restraint and hence the amount of development is the index of how much there is to be restrained. In her essay on Wallace Stevens, Miss Moore says that "the testament to emotion is not volubility." [12] But the poem "Silence" makes that point: " 'The deepest feeling always shows itself in silence; / not in silence, but restraint.' "

Jacques Maritain has deplored the scrupulous attention Miss Moore pays to "the world of sensory perception," and suggests that her modesty should yield to the pressure of what exists within.[13] The style certainly does not arise from any failure in feelings or from a lack in their intensity; on occasion Miss Moore has in fact yielded to her feelings to produce less characteristic poems. These, when considered in the light of her usual style, are remarkable in the lack of attention paid to the texture of the images, in the lack of restraint in feeling, and in the use of the faculty of the imagination.

As we have seen, one must be on one's guard against making too easy a distinction between kinds of poems—as if the imagination worked exclusively in one kind and the fancy in the other, the one turning litmus red and the other, blue. In fact, both faculties may be at work in one poem. Thus, in "A Carriage from Sweden," a poem mostly in Miss Moore's characteristic fanciful manner, the metaphorical "split / pine fair hair" works in the mode of the imagination; for not only is the split pine white, clean, fresh, and sweet scented, it conjures

[12] Marianne Moore, *Predilections* (New York: Viking Press, 1955), p. 36.

[13] Jacques Maritain, *Creative Intuition in Art and Poetry* (New York: Pantheon Books, 1953), p. 249 note.

up ideas of hard natural living, toughness, satisfaction in these qualities, and so on. And the metaphor detracts from our clear visual impression of the object. All the same, it does seem valid to distinguish from the great majority certain poems in which the images are predominantly used for the ideas they give rise to. "In Distrust of Merits," "What are Years?" and "Bulwarked Against Fate" are distinguished from Miss Moore's other work in the following passage by Roy Harvey Pearce:

> . . . the poem ["What are Years?"] is made to *argue* its case; and the figurative language functions as a controlling similitude, like an afterthought which reinforces, not develops, its substantial concern. It is significant, I think, that Miss Moore came to publish such a poem and others like it . . . after she had established her reputation as a descriptive-meditative poet —in the 1940's and after. Such poems have, besides their intrinsic merit, that of guiding us into an understanding of her *oeuvre*. Truth in these poems *is* an Apollo Belvedere [an allusion to "In the Days of Prismatic Colour"], formal; but the quality of its formality is somewhat eased when they are placed in their proper context.[14]

In "What are Years?" occurs the image of the sea in a chasm, which

> . . .   struggling to be
> free and unable to be,
>   in its surrendering
>   finds its continuing.
>   (CP, p. 99)

This image, whose development through earlier poems Kenneth Burke has traced,[15] is shot through with idea and gives no sen-

---

[14] Roy Harvey Pearce, *The Continuity of American Poetry* (Princeton, N.J.: Princeton University Press, 1961), p. 372.
[15] Burke, *A Grammar of Motives,* pp. 492ff.

sation of the upsurge and collapse of the water. Similarly, the
other image in the poem, in the lines

> . . . The very bird,
>   grown taller as he sings, steels
> his form straight up . . .

gives no more sensory detail than that supplied in the mere
designations. Both images contribute to the idea that the limitation that apparently inhibits transpires to be a kind of strength.
Lloyd Frankenberg says, "The word 'steels' is the crux of the
poem. In its literal and figurative meanings the ideas of im-
prisonment and liberation meet. The bird, in his mighty singing,
triumphs over captivity; he *becomes* the bars that confined
him." [16] This illustrates the trafficking in ideas and the fusion
between images (though in fact the bars do not appear in the
poem) that characterizes the work of the imagination.

"In Distrust of Merits" manifests unrestrained feeling more
than any other poem of Miss Moore's. She herself is unwilling
to call it a poem: although truthful—"it is testimony—to the
fact that war is intolerable, and unjust"—it is "haphazard"; "as
form," she says, "what has it? It is just a protest—disjointed,
exclamatory. Emotion overpowered me. First this thought and
then that." [17] The images are used by imagination for ideas,
and one of the more interesting of these is that precise judgments and feelings are lost in a turbulence of sentimental feeling. The subject and manner are matched; it is, I suppose, an
example of imitative form.

> . . . O tumultuous
>   ocean lashed till small things go
> as they will, the mountainous
>   wave makes us who look, know
>
> depth. Lost at sea before they fought! . . .
>
> (*CP*, p. 135)

[16] Lloyd Frankenberg, "Meaning in Modern Poetry," *Saturday Review of Literature*, XXIX (March 23, 1946), 5.
[17] *A Marianne Moore Reader*, p. 261.

This passage reminds us of the sea in "A Grave,"

> . . . looking as if it were not that ocean in
>   which dropped things are bound to sink—
> in which if they turn and twist, it is neither with volition
>   nor consciousness.

But in "A Grave," as we have seen, the poet is busy to avoid looking on the sea and attends rather to the finite things at the periphery or on the surface. Here, on the other hand, she does look and pays for so doing by knowing depth: she becomes immersed in the welter of emotion in which small things— judgments and feelings based on detailed perceptions—"go / as they will." Those who fought were already "lost," because they had been overwhelmed by the sea, the turbulent sentimental feelings that accompany war and confuse individual judgments. The idea returns later in the poem in the lines " 'When a man is prey to anger, / he is moved by outside things. . . . ' "

Once again, the image is used for the idea and not for itself, and again the poem departs from Marianne Moore's characteristic style. As Browning illustrated in and by his "One Word More," artists and poets before Miss Moore have dropped out of their characteristic styles to speak their minds in another vein. But speculation arises as to why this poet in this poem should so depart and demonstrate her competence in the vein of Dame Edith Sitwell's later work. The emotions, she says, overpowered her. But why? She deals elsewhere with strong feelings in the other manner; and, as we have seen, "The deepest feeling always shows itself in . . . restraint." It does not seem quite reasonable to think of her indignation rising to such a pitch that she abandoned the restrained procedures and, as it were, simply sent in the Seventh Fleet. Is not this new style rather a symbolic act of dispossession and self-deprivation insofar as it is a sacrifice of the advantages of the other style, which is an integral part of the poet's personality? The sentiment that

> . . . I must
> fight till I have conquered in myself what
> causes war . . .

calls for a sweeping distrust and questioning of *all* one's merits, including one's skill at controlling feeling. Perhaps in the face of the great catastrophe, the exercise of her habitual artistic strategy looked to her like a precious interest in personal cleverness.

IV

I have attended so far almost exclusively to the images in the poems of Miss Moore and to the operation of the fancy which permits them some independent development for the sake of restraint and precision of feeling and judgment. In connection with these same ends, however, other features of the poetry call for discussion: the quotations, which enjoy the same status as the imagery as sharp-edged entities; certain rhetorical constructions which contribute to restraint; and, on the other hand, the structural form, which tends to counterbalance the effects of these other features.

The quotation, like the image, Marianne Moore tends to present rather than to use, treating it as if it were simply an item from the heterogeneous objective world like the miscellaneous flora, fauna, jewels, and fabrics that supply her with texture. The extent of her portrayal of animals is due to the fact that, being less complicated than humans, they are more clearly self-expressive; similarly, the apt quotation is left untouched and presented as being clearly self-expressive in itself: "I've always felt," she says, "that if a thing had been said in the *best* way, how can you say it better?" [18] Thus, as with the image so with the quotation, she presents as much of it as appreciation and more than mere relevance demands. And naturally she gives credit. If, in connection with quotations,

---

[18] *Ibid.*, p. 260.

we think of "The Waste Land," we observe that Eliot's are much more closely built into the poem and are therefore usually modified, as Miss Moore's are usually not. Sometimes, but not always, Miss Moore's quotations are a means of controlling feeling, like the elaboration of an image or the proliferation of new ones. Certain passages in inverted commas for which no acknowledgment is made are, I suppose, the poet's own expressions, given by this means the quality of quotations and thus disinfected of the feeling that might otherwise attach to them. Or, as Bernard F. Engel says, they serve "to hold an observation up for examination and celebration" and they "subdue any impression of assertiveness." [19] Inverted commas occasionally reduce the immodesty of parading a flashy conceit. For instance, " 'born / of nature and of art' " (*CP*, p. 23) and " 'lit with piercing glances into the life of things' " (*CP*, p. 55) are disinfected of the taint of preciosity by the quotation marks. This is not a frequent usage; but such passages set off in inverted commas, whether or not they are the poet's own words, may thus supply a tonal effect which is almost precisely what Hulme described in his remark on classicism: "If you say an extravagant thing . . . yet there is always conveyed in some way at the end an impression of yourself standing outside it, and not quite believing it, or consciously putting it forward as a flourish." [20] Marianne Moore "would laugh," says William Carlos Williams, "with a gesture of withdrawal after making some able assertion as if you yourself had said it and she were agreeing with you." [21] Inverted commas, then, as well as indicating borrowed material, are directing the reader to set the words off from their context and giving them the tonal effect that words similarly enclosed have in Henry James. As R. P.

[19] Bernard F. Engel, *Marianne Moore* (New York: Twayne, 1964), pp. 29, 56.

[20] T. E. Hulme, *Speculations*, ed. Herbert Read (New York: Harcourt, Brace and Company, 1924), p. 120.

[21] "Marianne Moore" (1948), *Selected Essays of William Carlos Williams* (New York: Random House, 1954), p. 292.

Blackmur says, they "indicate a special or ironic sense in the material enclosed or as a kind of minor italicization, they are used as boundaries for units of association which cannot be expressed by grammar and syntax." [22]

The inverted commas in Miss Moore's verse frequently soften the full impact of the rhetorical meaning of the words. Another feature of the poems with the same effect is the obliquity of some of the statements. Often the statement is not made rhetorically at all but presented as an image, like the sign in "The Steeple-Jack" which says "Danger" and so labels the sentimental approach or like the statement about the killing effect of art embodied in the image of the swan that constitutes almost the whole of "No Swan So Fine." [23] There is also, however, the kind of obliquity in which the statement being made by the poem is offered as the speech or thought of a person or an animal or as what the animal reveals by its acts, as if not the poet herself but someone or something else were "the central intelligence." Very frequently constructions like the following occur: "the amateur is told; / 'mistakes are irreparable . . .'" (*CP*, p. 23); "Know that it [truth] will be there when it says, / 'I shall be there when the wave has gone by'" (*CP*, p. 49);

> . . . he revealed
> a formula . . .
> . . . the power of relinquishing
>   what one would keep; that is freedom
>   (*CP*, p. 143);

> wound themselves as if they knew love
> is the only fortress
> strong enough to trust to
>   (*CP*, p. 123);

"compelling audience to / the remark that it is better to be

[22] R. P. Blackmur, *Form and Value in Modern Poetry* (Garden City, N.Y.: Anchor Books, 1957), p. 227. See also p. 240.
[23] See Pearce, *The Continuity of American Poetry*, pp. 370–71.

forgotten than to be remembered too violently" (*SP*, p. 42);
"It knows that if a nomad may have dignity, / Gibraltar has
had more—" (*CP*, p. 88); "exclaiming . . . When you take
my time, you take / something I had meant to use . . ." (*CP*,
p. 61).

The virtuous restraint that results from Miss Moore's use of
images, the unassertiveness that comes from the use of quotations and oblique statements is balanced against the form of
the poems: for form, says Miss Moore, "is the outward equivalent of a determining inner conviction." [24] Form manifests itself in her poetry as the over-all shape of a poem achieved by
symmetries of sounds and meanings and also as the local fusing
of these two in the expressiveness of her sound effects. Either
of these achievements is, I suppose, a notification of the poet's
conviction. The latter is often unobtrusive and subtle and is
worth demonstrating: in a brief look at parts of "The Pangolin"
and of "The Jerboa" we can see something of the eloquence
of rhythms and rhymes which will serve as an example of the
expressive use this poet makes of the formal elements of
sound.

In "The Pangolin" (*CP*, pp. 118–21) the corresponding
lines in each of the nine stanzas are generally of an equal
number of syllables; lines 1 and 3 rhyme, more or less. But
within this regular pattern there is a variety of sound, and it
is this that is expressive. The poem is about grace: the possession
of grace requires that one be the master and not the slave of
time; and grace is associated with sculpture, in iron or stone,
and with hands. The pangolin is an ungraceful animal in the
usual sense of the word, and its description as such is aided
by the use of words clogged with consonants, especially stops,
and the use of internal rhymes, alliteration, and assonance.
The three places where the poet likens it to an artichoke will
serve to illustrate:

[24] Friar and Brinnin, *Modern Poetry*, p. 522.

. . . This near artichoke with head and legs and grit-equipped
gizzard. . .

.   .   .   .
. . .   the flattened sword-
edged leafpoints on the tail and artichoke set leg- and body-plates
quivering violently when it retaliates. . . .

.   .   .   .
. . .   this ant- and stone-swallowing uninjurable
artichoke which simpletons thought a living fable. . . .

The awkward and slow movement of such words and word
combinations as these conveys a sense of gracelessness. But it
is not simply this parallelism—awkward movement of verse
equals awkward animal—that form is effecting. The stumbling
movement of such lines as those quoted serves as a foil for
other more liquid lines which, come upon with the slight shock
of unusual ease, warn us that they point to something different
about the animal which its appearance belies. In the following
two passages, remarkable for their fluidity, the themes of grace,
which is associated with hands, and freedom from time are
respectively introduced:

> . . . [he] endures
>   exhausting solitary trips through unfamiliar ground at night,
>   returning before sunrise; stepping in the moonlight,
>   on the moonlight peculiarly. . . .

The fluid effect of these labials is perhaps only fully felt
when the passage is read in context. It closes with a reference
to hands:

> . . . that the outside
>   edges of his hands may bear the weight and save the claws
> for digging.

In the passage suggesting mastery over time, there are labials
and one line (the second one quoted below) in a perfect pattern of alternating stresses:

> . . . he can thus darken
> Sun and moon and day and night and man and beast
>   each with a splendour
>   which man in all his vileness cannot
>   set aside; each with an excellence!

It is not, once again, simply an easy equivalence—grace (elegance) equals grace (the gift)—that is at work here: the formal elements, the labials and the relatively regular lines, in *association* with "hands" and the motif of mastering time, *together* express the idea of grace.

Similarly, in "The Jerboa" (*CP*, pp. 16–22) there is more to the two sets of couplets than their easy equivalence to the animal's double leap. Lloyd Frankenberg writes,

> The rhymed couplets that begin and end each stanza—some regular; others rhyming an *on-* with an *off*-beat—re-create the double jump of the animal. The intervening section in each stanza suggests the poise of the jerboa gathering itself for the next spring.
>
> This springy verse-form has been preparing us, through the preceding twenty-five stanzas, for the three 'leaps' [in the last two stanzas] that bring the jerboa home.[25]

There is no doubt that Marianne Moore sometimes makes form serve this imitative purpose. It does so again, for example, in a passage in "The Plumet Basilisk," where the regular stanza form is disrupted and the rhymes emphasize the odd line lengths that imitate the action:

>   wide water-bug strokes,
>   in jerks which express
>   a regal and excellent awkwardness,
>
>   the plumet portrays
>   mythology's wish
>   to be interchangeably man and fish. . . .
>   (*CP*, p. 29)

[25] Lloyd Frankenberg, "The Imaginary Garden," *Quarterly Review of Literature*, IV (1948), 202.

But occasionally she is playing a more subtle game. In "The Jerboa," the form is not only imitating the sense but is part of a more comprehensive tactic. The first part of the poem, "Too Much," describes the lavish art, so-called, of the Romans and Egyptians. For both these races, art and living are contrived and are dependent upon the enslavement of men or animals, and the poet denigrates such art. The second part of the poem presents, in contrast to these races, Jacob and the jerboa: Jacob has an immediate grasp on reality: he does not act vicariously—his own natural hand holds a cudgel; he is at home with the stones. And vision is vouchsafed to him:

> Jacob saw, cudgel staff
> in claw-hand—steps of air and air angels; his
> friends were the stones. . . .

He provides a contrast to the king in the first part, who is separated from reality and whose servants will do his living for him:

> . . . Those who tended flower-
> beds and stables were like the king's cane in the
> form of a hand. . . .

Like Jacob, whose friends were the stones, the jerboa is natural: "It / honours the sand by assuming its colour." Its art is its leap; this is natural and free and the poet praises it.

And yet art *is* artificial and contrived. The leap of the jerboa and the animal itself are rendered in the poem in terms of artificialities: the former is "like the uneven notes / of the Bedouin flute"; the latter is a "three-cornered smooth-working Chippendale / claw." Likewise, of course, the artist is not free or (a favorite theme in Miss Moore) is only free when a slave to the proper, self-imposed controls, the apparent inhibitions which may, as we have seen, prove to be opportunities. And so, just as the natural animal is rendered in the unnatural simile and metaphor of art and artifact, throughout the poem the couplet, the artificial control, makes its own oblique statement countering the main statement, which is that art is free. The poem opens with a paradox:

> A Roman had an
> artist, a freedman,
>   contrive a cone . . . ;

the artist was a "freedman," but he worked to the bidding of the Roman. The couplet, the formal constraint, is extending one arm of this paradox; so that while the rhetoric is dispraising compulsory artificial art and praising the natural and real, the form is implicitly showing that the poet—this poet, anyway—is not really free or natural either. The play here between naturalness and artificiality reminds one of Robert Duncan's remark about this style: "Marianne Moore's natural style, an artifice / where sense may abound." [26]

Needless to say, other poems would show other and often less complicated functions of the sounds. For instance, in the fable "Bitch and Friend," the rippling half rhymes and assonances of the opening lines supply some of the sense of the wheedling Machiavellian trickery of the bitch:

> A bitch who approached each hutch with a frown,
> Since a-shiver to shelter an imminent litter,
> Crouched perplexed till she'd coaxed from a vexed benefactor
> A lean-to as a loan and in it lay down. [27]

Once she is in, it becomes difficult for the owner to regain possession. At the end of the description of the incident, in a slow rhythm and without the internal rhymes, the bitch's intentions are unmasked in straight declaration. There is no cleverness or trickery in the verse here:

[26] Robert Duncan, "The Maiden," *The Opening of the Field* (New York: Grove Press, 1960), p. 29.
[27] *The Fables of La Fontaine,* trans. Marianne Moore (New York, 1964), p. 40. Miss Moore has said that this poem and one other are her favorites among the fables (Engel, *Marianne Moore,* p. 128).

> "I'm prepared to depart and with my family
>   If you will turn us out of doors."
> The puppies were by then tall curs.

But here, surely, as often elsewhere, the sound effects of the opening are to be attributed at least in part simply to the poet's own delight in manipulating them, to her gusto.

These examples are intended to show that from sounds and sound patterns Miss Moore derives effects which contribute to meaning. More obvious, however, as the index of conviction is the "patterned arrangement" in which she says she tends to write[28]—the structural shape given by repetition of rhyme sounds and rhythms, and by reciprocation of sense. Not all Miss Moore's verse is so structured, however; there are poems in free verse in which a phrase may have the same freedom to develop as the imagery characteristically has. Robert Creeley once pointed to two of his poems that face each other in the volume *For Love,* saying that in the first the phrasing had not escaped the control of the rhythm whereas in the second it had:

> And I have left nothing behind in leaving
> because I killed him
>
> And because I hit him over the head with a stick
> there is nothing I laugh at.[29]

Here the rhythm controls the phrase; in the following it does not:

> If quietly and like another time
> there is the passage of an unexpected thing:
>
> to look at it is more
> than it was. God knows
>
> nothing is competent nothing is
> all there is. The unsure

[28] Friar and Brinnin, *Modern Poetry,* p. 522.
[29] Robert Creeley, "The Crow," *For Love: Poems 1950–1960* (New York: Scribner's, 1962), p. 30.

egoist is not
good for himself.[30]

Such a distinction would not be easy to make between phrases in Marianne Moore. Certainly, the phrases of poems in free verse are not necessarily free of rhythmic control, as some of the lines quoted above from "An Octopus" will readily show. But, on the other hand, the control exerted by the rhythm is light.

This we will find to be so with other formal features in the poetry. The form, which is the index of conviction, is, as such, in opposition to those elements in the poem that work toward tentativeness and restraint; and perhaps the imagery is permitted its individual waywardness because conviction is safely embodied in the structure. But the form, whose function is to press home what fancy is too shy to assert, is itself relatively unassertive. We are often unaware of it. Syllabic verse, of which especially in her earlier work Miss Moore has made much use, having no accents does not provide a strong form. Its basic rhythmic power and beauty, according to Robert Beloof, is in the firm sense of the length of the line which becomes a rhythmic unit used contrapuntally against the rhythm of the phrase. But, he says, Miss Moore uses this minimally.[31] She has spoken of being governed by "the pull of the sentence" as a formal principle;[32] but earlier she had said, "if a long sentence with dependent clauses seems obscure, one can break it into shorter units by imagining into what phrases it would fall as conversation." [33] So the formal tends to become informal.

Then again, rhyme, which gives a sense of form, is frequently inaudible in Miss Moore's poems, though it is visible. In "A Carriage From Sweden," for instance, how rarely if at all we

[30] "The Immoral Proposition," *ibid.*, p. 31.
[31] Robert Beloof, "Prosody and Tone: The 'Mathematics' of Marianne Moore," *Kenyon Review*, XX (Winter, 1958), 120.
[32] *A Marianne Moore Reader*, p. 263.
[33] Moore, *Predilections*, p. 3.

hear the rhymes between the third and final syllables in the first line and the first and last in the last line of each stanza. Or in "England," if the end rhymes between lines 1 and 3 of each stanza are just perceptible, how audible is the end rhyme or half rhyme between these lines and the last of the next stanza or next-but-one? On a number of occasions, on the other hand, rhyme does serve to bind a poem together; and one observes, though not as an unbreakable rule by any means, that the rhyme, the tissue of reciprocal sounds, is closer when there is less reciprocation in other features of the poem. A descriptive poem such as "Peter" needs no supplementary mechanism like the very limited rhyme it possesses to make it cohere; but where the various statements of the poem or the various images are disjunctive, or where there is paradox, or in difficult poems where the poet is getting subtle nuances out of the images, rhymes are more frequent or the rhyme scheme is more regular and, often, more artificially contrived.

We have already seen how the disjunctive images of "In the Public Garden" are united by rhyme—"a camel / from Hamadan, Iran." In "The Fish" the rhyme pattern is carefully, artificially adhered to; the poem is difficult partly because its images are derived from optical illusion and partly because it deals in open paradox. That fish wade through jade, that barnacles encrust the side of the wave, and that water drives a wedge of iron through the cliff are illusions that result from the refraction of water. The difficulty thus caused is less than that of the paradox with which the poem closes:

> . . . the chasm-side is
>
> dead.
> Repeated
>   evidence has proved that it can live
>   on what can not revive
>   its youth. . . .
>
> (CP, p. 38)

The structure is held firm in the rhymes, however, as some trees live only in their bark. Similarly, a stanza scheme in which first and last lines rhyme may serve to bring to order—strictly speaking, to a spurious unity—a poem such as "The Hero" and compensate for the broad modulation and the heterogeneous imagery. Or again, tight rhymes, couplets in fact, bind together the wayward ideas in "An Egyptian Pulled Glass Bottle in the Shape of a Fish."

This poem is complex; it is mentioned by Louis Zukofsky as an example of objectivist poetry in the issue of *Poetry*[34] devoted to this mode, but the reasons for its having been included are obscure. The complexity of the poem centers around the word "perpendicularity" in the first of the two stanzas:

> Here we have thirst
> And patience, from the first,
> > And art, as in a wave held up for us to see
> > In its essential perpendicularity. . . .
>
> > > (CP, p. 90)

Is it the bottle or art or the wave that is held up in its essential perpendicularity? It is all three. First, the bottle is naturally and functionally perpendicular. Second, the wave, a favorite image in Miss Moore, is not a wave when it is not perpendicular; and yet its perpendicularity—its quiddity—is a momentary thing only, maintained in a momentary equilibrium, one may say, by various opposing forces. Thirdly, art is similarly the result of a momentary equilibrium of contrary forces, two of which are "thirst" and "patience." In the process of art, the fish which is essentially *not* perpendicular might seem to have lost its nature and been frozen into an art form. The poet implies otherwise in the second and last stanza:

> Not brittle but
> Intense—the spectrum, that

[34] Louis Zukofsky, "Program: 'Objectivists' 1931," *Poetry*, XXXVII (February, 1931), 268.

Spectacular and nimble animal the fish,
Whose scales turn aside the sun's sword with their polish.

The animal has not been lost to brittleness in a frozen art form, but one aspect of it, its spectrum-like color, has been intensified by the iridescence of the glass of the bottle.

The concentration in this eight-line poem of these widely disparate and ramifying ideas is brought about, or at least assisted, by the rhyme, which serves to bring all into unity. That the rhymes perform this sort of function in complex poems seems clear enough, even though other poems which are not especially complex may also have neat rhymes: a simple descriptive poem like "The Wood-Weasel," which has no serious complexities, is bound together by couplets that are even tighter than those in "An Egyptian Pulled Glass Bottle"; and the translations of La Fontaine's fables are closely rhymed, although they are, of course, adequately unified by their narratives. In another poem one single rhyme supplied by the last word binds together disparate elements: "Voracities and Verities Sometimes are Interacting" closes with the lines "One may be pardoned, yes I know / one may, for love undying" (*CP*, p. 147). The last word, with "trying" at the end of the first stanza, forms the strongest rhyme in this short poem. And its effect is like the last element in a periodic sentence, sealing, as it were, what has gone before. Rhyme, which is part of the measure of Miss Moore's conviction, may serve also to buy the reader's.

Rhyme is not characteristically assertive in Miss Moore; she states that concealed rhyme is better than open.[35] Often the rhyme that *is* asserted is a bad rhyme and a point of wit. The rhymes, for instance, in "The Arctic Ox (or Goat)" which, playing on the association of the word *cordial* with earlier comments on warmth, ends as follows:

. . .   If we can't be cordial
to these creatures' fleece,

[35] Moore, *Predilections,* p. 8.

> I think that we deserve to freeze. . . .
>
> > (*Dragon,* p. 24)

Or the lyrical rhyming in "Spenser's Ireland,"

> the guillemot
> > so neat and the hen
> of the heath and the
> linnet spinet-sweet,
>
> > (*CP,* p. 115)

draw light ridicule upon aspects of Ireland by which the poet is most demonstrably not going to be taken in!

Thus, in general, form which asserts the conviction is by no means allowed to dominate: the instinct which scrambles the feeling through associated images controls likewise the notification of the conviction. All these techniques I take to be caveats and guards indicative of the poet's terrible sense that truth is a high hill, unassailable by the crude advance, and that one "about it and about must go."

✍ CHAPTER IV ੧

WILLIAM CARLOS WILLIAMS

LIKE MISS MOORE, William Carlos Williams depends very much for his poetry upon his clear vision of the real world. She, as we have seen, resorts to a minute study of individual images to preserve herself from the danger of the grand poetic gesture. Williams, throughout most of his career, keeps close to the concrete world: he may turn away from it temporarily at the time of his repudiation of imagist and objectivist verse and work a little with abstraction and learned reference,[1] but with the newspaper clippings in *Paterson* or later the solid chunks of reported fact in "The Desert Music" he comes back to keep himself within reach of reality, like an Antaeus who knows the source of his strength. He is faithful, too, in his poetry to the phrasing of speech, and he is anxious to draw out and use its rhythms; and he is also faithful to the unformalized movements of his own thought. These fidelities establish him as the forefather of open verse: in the long poem his verse is directed to an end, but it is unconfined by structural requirements im-

[1] See Louis L. Martz, "William Carlos Williams: On the Road to *Paterson*," *Poetry New York*, No. 4 (1951), pp. 31–32.

posed from without; it is open to digression, if new meanings or new potential meanings should arise in the course; it is willing at any point to sacrifice the reader's expectations to express the fullness of experience or artistic coherence for the sake of encompassing a realistic complexity.

His poetry reflects our world in its images, but only to a meager extent does it give that world prismatic color; it recreates our experiences but shapes and orders them only minimally; it speaks to the life we know, but does not render it in the lovely distortion of art. Such poetic activities as occur in traditional and more opulent work are eschewed out of the poet's uncompromising devotion to the world he knows in his sensory receptors; "the effect of a 'thing,'" as he says to Louis Zukofsky, "surpasses all thought about it." [2]

His belief in poetry and the claims he made for it were as exorbitant as Shelley's. "We begin to see," he says, speaking of his patients in the *Autobiography,* "that the underlying meaning of all they want to tell us and have always failed to communicate is the poem, the poem which their lives are being lived to realize." [3] Again in the *Autobiography,* "the reconstruction of the poem" is "one of the major occupations of the intelligence in our day" (p. 332). In "The Desert Music," he says,

> Only the poem
> only the made poem, to get said what must
> be said. . . .[4]

In "Asphodel, That Greeny Flower,"

> It is difficult
> to get the news from poems

[2] William Carlos Williams, *Selected Letters* (New York: Random House, 1957), p. 102. Hereafter *SL.*

[3] *The Autobiography of William Carlos Williams* (New York: Random House, 1951), pp. 361–62.

[4] William Carlos Williams, *Pictures from Brueghel and Other Poems* (Norfolk, Conn.: New Directions, 1962), p. 109. Hereafter *PB.*

                    yet men die miserably every day
                              for lack
          of what is found there.

                                        (*PB,* pp. 161–62)

And in *Paterson,* Book II, the strongest claim of all:

                    . . . without invention
                    nothing lies under the witch-hazel
                    bush. . . .[5]

His concept of what poetry was, however, Williams never
exactly, directly, or completely expressed; and as far as one can
tell, it would by its very nature have resisted definition, if only
because his whole career was a series of poetical experiments.
But from his various dicta and from the poetry itself we may
deduce broad poetic principles which will, I believe, reveal in
part what he was about.

                                I

    The first principle is that Williams works by fancy rather
than imagination. Fancy is associated with the control of feeling, as it is in the poems of Miss Moore; but it is a strategy
used generally throughout: images are sharply presented; there
are no "smears of mystery," to use for his own work the phrase
he used for Miss Moore's; and neither the images nor the
larger elements in the poems are made to blend with one another. One of Williams' earliest statements about technique
appears in the prologue to *Kora in Hell,* which introduces the
book and provides both the artistic rationale for such a species
of literature and Williams' motives in writing it. The book consists of twenty-seven improvisations in prose, written during
the war when "everything [he] wanted to see live and thrive
was being deliberately murdered in the name of church and
state" (*Autobiography,* p. 158). Each improvisation is divided

    [5] William Carlos Williams, *Paterson* (Norfolk, Conn.: New Directions,
1963), p. 65.

into three parts, each part varying in length from about twenty-five words to over five hundred. They are all spontaneous observations, or ideas, or even small narratives rendered in imagery, or brief streams of consciousness. Here and there among them is an italicized passage—a "brief moralistic statement" as Williams calls it—which, he says, "interprets" the imagery or whatever of the preceding passage; but it is sometimes less of an interpretation than an additional statement in a similar style counterpointing the earlier. Also, there are comments in the prologue upon various parts of the improvisations, certain of which are quoted from below. Here is a sampling from one improvisation, Number XXIII:

> Baaaa! Ba-ha-ha-ha-ha-ha-ha-ha! *Bebe esa purga.* It is the goats of Santo Domingo talking. *Bebe esa purga!* Bebeesapurga! And the answer is: *Yo no lo quiero beber!* Yonoloquierobeber!

The italicized snatches of what is presumably the real language of men mean respectively, "Drink that laxative" and "I will not drink it." In the interpretation that follows, Williams speaks of the difficulty of writing poetry: *"It is something of a matter of sleight of hand . . . it's a kind of alchemy of form, a deft bottling of a fermenting language."* The second part of the improvisation and its interpretation are as follows:

> The red huckleberry bushes running miraculously along the ground among the trees everywhere, except where the land's tilled, these keep her from that tiredness the earth's touch lays up under the soles of feet. She runs beyond the wood   follows the swiftest along the roads   laughing among the birch clusters   her face in the yellow leaves   the curls before her eyes   her mouth half open. This is a person in particular   there where they have her—and I have only a wraith in the birch trees.

> ――――――――

> *It is not the lusty bodies of the nearly naked girls in the shows about town, nor the blare of the popular tunes that*

make money for the manager. The girls can be procured rather more easily in other ways and the music is dirt cheap. It is that this meat is savored with a strangeness which never loses its fresh taste to generation after generation, either of dancers or those who watch. It is beauty escaping, spinning up over the heads, blown out at the overtaxed vents by the electric fans.[6]

The third part of the improvisation is itself in italics; it describes the cheap prints that embellish the walls of poor and sentimental households. Some of them bear words pertaining to love, which are appropriate enough "when the bed is new and the young couple spend the long winter nights there in delightful seclusion" but which later, after childbirth, are ironic.

This much of one improvisation of the book must serve to illustrate the process for which the prologue provides commentary. Before considering it as an example of the working of the fancy, I wish to look in some detail at what seems to me to be the most important passage of the prologue, bearing in mind that the prologue was written to accompany a series of spontaneous, experimental pieces, completely unplanned, jotted down from day to day—every day, Williams says, "be it nine in the evening or three in the morning"—and published, albeit with much thrown out, without the change of a word.

In the passage from the prologue that I wish to quote at length, Williams speaks of the "imaginative category," which proves to be the product of the fancy:

The true value is that peculiarity which gives an object a character by itself. The associational or sentimental value is the false. Its imposition is due to lack of imagination, to an easy lateral sliding. The attention has been held too rigid on the one plane instead of following a more flexible, jagged resort. It is to loosen the attention, my attention since I occupy part

<hr>

[6] William Carlos Williams, *Kora in Hell* (San Francisco, Calif.: City Lights Books, 1964), pp. 72–73.

of the field, that I write these improvisations. Here I clash with Wallace Stevens.

The imagination goes from one thing to another. Given many things of nearly totally divergent natures but possessing one-thousandth part of a quality in common, provided that be new, distinguished, these things belong in an imaginative category and not in a gross natural array. To me this is the gist of the whole matter. It is easy to fall under the spell of a certain mode, especially if it be remote of origin, leaving thus certain of its members essential to a reconstruction of its significance permanently lost in an impenetrable mist of time. But the thing that stands eternally in the way of really good writing is always one: the virtual impossibility of lifting to the imagination those things which lie under the direct scrutiny of the senses, close to the nose. It is this difficulty that sets a value upon all works of art and makes them a necessity. The senses witnessing what is immediately before them in detail see a finality which they cling to in despair, not knowing which way to turn. Thus the so-called natural or scientific array becomes fixed, the walking devil of modern life. He who even nicks the solidity of this apparition does a piece of work superior to that of Hercules when he cleaned the Augean stables.[7]

The reader may feel he is on a darkling plain where ignorant metaphors clash by night: the "imposition" of false values is due to "lateral sliding" because attention has been held "too rigid"; a "certain mode" has "members" lost in a "mist of time." But, if I interpret it right, this passage does demonstrate how Williams departs from a more familiar, earlier poetic and particularly from that of Coleridge. It comes fairly early in his career (1920), but by and large the ideas it expresses remain with him: when some thirty years later, in *Paterson*, Book IV (p. 208), he opposes "antagonistic cooperation" to love, he is speaking in the same vein.

[7] *Selected Essays of William Carlos Williams* (New York: Random House, 1954), pp. 11–12. Hereafter *SE*.

The statement is concerned with a way of looking at the world by means of which an object will reveal its true value. The true value is not revealed when, by association or sentimentality, the object always calls forth the idea—one stereotyped response. The attention must be shaken out of this fixed posture by the imagination. Representations of entirely disparate parts of the world, Williams says, belong in an "imaginative category" by virtue of each possessing only one-thousandth part of its nature in common with the others. The gathering of images into an imaginative category will preclude us from making a stereotyped response to each; and the context releases each object from its natural, dull, scientific "meaning."

Part of this sounds oddly like Coleridge: Williams wants to lift to the imagination those everyday phenomena "which lie under the direct scrutiny of the senses"; the imagination, for Coleridge, was among other things the agency by which "Mr. Wordsworth . . . was . . . to give the charm of novelty to things of every day" and direct the mind's attention "to the loveliness and wonders of the world before us." This is exactly Williams' intention and sometimes his effect over and over again in his poetry: imagination, he says, is a faculty which makes use of reality and yet presents it as detached.[8] This kinship with Wordsworth's intentions (or those Coleridge attributed to him) will be worth bearing in mind when we consider Williams as a romantic. And yet Williams with his reverence for actuality would never have spoken, as Coleridge does with his ulterior motives, of the "modifying colours of the imagination." And the world before Williams is not selected as Wordsworth's was: in fact, in "Notes in Diary Form" in which he shows the reader what vivid untidy chunks of realism are to be enjoyed adjacent to the Ajax Aniline Dye Works in Fairfield, he sneers at a popular habit Wordsworth would have approved

[8] See William Carlos Williams, *Spring and All* (Contact Publishing Co., no place, n.d.), p. 34.

—taking the car out into the country, "To 'nature' to breathe her good air. Jesus Christ" (*SE*, p. 66).

It is from Coleridge's use of imagery, however, that Williams' practice is sharply distinct. The imaginative category does not find in its members such an unlimited list of similarities as those which relate images under the influence of the Coleridgean imagination; they need only have one-thousandth part of their natures in common. "Although it is a quality of the imagination that it seeks to place together those things which have a common relationship," says Williams in another passage in the prologue, "yet the coining of similes is a pastime of very low order, depending as it does upon a nearly vegetable coincidence. Much more keen is that power which discovers in things those inimitable particles of dissimilarity to all other things which are the peculiar perfections of the thing in question" (*SE*, p. 16). Nor is there any blending and fusion of the images in Williams' category; there is indeed an effort to avoid just that process that Coleridge looked for as the function of the imagination. The expression of esteem in the passage above for the power that discovers the haecceity of things is shortly followed by an analogy:

> . . . one does not attempt by the ingenuity of the joiner to blend the tones of the oboe with the violin. On the contrary the perfections of the two instruments are emphasized by the joiner; no means is neglected to give to each the full color of its perfections. It is only the music of the instruments which is joined and that not by the woodworker but by the composer, by virtue of the imagination [*SE*, p. 16].

Nor is the imagination a "shaping power" in Williams. The clash with Wallace Stevens referred to above is due to Stevens' advocacy of the fixed point of view. "Given a fixed point of view, realistic, imagistic or what you will," Stevens says in a letter quoted in the prologue, "everything adjusts itself to that point of view." Stevens is complaining of the casualness and miscellaneousness of Williams' *Al Que Quiere*; but Williams accepts the criticism as holding good for each of the improvisations in *Kora in Hell* "if not for the *oeuvre* as a whole." The improvisations are not governed by anything so rigid that "everything adjusts itself" to it; Stevens is objecting to a flexibility at the heart of Williams' notion of the imagination, which seems to work for him as an *un*shaping power, freeing the mind from any single scheme, such as that which the obsessive spirit of Coleridge's imagination imposes upon phenomena. Williams uses no blue guitar, upon which "things as they are" are changed. Imagination in his sense, then, does not blunt the edge of the images and shape them into an overwhelming coherence; it goes rather, like Coleridge's fancy, "from one thing to another."

To turn from the prologue back to the book itself: the example above from *Kora in Hell* may now be seen to illustrate the fanciful relationship between items in an imaginative category. The feature common to all parts is the slightest: each part in its own way speaks to a kind of beauty that can only with difficulty and perhaps loss be brought into expression. The first part is an effort to catch and preserve alive on paper a snatch of living speech, and the interpretation renders this difficult operation as "a deft bottling of a fermenting language." In the second part, the touch of the earth would depress the spirit-like girl, who is to some people a real girl but to the poet "a wraith in the birch trees"; the italicized interpretation describes the attraction of the strippers as that of "beauty escaping." The third part describes the ultimately ironic effect of a tender sentiment when it is congealed into permanent expression. Each individual presentation makes a point scarcely or not at all; together, in juxtaposition, by interaction, a point is conveyed, the above articulation of which is, of course, necessarily crude.

On account of the "one-thousandth part of a quality in common" between the passages in *Kora*, they may not be considered to react together in what Philip Wheelwright calls a purely diaphoric manner, in which a meaning completely absent from any of the individual elements emerges from their juxtaposition.[9] But although not pure, a diaphoric process is consistently in operation both here in *Kora* and elsewhere in Williams' poems: elements fancifully related, which do not blend with one another, produce meaning by their juxtaposition, the principle insisted upon by Ford Madox Ford as supporting "the whole fabric of modern art." [10] The process might be illustrated early and late, the fanciful similarity between elements being more or less manifest. Sometimes the juxtaposition of elements produces a theme, as in the above improvisation and in *Paterson*; sometimes, as in "An Elegy for D. H. Lawrence" [11] or in the book *Yes, Mrs. Williams,* it produces a character. "Asphodel, That Greeny Flower" (*PB*, pp. 153–82), proceeding by elements fancifully juxtaposed, produces the theme of love and also reveals the character of the poet.

Finally, there is in *Kora in Hell* one part of an improvisation which is perhaps a deliberate allegory of the principle of juxtaposition:

> *There are divergences of humor that cannot be reconciled. A young woman of much natural grace of manner and very apt at a certain color of lie is desirous of winning the good graces of one only slightly her elder but nothing comes of her exer-*

[9] Philip Wheelwright offers the following as a rare example of purely diaphoric juxtaposition:

> My country 'tis of thee
> Sweet land of liberty
> Higgledy-piggledy my black hen.

He says that "in this combination of elements, and by their combination alone, the writer manages to convey what is not expressed by either of the parts" (*Metaphor and Reality* [Bloomington: Indiana University Press, 1962], p. 78).

[10] Quoted by Hugh Kenner, *Gnomon* (New York: McDowell Obolensky, 1958), p. 146 note. On juxtaposition in a short poem by Williams, see Linda Wagner, *The Poems of William Carlos Williams: A Critical Study* (Middletown, Conn.: Wesleyan University Press, 1964), p. 40 note.

[11] *The Collected Earlier Poems of William Carlos Williams* (Norfolk, Conn.: New Directions, 1951), pp. 361–64. Hereafter *CEP*.

*tions. Instead of yielding to a superficial advantage she finally
gives up the task and continues in her own delicate bias of
peculiar and beautiful design much to the secret delight of
the on-looker who is thus regaled by the spectacle of two exquisite and divergent natures playing one against the other*
[p. 78].

II

The most significant thing about Williams' poetry is, I believe, that he worked according to the fancy and not the
imagination as Coleridge used this word. The next principle I
wish to consider is that the poetic act in Williams consists in
setting a part of the real world in a new context and giving it
thereby a new role and possibly a new meaning. The effect of
the juxtaposition of images or snatches of idiomatic speech or
descriptions of actions may be thought of in this way: they are
endowed with meaning or new meaning by the context. Thus,
for instance, the image of the wraith-like girl in *Kora* means
something in its context in the improvisation that it would not
or would scarcely mean alone. It will be useful to think of
juxtaposition as part of this broader technique.

Williams suggests this as a poetic principle in his *Autobiography:* after quoting the long passage from Charles Olson's essay
on projective verse as an "example" of "the reconstruction of
the poem as one of the major occupations of the intelligence in
our day," he relates an anecdote which gives us some indication
of what kind of object the poem is. Charles Sheeler, the painter,
took over the gardener's cottage of a destroyed estate and made
it his house. Williams gives a few details: the willfully destroyed, sixty-room building of the former Lowe estate, the
barns, the maples, purple beeches, and so forth. Then he interprets the allegory: "The poem is our objective, the secret at
the heart of the matter—as Sheeler's small house, reorganized,
is the heart of the gone estate of the Lowes—the effect of a
fortune founded on tobacco. . . ." The artist took "the one rare
object remaining more or less intact . . . and proceeded to live

in it. . . . It is ourselves we organize in this way not against the past or for the future or even for survival but for integrity of understanding to insure persistence, to give the mind its stay" (*Autobiography*, pp. 332–33).

Only the one implication which will be useful in reconstructing the nature of poetry need be drawn out of this anecdote. The cottage, Williams makes clear, is the poem. The making of the poem consisted in Charles Sheeler's abstracting from its original context (the wrecked estate) a part of reality (the cottage) which he could use in another context (his own life). Intrinsically the cottage remained exactly what it had been, but in its new context it played a new role and from it derived a new meaning.

This seems a valid way of describing the poetic act in much of Williams' work: to speak generally, in the earlier poems reality is characteristically modified by a context of rhythm, for which no modern poet had a better ear than Williams; in the later, by a context of new meaning. A passage in "Two Pendants: for the Ears" will serve as a useful example of the transformation of reality by rhythm into a fragment of a poem, since it was subsequently discussed in a television interview:

> 2 partridges
> 2 Mallard ducks
> a Dungeness crab
> 24 hours out
> of the Pacific
> and 2 live-frozen
> trout
> from Denmark.[12]

In the interview, which becomes a part of *Paterson V*, the questioner says, "Now, that sounds just like a fashionable grocery list!"

[12] *The Collected Later Poems of William Carlos Williams* (Norfolk, Conn.: New Directions, 1950), p. 222. Hereafter *CLP*.

A[nswer]. It is a fashionable grocery list.

Q. Well—is it poetry?

A. . . . It is the American idiom. Rhythmically it's organized as a sample of the American idiom. It has as much originality as jazz. If you say '2 partridges, 2 mallard ducks, a Dungeness crab'—if you treat that rhythmically, ignoring the practical sense, it forms a jagged pattern. It is, to my mind, poetry.

Q. But if you don't 'ignore the practical sense' . . . you agree that it is a fashionable grocery list.

A. Yes. Anything is good material for poetry. Anything. I've said it time and time again.

(Paterson, p. 262)

Conceived of pragmatically the elements constitute a fragment of reality—a grocery list; conceived of rhythmically—in a rhythmical context—they constitute a part of a poem.[13] One ought not to think necessarily of the rhythm being imposed upon previously nonpoetic words; rather the disposition of pauses marked by the arrangement of the words on the page will, here as elsewhere in Williams, permit inherent rhythms to be heard. They may be actual rhythms of speech or rhythms reflecting the movement of an object, such as the water in the fountain, in "Spouts":

> . . . the rocking water
> in the basin
> turns from the stonerim
> back upon the jet
> and rising there
> reflectively drops down again.
>
> (CEP, p. 222)

Such rhythms do not necessarily form a pattern.

[13] Compare the following remark of Gerard Manley Hopkins about a line in "The Loss of the Eurydice," in a letter to Robert Bridges, May 21, 1878: "The line 'she had come from a cruise training seamen' read without stress and declaim is mere Lloyd's Shipping Intelligence; properly read it is quite a different thing. Stress is the life of it" (*Letters of Gerard Manley Hopkins to Robert Bridges*, ed. Claude Colleer Abbott [London: Oxford University Press, 1935], I, 51–52).

The difference between this poetic process, which merely submits words to rhythmical context, and the more orthodox one is, I suppose, a difference of degree. In this process rhythm is the only poetic agent; normally the most important agent, whether rhythm is present or not, is the selection of images and the demonstration of certain relationships among them. The effect of this latter agent in the more familiar poetic process is a more or less strong distinction—in much modern poetry less strong—between the reality we recognize as we get on with our lives and that which appears in a poem. In the lines quoted above, where only rhythm is at work as a poetic agent, it is certainly questionable whether there is any distinction at all.

This single principle, the placing in a new context of images from the world, will carry us some way into the poetry. There is, for eminent example, "The Red Wheelbarrow," which consists almost exclusively of images of ordinary real things. The new context to which these are assigned is rhythm, as it is in the poetization of the grocery items. The rhythm is beautifully contrived (or seems so—one must avoid suggesting that Williams always took time and pains over his poems). In each stanza the break imposed by the line ending separates words which sense normally runs together: "depends / upon," "wheel / barrow," "rain / water," and to a lesser extent "white / chickens." Even to mention such a small feature is to overemphasize its role. But it is exactly this movement which supplies a new context for the things from the chicken run; and it is by virtue of this movement, which treats the four things in the poem analogously, that the wheelbarrow, its vividness ("glazed"), its background ("chickens"), and its importance ("so much depends / upon") are annealed. One might also properly point to (what again is nearly too small to mention) the variety in the arrangement of stresses in the two-stress, longer lines and the assonance in "glazed" and "rain" and in "beside" and "white" as parts of the artificiality of the new context.[14] But the artificiality is minimal:

---

[14] The existence of the end-line pause upon which this concept of the poem

the objects remain in their native state—shining, perhaps, but not with the light that never was, on sea or land.

The poem is pure simplicity rendered simply. Philip Wheelwright finds that simplicity cannot be conveyed as such: ". . . the peculiar character of this or that experienced simplicity has been made possible by an indeterminate network of psychic associations that is never the same in any two individuals." [15] "The Red Wheelbarrow," he says, is an example of the failure "of the attempt to convey a simple experience through sheer simplicity of statement. . . ." Again, "What the red wheelbarrow poem lacks . . . is a more tensive presentation. Why? Because when two imagistic elements are put in a tensive relation to each other a slight pattern is established—a flexible, unobtrusive pattern—and this is something that can be communicated." [16]

Wheelwright notes that for Dr. Williams himself the scene was "of arresting and retaining importance." For many of the very recent generation of American poets also there have been scenes and visions of arresting importance; and Wheelwright's comments may be relevant to their failure to communicate significance by the naked presentation of such scenes. But I am not sure that "The Red Wheelbarrow" is in the same category

---

rests is not accepted by Mary Ellen Solt, who says, "To stop at the end of the single line produces distortion of stress and does violence to pronunciation. This is completely opposed to the poet's stated intentions . . ." ("William Carlos Williams: Poems in the American Idiom," *Folio,* XXV [Winter, 1960], 21). Winifred Nowottny, on the other hand, says, "If the line and stanza endings were nullified by reading out the poem, to someone who had never seen it on the page, as though it were continuous prose, the poem would lose its point" (*The Language Poets Use* [London: Athlone Press, 1962], p. 120). Elizabeth Drew says the poem "should not be called 'verse,' since that word means that the rhythm 'turns' and repeats itself" (*Poetry: A Modern Guide to Its Understanding and Enjoyment* [New York: W. W. Norton, 1959], p. 36). It seems to me that, although there is variation in the placing of stresses, there is audible repetition in the rhythm: "glazed with rain / water // beside the white / chickens." This reading again assumes the existence of an end-line pause.

[15] Wheelwright, *Metaphor and Reality,* p. 159.
[16] *Ibid.,* p. 161.

or that a tension between images is exclusively necessary. The fallacy that simplicity can convey simplicity is similar to the fallacy of expressive form as R. P. Blackmur describes it in his essay on D. H. Lawrence's poetry: ". . . that if a thing is only intensely enough felt its mere expression in words will give it satisfactory form, the dogma, in short, that once material becomes words it is its own best form." [17] But whereas Wheelwright claims that two imagistic elements in a tensive relationship are necessary for the creation of a pattern which is something that can be communicated, Blackmur suggests that "the craft and conventions of the art of poetry" or the fact of being "ordered in a form external to the consciousness that entertained it in flux" [18] will render the private experience intelligible. One might consider the rhythm of "The Red Wheelbarrow" such an external form, though an unimpressive one, as renders its scene publicly intelligible.

The movement of the poem is an artifice; the rest is rude nature. Such a poetic practice, I suppose, is prescribed in "Tract," the poem in which Williams describes how a funeral should be provided for. The proceedings are to be extremely, almost absolutely simple; the hearse is to be not merely undecorated but rough, there are to be no curtains, no flowers, none of the celebrated, expensive embellishments of the trade. But the wheels of the hearse, if there are to be any, are to be fine:

> Let it [the hearse] be weathered—like a farm wagon—
> with gilt wheels (this could be
> applied fresh at small expense)
> or no wheels at all:
> a rough dray to drag over the ground.
> (CEP, p. 129)

The imagery, according to this allegorical prescription for poetry,

---

[17] R. P. Blackmur, "D. H. Lawrence and Expressive Form," *Form and Value in Modern Poetry* (Garden City, N.Y.: Anchor Books, 1957), p. 256.
[18] *Ibid.*, pp. 254, 262.

should be as naked as it can be; but the anomalous gilt wheels, concerned as they are with movement, are a figure for the rhythm of the poem, which should be fine. Otherwise let the expression be prose—"a rough dray to drag over the ground."

Many small pieces in Williams will be found to contain as fundamentals the two features of "The Red Wheelbarrow" emphasized above: familiar idioms or images of familiar objects nakedly presented and rhythms that give them new context. And the rhythm may be too subtle to strike immediately an ear less fine than Williams'

III

We have not finished with "The Red Wheelbarrow," however, when we have described it as a collation of things from the world in a new context. We should look to the meaning of the poem, but before we do so another principle—the third—must be invoked: the idea that a poem is an invention, an object, says Williams, that occupies the same place "as that where bricks or colored threads are handled." [19] Again the *Autobiography* yields a discussion of Williams' concept of the poem as such an object. It is embodied in another anecdote: a lady about to purchase a painting in the Daniel Gallery asked Alanson Hartpence, "What is all that down in this left hand lower corner?" and Hartpence, after examining the area closely, replied, "That, Madam, is paint." "This story," says Williams, "marks the exact point in the transition that took place, in the world of that time, from the appreciation of a work of art as a copying of nature to the thought of it as the imitation of nature" (*Autobiography*, p. 240). Artists, including poets, do not copy nature, we are given to understand; they invent, imitating in their own medium only nature's creativity. Aristotle's real meaning has been missed for over two thousand years; Shakespeare's

---

[19] "Marianne Moore" (1931), *SE*, p. 125.

"To hold the mirror up to nature" is "as vicious a piece of bad advice as the budding artist ever gazed upon." This conception of imitation in poetry and art means a rather sweeping renunciation of traditional views, and we must try to adjust our responses to Williams' poetry in accordance with it. The invented poem is built up with words that are conceived of not as signs but as objects. Williams praises Louis Zukofsky's poems, for instance, as being "thoughtful poetry, but actual word stuff, not thoughts for thoughts." He goes on: "It escapes me in its analysis (thank God) and strikes against me a thing (thank God)" (*SL*, p. 94). He believed that in making a poem one should not start with an idea and then seek words to express it; one should start with words as objects and then dispose them in the hope that they will produce ideas. Here, in his review of *The Phoenix and the Tortoise*, is the complaint he makes about Rexroth's procedures:

> Concerning the poetry one might object to everything in the book on the basis that Rexroth has learned nothing from the concept of verbalism—purloined by Gertrude Stein and capitalized by Joyce but really the genius of a generation, the concept of words as things. . . .
>
> [T]o Rexroth words have absolute meanings synonymous with the context of ideas, which he accepts. Dangerous ground. Rather, for the poet words come first and the ideas are caught, perhaps, among them. The poet invents his nets and catches the birds and butterflies of philosophy. It does not go the other way.[20]

When now we turn back to "The Red Wheelbarrow," bearing in mind this concept of the poem as an invented thing rather than an imitation, we should not expect, since it is an object, that it will be able to describe the world beyond itself in quite

[20] William Carlos Williams, "In Praise of Marriage," *Quarterly Review of Literature*, II, No. 2 (1944), 147.

the same way as a poem that is simply communication. Being an object does not render it inexpressive; but its expression is only an aspect of its being. It is an object, Williams says, "that in itself formally presents its case and its meaning by the very form it assumes" (*Autobiography*, p. 264).

It is quite possible to ascribe meanings of a limited kind to inventions such as collages and abstract sculpture; it is not so easy to conceive of the meaning of a poem in an analogous way, since the words, the elements of the form, have their own denotations. But we should at least correct our normal reading procedures by thinking of the meaning which gets "caught" in the words more as the product of the form and less as that of their denotations: in a Williams poem we should dwell less on the reference of words to what is outside the poem and more on their formal arrangements within.[21] H.D. in her poem "Heat," speaking of the blunt ends of pears, reminds us of our previous experience in which we have seen such things, and by appealing to this memory she evokes the feeling of torpor that the poem conveys. In Williams' "Red Wheelbarrow" it is not so much in the existence outside the poem of the arrayed objects but in the fact of their arrangement within the poem

[21] I don't want to go as far as J. Hillis Miller, who claims that Williams never uses words to "represent" things (*Poets of Reality: Six Twentieth-Century Writers* [Cambridge, Mass.: Harvard University Press, 1965], p. 290)—a statement he qualifies a little later, allowing that "Williams cannot escape the referential meaning of words" (p. 305). In his general presentation Miller seems to call for a modification of our usual responses to poetry far more radical than I do, though often, I believe, it is only his statement that is more radical. For example: "All these images urge the reader to respond to the words with subliminal movements of his muscles mimicking the energy of trees, yachts, plants, or water" (p. 315). This is a pretty unusual exercise to demand of a poetry reader; on the other hand, as will appear below, I think *something of the kind* may be said to be part of a proper response to some of Williams' poems or parts of poems. It must, of course, be immediately added that in their own contexts such statements as these are less sensational than they appear here. And I must also add that if I had had the advantage of reading *Poets of Reality* before I wrote this essay my task would have been easier and I would have written better.

that the meaning resides. And they could be other things—a green garden hose, say, lying among nettles; since "anything is good material for poetry," and the meaning lies in the formal arrangement. "The rhythm of 'The Red Wheelbarrow,'" Marianne Moore quotes Williams as saying, "though no more than a fragment, denotes a certain unquenchable exaltation." [22]

"The Red Wheelbarrow," then, becomes an object which expresses in itself the poet's joy at poetic achievement: the words "so much depends" are equivalent to the lines near the end of "The Desert Music" where, after a poetic act more complex but similar in kind, Williams exclaims, "I *am* a poet! I / am. I am." We must observe also that as Williams continuously invents and renews his world, he does so, to a great degree, in order to create himself within it and to wonder at the product. This wonder is the "meaning" of "The Red Wheelbarrow." The poet's practice of weaving himself into the tapestry of the created world and delighting in the product appears again and again; it is, in fact, a major feature of his poetry, which seems so often to be saying, in Roy Harvey Pearce's nice phrase, "Brave new world . . . that has me in it!" [23]

The concept described here of the poem as an invented thing which is to be looked at for its formal beauty and which offers only the limited meaning that one may derive from abstract sculpture serves, I believe, not so much as a rigid principle to be followed in reading Williams but as a corrective. It should not be a kind of fifth amendment by means of which we can write off our responsibility to the meaning of a poem: we may not dismiss "The Desert Music," for instance, by discovering that its meaning is simply the poet's delight in his own power, writ large. On the other hand, we must always take into full consideration in this poem and others the possibility, to say

[22] Marianne Moore, *Predilections* (New York: Viking Press, 1955), p. 3.
[23] Roy Harvey Pearce, *The Continuity of American Poetry* (Princeton, N.J.: Princeton University Press, 1961), p. 346.

the very least of it, that the meaning will emerge in consideration of the poem as an object with its own internal relationships and consistencies.

IV

In considering "The Red Wheelbarrow," its rhythms and its meaning, we have been led away from the discussion of the second principle in Williams' poetry—that the poetic act consists in setting a part of the world in a new context. In many poems, that new context is supplied not by rhythm or not by rhythm alone but by the over-all meaning of the poem, which incorporates the parts of the world as metaphors. As Charles Sheeler exemplified the making of a poem by giving the cottage on the estate a new context and a meaning, so Williams takes parts of reality and gives them meanings in new contexts, a process he has spoken of as "the lifting of an environment to expression" (SL, p. 286). The process is more apparent in his later verse than in his earlier. It will appear at once that Williams has no patent for it, since throughout the whole heritage of literature phenomena of the real world are used as metaphors and symbols: as Susanne Langer says, "It is actually harder to associate roses with vegetables than with girls." What is more peculiar to Williams is that frequently the poem is largely given over to the purpose of finding the metaphors; it is a conscious and deliberate process; and frequently the poet is there in the poem supervising it, as it were.

Williams tends to present the real phenomena of the outside world first of all as they actually are, with as much realism and as little distortion as the poetic or prosaic medium permits, and then later to bring them back again into the poem as metaphors. A short poem, "Prelude to Winter," illustrates this procedure, which is characteristic of a broad expanse of Williams' work:

> The moth under the eaves
> with wings like

the bark of a tree, lies
symmetrically still—

And love is a curious
soft-winged thing
unmoving under the eaves
when the leaves fall.
                    (*CLP,* p. 55)

In *Paterson* there are "no ideas but in things"; early in the poem
Williams presents some of the things; later he draws on them
for metaphor in order to reveal the ideas. For example, the facts
of Mrs. Cumming's tragedy and of Sam Patch's exploits and
death are first seen in prose reports. Later, they are found to
have symbolic meanings: Mrs. Cumming's fall becomes a symbol for artificiality swept away by the real; Sam Patch, who
met his death in a foreign river, becomes a symbol for a kind of
sterility, the kind that can

                    . . . run off
                  toward the peripheries—
                  to other centers, direct—
                  for clarity (if
                  they found it)
                              loveliness and
                  authority in the world,
                              (p. 48)

a passage Louis L. Martz has described as a protest against the
foreign aspects of the poems of Pound and Eliot.[24] "Not until
the following spring," says the prose report, "was the body
found frozen in an ice-cake." And this detail, referred to later
in the poem, becomes, I suppose, a metaphor for Pound's and
Eliot's work, which Williams seems to condemn to a kind of
museum status, frozen like Sam Patch's body.

[24] Louis L. Martz, "The Unicorn in Paterson: William Carlos Williams,"
Thought, XXXV (Winter, 1960), 544.

The prose passages of these two incidents contain suggestions as to the meanings with which they are later revealed to have been endowed; these are the florid style of the passage describing Mrs. Cumming and the following hint from the report on Sam Patch: "But instead of descending with a plummet-like fall his body wavered in the air—Speech had failed him. He was confused. The word had been drained of its meaning." But even if, as Roy Harvey Pearce suggests, "the meaning is immanent in the perceptive act," [25] the first appearance of these phenomena is predominantly as solid parts of the world; only in later passages do their metaphorical values clearly emerge.

The same practice is apparent in the last poems: in "The Yellow Flower," for instance, or in "Asphodel, That Greeny Flower." In the latter, the sea appears first as the real thing (its appearance is enriched by a metaphor; it is not itself one):

> . . . the sea
> which no one tends
> is also a garden
> when the sun strikes it
> and the waves
> are wakened.

Later, it becomes a metaphor for love:

> There is no power
> so great as love
> which is a sea,
> which is a garden. . . .
> (PB, pp. 156, 166)

Again, at first mention lightning naturally "plays about the edges of the clouds"; later, light, which has the characteristics of lightning, becomes the imagination:

[25] Roy Harvey Pearce, "The Poet as Person," *Yale Review*, XLI (Spring, 1952), 431.

Light, the imagination
    and love,
                in our age,
    by natural law
            which we worship
                    maintain

    all of a piece
            their dominance. . . .
    The light
            for all time shall outspeed
                    the thunder crack.
            (*PB,* pp. 157, 180, 181)

T. S. Eliot, in characteristic practice, would have made use on all these occasions of the later passages only, where the items have lost something of their sharp realism through having been already transformed into metaphor. And the object would not most likely be a quotidian thing or a local matter but one of public interest or an item from the cultural heritage. One responds to "the roots that clutch," "the ships at Mylae," or "the change of Philomel," not by imagining the appearance of roots or ships or a woman becoming a bird but by immediately capturing their meaning. Marianne Moore, on the other hand, typically chooses an object, a plant or animal generally, which, although no less solid or real than any object in Williams, renders a moral naturally when it is studied carefully enough without the deliberate resetting as metaphor in which Williams engages.

The procedure described here, in which Williams presents an image first for its own sake and only then as a metaphor, is characteristic. But we may not close our eyes to certain important exceptions: in some poems images are used metaphorically without a previous literal appearance; such poems have an intensity which is atypical of Williams, and they seem to have been attractive to anthologists. For example, "To Waken an Old Lady" begins,

> Old age is
> a flight of small
> cheeping birds. . . .
> (CEP, p. 200)

The rest of the eighteen-line poem is given over to a description of those of the birds' activities that speak to the condition of old age. But the details survive in themselves despite their metaphoric function:

> On harsh weedstalks
> the flock has rested,
> the snow
> is covered with broken
> seedhusks
> and the wind tempered
> by a shrill
> piping of plenty.

In "The Widow's Lament in Springtime" (CEP, p. 223) the details do not so survive. The poem opens as the other with a bold, unabashed metaphor which withdraws our consideration of the image as the reflection of a material thing: "Sorrow is my own yard." The items in this yard have similarly lost most of their power to force their sensuous appearance upon us: the "new grass / flames," but our attention is given to it as a source of pain and not as mere grass; if the poet had said that the new grass flickered, something of the sensuous appearance of the grass would have been retained; but it "flames" because it is one among other items that were formerly the widow's joy, and there is no greater pain—*nessun maggiore dolore*—than in the remembrance of that joy.

> The plumtree is white today
> with masses of flowers.

> Masses of flowers
> load the cherry branches. . . .

Here again it is not the trees as such that claim our attention but the whiteness associated with the widow's wedding and the "masses" associated with the masses for the dead (compare "Thousands of glittering small leaves / that no church bell calls to Mass / —but there will be a mass soon / on the weighted branches" [26]).

Another small poem frequently anthologized where metaphoric usage blurs the reader's perception of the image is "Queen-Ann's-Lace" (*CEP,* p. 210). The metaphor is not completely developed; but one may summarize roughly that the body of the woman in this poem is a field of Queen Anne's lace which at the places where her lover touches it becomes anemones. Within the broad metaphoric scheme and disturbing it there are the kind of irrelevant developments that appear in Donne: the likeness between the center of an anemone and a purple mole on the skin, presented as if the poet could not resist introducing a complexity which disrupts his large analogy; and the fact that the blossoms of the Queen Anne's lace are a "hand's span" in dimension, troubling the announcement that

> . . . Wherever
> his hand has lain there is
> a tiny purple blemish. . . .

These last two pieces are fairly popular; they are, I think, more *immediately* exciting than Williams' staple kind of work. But they are atypical; and their repeated reprinting may have led to a wrong general impression of this poet. His poetry is usually different.

v

We will be on the right lines if we approach *Paterson* in the light of the three principles discussed above: procedure by

[26] "Two Pendants: for the Ears," *CLP,* p. 217.

fanciful likeness; the setting in context of parts of the world; and the poem as a thing. To consider the second of these first: *Paterson* is a poem in which facts and concrete objects, initially presented simply as such, are woven into a fabric by virtue of the meanings they assume as metaphors. It is a poem about the making of poetry. Many of its elements are made, by the total context, to contribute to the major theme, the poet's relation to reality. At the beginning of the poem, we are presented with the giant Paterson sleeping with the giantess, and among minor meanings imposed upon these two is the major one of poet and reality, respectively. A host of otherwise irrelevant entities, many of them sexual episodes, are made to contribute to this theme.[27] The concept of poetry as fulfilling reality appears often in Williams' various writings. He speaks, for example, as we have seen, of the "lifting of an environment to expression"; or he says, "Until your artists have conceived you in your unique and supreme form you can never conceive yourselves and have not, in fact, existed." [28] Or, "The world of the senses lies unintelligible on all sides. It is only interpretable by the emotions. It only exists when its emotion is fastened to it." [29] Or he speaks of poetry as marriage.[30] And the result of the poet's act of fulfillment upon reality is, as mentioned above, a brave new world with WCW in it.

It would be boring to dwell on all the occasions in *Paterson* which are brought into context by and given meanings contributory to the sexual theme; but a few places should be adduced. In Book I, Part I,

[27] The sexual analogy of the poet's relationship to his world is not remote: Ezra Pound speculated on it in his "Translator's Postscript" to Rémy de Gourmont's, *The Natural Philosophy of Love* (New York: Liveright, 1942), p. 297, speaking of "driving any new idea into the great passive vulva of London" as "a sensation analogous to the male feeling in copulation."

[28] Address to members of the English Institute, 1948. Quoted from Sister M. Bernetta Quinn, *The Metamorphic Tradition in Modern Poetry* (New Brunswick, N.J.: Rutgers University Press, 1955), p. 116.

[29] William Carlos Williams, "Notes from a Talk on Poetry," *Poetry*, XIV (July, 1919), 213. Quoted in Quinn, p. 106.

[30] Williams, "In Praise of Marriage," p. 149.

> The flower spreads its colored petals
> wide in the sun
> But the tongue of the bee
> misses them
> They sink back into the loam
> crying out. . . .
>
> (p. 20)

Randall Jarrell suggests that "the people are like flowers that the bee misses," [31] and we recall Williams' own remark that the poem is "the underlying meaning of all they want to tell us and have always failed to communicate. . . ." Later in the poem the bee and the flower become the seaplane and the landlocked bay of Port au Prince (p. 37), and here the seaplane successfully enters. The passage in which "we" sit and talk and "I" wish to be abed with "you" and the one expressing the unacknowledged desire of the environment to be fulfilled (pp. 35, 36) are parts of this theme. Then an important contributing passage opens Part III of Book I:

> How strange you are, you idiot!
> So you think because the rose
> is red that you shall have the mastery?
> The rose is green and will bloom,
> overtopping you, green, livid
> green when you shall no more speak, or
> taste, or even be. My whole life
> has hung too long upon a partial victory.
>
> (p. 41)

The poet voices here his failure, which was earlier expressed in the image of the bee and the flower, to fulfill the world: always beyond the area of his mastery is one that the poetry cannot, or cannot yet, or will not occupy. And yet, as will appear in a later part of this chapter, this world, which remains virginal to his approaches and with which he has apparently failed, is, in fact,

---

[31] Randall Jarrell, *Poetry and the Age* (New York: Alfred A. Knopf, 1955), p. 208.

a component of his poetry, and it is of some importance to him.

The strongest statement of the theme of fulfillment (one might call it the climax if this did not suggest a structure different from that which *Paterson* possesses) comes in the description of Madame Curie in Book IV. Madame Curie is related to the nature she is probing as the male is related to the female and the poet to the world. There is a beautiful skein of associations between the images in the following passage, made possible by the meanings that the context has endowed them with:

> Paris, a fifth floor room, bread
> milk and chocolate, a few
> apples and coal to be carried,
> *des briquettes,* their special smell,
> at dawn:　Paris　　　　　.
> the soft coal smell, as she
> leaned upon the window before de-
> parting, for work　　　　.
>
> —a furnace, a cavity aching
> toward fission; a hollow,
> a woman waiting to be filled
>
> —a luminosity of elements, the
> current leaping!
> Pitchblende from Austria, the
> valence of Uranium inexplicably
> increased. Curie, the man, gave up
> his work to buttress her.
> But she is pregnant!
>
> 　　　　　　　　　(pp. 206–7)

The passage has a narrative coherence: the first eight lines describe Marie Curie's domestic situation in Paris; the rest, her work, except for the last line quoted, which refers again to her domestic life, the ironic effect of Curie's assisting her in her work. But a number of the details from the two parts are related by association; they belong in Williams' "imaginative category." Marie Curie leans on the window sill looking over Paris breathing the smell of the soft coal (one guesses that this is a detail culled from Williams' own experience, since Dr. Evans had breathed the same scent in *his* Paris room, in *A Voyage to Pagany*). And yet there is an exquisite network of associations between Paris and the coal, the furnace and the pitchblende: Paris, primarily the city as seen from the fifth-floor window, is the example to hand of the uninformed chaos, the feminine principle of the world (in the letter which precedes these lines, A.G. speaks of his "struggle to love and know his own world-city"); hence Paris is the "furnace, a cavity aching / toward fission" and also the "woman waiting to be filled." It is the reality which the poetic principle must fulfill. But the pitchblende also is a material awaiting refinement; and Marie Curie herself, while pregnant with the idea of radium, is a woman who has been fulfilled by her husband and is "aching / toward fission." The phrase, "the / current leaping," not only referring to the electric current but alluding back to the Passaic River as described in Book I of the poem, relates the whole endeavor of Madame Curie to that of *Paterson*.

The theme of fulfillment appears again in the passages about the whore and the virgin, in Book V, who are "an identity" inasmuch as they are both womanhood ("the joint symbol of woman—Mary Magdalene against Mary the Mother of God"[32]) and who are both metaphorically the world—the virgin, the untouched reality that is "green, livid / green" which the poet has not mastered, and the whore, that which he has. It is the green world that most endures:

> —the virgin and the whore, which
> most endures? the world

[32] John C. Thirlwall, "William Carlos Williams' 'Paterson': The Search for the Redeeming Language—A Personal Epic in Five Parts," *New Directions in Prose and Poetry* 17 (Norfolk, Conn., 1961), p. 258.

of the imagination most endures. . . .
(p. 248)

The green world is represented earlier by the youngest of the nine African wives who awaits fulfillment:

> . . . the uppointed breasts
> . . . tense, charged with
> pressures unrelieved   .
> (p. 23)

And the mastered world appears as the oldest wife, at the bottom of the "scale of freshness." The theme of fulfillment is present also, by negation, in passages about sexual failure, notably those in the beginning of Book IV.

In the first four books another theme interlaces with that of fulfillment: the "reply to Greek and Latin with the bare hands," which is Williams' description of the poem, is to be a poetic act upon a bare reality, nothing intervening between poet and his world. Thus the following situation is as inappropriate as it is grotesque:

> He   Me with my pants, coat and vest still on!
> She   And me still in my galoshes!
> (p. 104)

An earlier part of the poem reads,

> . . . unless there is
> a new mind there cannot be a new
> line, the old will go on
> repeating itself with recurring
> deadliness. . . .
> (p. 65)

This smaller motif of newness and nakedness incorporates the passages where a male is bidding a female to remove her clothes (pp. 128–29, 162–63) and those where a naked encounter replaces a relationship via books (p. 221). Another agency by which reality is unclothed is the fire, in Book III. It burns the library, the artificiality that has obscured reality, the beautiful thing. And it creates anew the old bottle (p. 143); the poet also, with "a second flame, surpassing / heat," brings the bottle back to a condition of being newly created. Then, furthermore, there is a sense of continuous sequence wherein the world is clothed in poetry which, as it becomes outmoded, is to be removed to make way for a new fulfillment by the poet of a new and naked reality, as the nine wives of the African chief are successively fulfilled. In *Spring and All*, Williams imagines a colossal holocaust of destruction which is followed by the renovation of spring.[33] The motif is more familiar, however, in the poetry of Wallace Stevens, where the stripping away of the accretions of the old myth is followed by the constant production of the imagination and, again, the constant dissolution of its product.

In Williams the achievement of wisdom by the poetic clothing of reality alternates with the despair attending the descent to the original bare reality itself. But the recalling of that original is not entirely a defeat, for it opens up possibilities "heretofore unrealized," and there is

> a new awakening :
> > which is a reversal
> of despair.
> > > (*Paterson*, p. 97)

This, I believe is one meaning that may be derived from the long passage "The descent beckons" (pp. 96–97) and from the following lines, which occur a little later "—the descent follows the ascent—to wisdom / as to despair" (p. 104).

Other motifs are interwoven in *Paterson*: that of language runs through the whole poem and has been dissected out by a number of critics; the image of the dog appears and reappears; the poet as dwarf, the poet as crow, and credit and usury give a local context to a number of details. But if we look to one or

[33] Williams, *Spring and All*, pp. 4–8.

another or all of these motifs for the meaning of the poem, we omit one stage in the interpretive procedure. Once again the poem means what it does through first being what it is. To Williams, direct statement is as much an anathema as the finished form: "Kill the explicit sentence, don't you think?" he says, "and expand our meaning—by verbal sequences" (*Paterson*, p. 222). If he had wanted one single, clear, un-equivocal descriptive meaning to shine forth, he would have proceeded otherwise. "It isn't what he [the poet] says that counts as a work of art," says Williams, in "The Wedge," "it's what he makes, with such intensity of perception that it lives with an intrinsic movement of its own to verify its authenticity" (*CLP*, p. 5). One small instance of an interlacing motif—more literally a motif than the others mentioned, since it is a matter of sound—may stand for all in this respect. In Book I (*Paterson*, p. 31) there is the anticipation and the echo of the redbreast's call created by the repetition of words to which Randall Jarrell has drawn attention. But we cannot deduce a meaning from this—not from the fact of the sound effects themselves.

I think it is proper to consider the whole poem in the same way: a tissue of interwoven sounds, themes, images, and speech from the outside world. We must, as the poem tells us, "Go . . . to the river for relief from 'meaning'" (p. 135); and when we do, we find that the parts of *Paterson* are related in the same way as Paterson's thoughts, which

> interlace, repel and cut under,
> rise rock-thwarted and turn aside
> but forever strain forward—or strike
> an eddy and whirl, marked by a
> leaf or curdy spume, seeming
> to forget   .
>
> (p. 16)

This is exactly a description of the poem. The river runs eventu-ally to the sea—Williams cannot help the natural habits of rivers; but the sea gives no completion of form or crystallization of meaning: ". . . the sea is not our home." And Paterson makes his way back inland.

VI

The themes of *Paterson* are woven, one might say, into a pattern. But to say so would be to speak loosely; the metaphor needed is one that would describe a "pattern" that is constantly enlarging. It is said that in the making of Persian carpets the errors made against symmetry are incorporated in the larger design. But whereas the rug is eventually finished, *Paterson* is not. Williams, I am sure, did not want it to be. His respect for detail is incompatible with an equal respect for a completed structure: he, like Miss Moore, would be quite out of sympathy with the steam roller as it appears in her poem, leveling down details to make them fit the large conception. Nor are his ideas about order consonant with completeness. He says, not specifically about *Paterson*, "Order is what is discovered after the fact, not a little piss pot for us all to urinate into—and call ourselves satisfied" (*SL*, p. 214). A poem of his is not perfected like a sonnet; there is always the sense, arising sometimes from the omission of a final period,[34] that there is something more to follow the poem. A poem is not a self-contained structure but rather "a moment of the mind, a temporary surfacing of the stream of consciousness, or perhaps just the beginning of an endless poem." [35] Such is the shape of a life: not planned ahead, but discovered later. Williams' practices result in a poem that is not a completed statement but rather a field of possible choices. Poetry to him is not a game in which you set a pattern and conform to it; and "when you conform to it successfully, you overcome it and it serves your purpose." Such a game is like fishing with an unbarbed

[34] See Glauco Cambon, "William Carlos Williams and Ezra Pound: Two Examples of Open Poetry," *College English*, XXII (March, 1961), 389.
[35] Glauco Cambon, *The Inclusive Flame: Studies in American Poetry* (Bloomington: Indiana University Press, 1963), p. 217.

hook and a thin leader—the sport advocated in Lionel Trilling's *The Middle of the Journey* by John Laskell, who, speaking of sonnets, makes the remark above and earns the contempt of the pragmatists, Nancy Croom and Duck Caldwell. Duck fished because he wanted fish. Williams too wants fish; what prizes there are to be won in the poem's struggle against its own shape are not for him. A propos of *Paterson,* he says: "I had thought about it all a long time. I knew I had what I wanted to say. I knew that I wanted to say it in *my* form. I was aware that it wasn't a finished form, yet I knew it was not formless. I had to invent my form, if form it was." [36] To have a form, however, which is not a "finished form" seems to me to be tantamount to having no structural form at all. That which is not finished must be said, without undue asperity, to lack a structural form. A poem that ends, as *Paterson* ends, in jottings posthumously collected has in fact no end and hence no over-all shape. If Williams had concluded the poem with Book IV with the echo of the Neo-Platonic return to the source of being, we should have had an ending somewhat conclusive. But characteristically he did not. "In 1953," says John C. Thirlwall, "it was clear that *Paterson* was not ended, since Williams' education in life was not ended." [37] But nobody's education—not even Milton's—is ever ended. In the 1963 edition of *Paterson,* Williams says:

> [since completing *Paterson, Four*] I have come to understand not only that many changes have occurred in me and the world, but I have been forced to recognize that *there can be no end* to such a story I have envisioned with the terms which I had laid down for myself. I had to take the world of Paterson into a new dimension if I wanted to give it imaginative validity. Yet I wanted to keep it whole, as it is to me. As I

[36] *I Wanted to Write a Poem,* ed. Edith Heal (Boston: Beacon Press, 1958), p. 74. Quoted by Gordon Grigsby, who discusses the matter further in "The Genesis of Paterson," *College English,* XXIII (January, 1962), 279.
[37] Thirlwall, "Williams' 'Paterson,'" p. 282.

mulled the thing over in my mind the composition began to
assume a form which you see in the present poem, keeping,
I fondly hope, a unity directly continuous with the Paterson
of *Pat. 1* to *4*. Let's hope I have succeeded in doing so.[38]

This is not, probably, a carefully meditated pronouncement; but
it is noticeable that to Williams the concept of unity is not related to completion and wholeness but something that can be
continuous—like tone, perhaps. When, in addition, we learn
from John C. Thirlwall that "the long poem 'Journey to Love'
. . . was originally entitled 'Paterson V,' " [39] we realize that if
Williams was seeking unity with this addendum also he must
have conceived of it as a very flexible quantity.

What surely accounts for the continuation of *Paterson* into
Book V is Williams' instinctive avoidance of conclusiveness.[40]
And inconclusiveness in general, which is related to it, is the
fourth principle of his poetry that I wish to present. A poem of
Williams' as published—the words we have on the page—is
not so much a finished thing as the chartering of an area in
which the poem might exist or in which it exists potentially.
This principle, again, ought to be thought of not as rigid but as
a corrective to more normal expectations.

There is a dislike or perhaps more accurately a distrust of
finality in many of Williams' utterances. He thinks of summer
as representing a kind of finality, and he celebrates it in his
poems much less than early spring; March, with its "hard-edged
light," is his favorite month. His delight in spring is seen
throughout; in the title *Kora in Hell*, he even identifies himself with it.[41] In early spring, the high midsummer pomps are
found as possibilities only about to be realized, not yet formed,
fixed, and dying. And his work, insofar as it is unfinished, is like
spring at the time of its "stark dignity of entrance." Williams

[38] "Author's Note." Italics in first sentence mine.
[39] Thirlwall, "Williams' 'Paterson,' " p. 295.
[40] Over-all structural form in Williams is discussed in Chapter 5; see pp.
172–83.
[41] *I Wanted to Write a Poem*, p. 29; *Autobiography*, p. 158.

has always been busy to avoid completion and permanence: he says, for instance, "It is to the inventive imagination we look for deliverance from every other misfortune as from the desolation of a flat Hellenic perfection of style" (*SE*, pp. 10–11). In this respect he is reminiscent of T. E. Hulme, who says, "We no longer believe in perfection, either in verse or in thought, we frankly acknowledge the relative. We shall no longer strive to attain the absolutely perfect form in poetry." [42]

The antipathy toward perfection and the singling out of the Greeks as perpetrators of it remind us of D. H. Lawrence, who says, "One wearies of the aesthetic quality—a quality which takes the edge off everything, and makes it seem 'boiled down.' A great deal of pure Greek beauty has this boiled down effect. It is too much cooked in the artistic consciousness." [43] Again like Lawrence, Williams thought of the poem as ephemeral; in a late poem, "Come On!" there is the joke of the sergeant exhorting the men—

> Come on!
>   Do you want to live
> forever?—
>   That
>   is the essence
> of poetry. . . .
>
>   (*PB,* p. 139)

The aim of avoiding the finished form is abetted by carelessness. Carelessness will guard the poet against offering what is fixed and definite, which may then occupy the mind with error. "A chance word, upon paper," he says in the opening of Part III of *Paterson,* Book III, "may destroy the world. Watch carefully and erase, while the power is still yours. . . ." Then:

[42] *Further Speculations by T. E. Hulme,* ed. Sam Hynes (Minneapolis: University of Minnesota Press, 1955), p. 71.

[43] D. H. Lawrence, *Etruscan Places* (New York: Viking Press, 1932), pp. 185–86.

"Only one answer: write carelessly so that nothing that is not green will survive."

The presence of the prose passages in *Paterson* must be accounted for partly as the result of Williams' antipathy toward the perfect and the complete. Although

> . . . without invention
> nothing lies under the witch-hazel
> bush . . . ;

on the other hand, paradoxically, "The rose is green and will bloom . . . when you shall no more speak, or / taste, or even be." Beyond the world the poet has invented, or fulfilled, there is the green world, which held a romantic appeal to Williams. It is the world in which the pink church exists, as pristine as

> the nipples of
> a woman who never
> bore a
> child,[44]

not to be touched by philosophy. One world the poet has rendered: "every married man," he says,

> . . . carries in his head
> the beloved and sacred image
> of a virgin
> whom he has whored   .
> (*Paterson*, p. 272)

The other world, the one that most endures, is beyond poetry; as, in Wallace Stevens, "The plum survives its poems." [45] It is to the virgin world—the world with which he registers his failure—that Williams constantly looks to deliver him from the finished perfection of a completed poem.

[44] "Choral: the Pink Church," *CLP*, pp. 159–62.
[45] "The Comedian as the Letter C," *The Collected Poems of Wallace Stevens* (New York: Alfred A. Knopf, 1957), p. 41.

There are interesting implications in the fact that Williams chooses to operate in this closely guarded way, desiring to relate himself to the virgin in invention and yet eschewing the whore of fulfillment, rather as Wallace Stevens operates between the wilderness and the statue. One reason for the choice is that a complete pattern or an unblemished harmony precludes discovery. In *Paterson*, the sea, symbol of wholeness, is not our home; the poet withdraws from it to begin again.

> —you cannot believe
> that it can begin again, again, here
> again   .   here
> Waken from a dream, this dream of
> the whole poem . . . .
>
>   (p. 234)

The sea is not our home because our home, our lot, is the river, continuing discovery. Toward this, the harmony of the sea will not lead; but dissonance will: as we have already seen,

> A dissonance
> in the valence of Uranium
> led to the discovery. . . .

In a letter to Sister Bernetta Quinn, Williams speaks of the necessity of incorporating in the poem elements whose inclusion reason does not sanction (*SL*, p. 309). He leaves the poem not a rounded whole but incomplete, straining outward toward a wider encompassing and more comprehensive completion.

Many of the prose passages have a fanciful relationship to the interlacing themes of the poem; it is possible to regard them also as contributing to the large rhythm or as part of the collage effect, like the wine labels Picasso stuck on to his paintings.[46] But as Ralph Nash has pointed out, they are partly intended "as a forceful marriage of his poem's world with that world of

[46] Guy Davenport, "The Nuclear Venus: Dr. Williams' Attack upon Usura," *Perspective*, VI (Autumn–Winter, 1953), 183–90.

reality from which he is fearful of divorcing himself." [47] In a
letter to Nash, endorsing the perceptions in his article, Williams
says, "A man must, without relinquishing any of the reasons for
the poetry with which he surrounds himself and with which
the great of this world, at their most powerful, surround him,
fight his way to a world which breaks through to the actual"
(*SL*, pp. 323–24). Naturally when the poet, in the midst of his
invention, fights his way toward the uninvented world, the bits
and pieces of that world are irrelevancies that have seemed to
some critics like grit in the teeth. "Should so much of this book,"
asks Randall Jarrell of *Paterson II*,

> consist of what are—the reader is forced to conclude—real
> letters from a real woman? One reads these letters with in-
> volved, embarrassed pity. . . . What has been done to them
> to make it possible for us to respond to them as art and not
> as raw reality? to make them part of the poem *Paterson?* I
> can think of no answer except: *They have been copied out
> on the typewriter.* Anyone can object, *But the context makes
> them part of the poem;* and anyone can reply to this objection,
> *It takes a lot of context to make somebody else's eight-page
> letter the conclusion to a book of a poem.*[48]

Certainly it is a large lump of world that we are invited to digest.
And although I think the explanation is correct, it may seem
lame or even a spurious accounting to claim that the context to
which we must look to justify the inclusion is not just the poem
itself but Williams *and* the poem, or Williams *making* the poem.
Williams himself does not quite know how such irrelevancies
belong. He writes to Sister Bernetta, "The irrational enters the
poem in those letters, included in the text, which do not seem
to refer to anything in the 'story' yet do belong somehow to the
poem—how, it is not easy to say" (*SL*, p. 309). The practice,

---

[47] Ralph Nash, "The Use of Prose in 'Paterson,'" *Perspective,* VI
(Autumn–Winter, 1953), 194.
[48] Randall Jarrell, "A View of Three Poets," *Partisan Review,* XVIII
(November–December, 1951), 699.

however, of dragging in a piece of actuality related only by slender threads of association is not peculiar to Williams: we have seen Marianne Moore moving along similarly fanciful tangents; and we may observe a practice closely akin in a very different kind of poet. In "Birches," the process of describing birch swinging, the manifest business of the poem, is quite explicitly laid aside while Robert Frost describes how ice storms cripple these trees. Then, reintroducing the subject, he suggests that actuality had momentarily forced itself upon him and deflected the poem: "But I was going to say when Truth broke in / With all her matter-of-fact about the ice-storm. . . ." Williams goes in for a modulation much more extreme than this; but we can register the basic similarity in procedures: truth, or actuality, must be given a hearing at the cost of relevance or structural tidiness. It is interesting that Frost remarks the same process in Emily Dickinson, who is prepared to dispose of her regular, structurally relevant processes in order to make way for the truth.

VII

The four principles described above—the operation of fancy, the endowment of context, the poem as an invented thing, and the eschewal of completeness—are, I believe, all valid to some degree for all Williams' poetry; but they are not all equally valid all the time. There are differences between the early verse and the later, which can be seen by considering the change in Williams' purposes as a poet and, associated with this, the changes in the poet's own position in the poem and in his tolerance of the romantic. One early statement concerning purpose comes in the prologue to *Kora in Hell* (1920), a work which, as we have seen, is a yoking together of heterogeneous images with a violence that makes John Donne seem tender. Williams considers it primarily an exercise of the will: "All is confusion," he says, "yet it comes from a hidden desire for the

dance, a lust of the imagination, a will to accord two instruments in a duet" (*SE*, p. 16). Earlier still Williams had said,
"The world of the senses . . . is only interpretable by the
emotions." Back of these remarks is the desire to relate the world
to the mind of the poet. And this purpose is consonant with the
poet's presence in the poem as we have noticed it. In the earlier
poems, this presence has only the slightest notification: by the
phrase, "so much depends," for instance, or by the rhythms the
poet has discovered in his materials or imposed upon them, of
which a fine example to be discussed more fully below is the
series of trochees in the third section of "By the Road to the
Contagious Hospital,"

> All along the road the reddish
> purplish, forked, upstanding, twiggy
> stuff of bushes. . . .
> (*CEP*, p. 241)

The presence of the poet in the later poems, however, is different and bespeaks a purpose other than the "hidden desire for
the dance." This later purpose is more nearly expressed by the
sentence in the anecdote about Charles Sheeler, "It is ourselves we organize in this way . . . for integrity of understanding to insure persistence, to give the mind its stay," than
by the statements I have quoted immediately above.

The poems in *The Desert Music*, partly because they were
written after Williams had had a stroke and partly because of
the threat of the bomb, are pervaded by themes of fear, pain,
suffering, and survival. By the same act that sets parts of the
world in new context the poet is bent on managing his pain.
The last lines of "The Orchestra" show that the poem has been
directed toward setting a phenomenon in context:

> The birds twitter now anew
> but a design
> surmounts their twittering.

It is a design of a man
    that makes them twitter.
      It is a design.

                    (*PB*, p. 82)

The poem has been concerned to find a context for suffering, more precisely, for fear, since to discover a context for it is to manage it. The poem describes the progress of a musical work in which, at first, the instruments are "together, unattuned / seeking a common tone"; and the common tone is love. But the "wrong note" must also be accommodated by the orchestration:

    The purpose of an orchestra
        is to organize those sounds
           and hold them
  to an assembled order   .
      in spite of the
         "wrong note."

Near the end of the poem we learn what the "wrong note" figures: "Man has survived hitherto because he was too ignorant to know how to realize his wishes. Now that he can realize them, he must either change them or perish." But the poem has done its work:

    Now is the time   .
      in spite of the "wrong note"
        I love you. . . .

And the birds "twitter now anew."

"The Yellow Flower" also seeks to manage pain. It is a special instance of Williams' characteristic way of presenting an object first literally and then symbolically. The flower is presented as in itself it actually is, though the poet's confusion as to its species hints of meaning in the act of perception;

                . . It is
  a mustard flower

and not a mustard flower,
a single spray
topping the deformed stem
of fleshy leaves. . . .
(PB, p. 89)

But preceding these lines there is a panegyric of the flower,

which only to look upon
all men
are cured

and

for which all men
sing secretly their hymns
of praise. . . .

The flower, we learn subsequently, is being viewed in a store window whither it had been transplanted from its natural environment. Thus an object in an artificial context is a symbol for a poem, and as such it receives the poet's unqualified praise. But since the flower is twisted and deformed it symbolizes also the poet's torture. And by its means he feels his ability to give context to his suffering—to make a poem of it—and thus to be liberated from it: although he sees ruin for himself, he sees also

through the eyes
and through the lips
and tongue the power
to free myself
and speak of it. . . .

This treatment of suffering may be reminiscent of that of another poet who managed pain by setting it in a beautiful context: ". . . yet there the nightingale / Filled all the desert with inviolable voice. . . ." But if in this one respect Williams comes close to Eliot, the differences are characteristic: Eliot appeals to a public myth, Williams to a small and private incident in everyday life.

The suffering animal in "To a Dog Injured in the Street" is immediately made a symbol for the suffering poet. The poem opens:

> It is myself
>> not the poor beast lying there
>> yelping with pain
> that brings me to myself with a start. . . .
>> (PB, p. 86)

Again the poem seeks to deal with pain. The poet appeals to René Char whose suffering

> . . . brought him
>> to speak only of
> sedgy rivers,
>> of daffodils and tulips
>>> whose roots they water . . .

and such objects. Williams does not actually say so, but we assume that René Char had succeeded in subordinating his personal pain, his "wrong note," to a design and was thus liberated from it to speak lyrically of the beauty of the natural order. The poet then recalls two other incidents in which he had suffered, as he is suffering now, as a witness of, respectively, pain and indignity meted out to animals. After the second of these he says,

> Why should I think of that now?
>> The cries of a dying dog
>>> are to be blotted out
> as best I can

—the lines are not heartless, because the cries of the "dying dog" are the poet's own. And he then appeals again to René

Char, who believed in "the power of beauty / to right all wrongs." The poem is a testimony to Williams' faith that with the human power of poetry, which sets it in context, suffering can be overcome.

> With invention and courage
>> we shall surpass
>>> the pitiful dumb beasts. . . .

There is a substantial difference between these later poems and the earlier in the way and in the degree to which the poet is in the poem. And this change is accompanied by others, all of which together suggest a movement toward romantic poetry.

I do not know why one should be anxious to avoid calling Williams a romantic, or if one were how one would do so. His early poem *The Wanderer* seems to me to be closer to Shelley's *Alastor*[49] than any other poem in this century, except possibly parts of *The Bridge*. In it, the river enters the poet's heart—an implantation which exfoliated thirty years later in *Paterson*. After *The Wanderer* he balanced the romantic with the anti-poetic, though when Wallace Stevens pointed out this practice in his preface to the *Collected Poems* of 1934 Williams was irritated and was irritated again and again thereafter when Stevens' dialectic was cited. In the later work the romantic voice is heard clearer than before. In the kind of poetry Williams had established as his own in his earlier career much depended on insignificant concrete objects, such as a red wheelbarrow, a grocery list, his wife's bedroom slippers, sparrows, a dish of plums, or whatever. And his poems on these were jottings, not recollections in tranquillity.[50] All through his early career, like the cubist painters he admired so much, he kept his

---

[49] Though it was "Hyperion," "Aucassin and Nicolette," Bocklin's "Insel des Todes," and *Don Juan* that he says he had been reading at the time (Thirlwall, "Williams' 'Paterson,'" pp. 257–58).

[50] See the remark in *Spring and All*: ". . . this moment is the only thing in which I am at all interested" (pp. 2–3).

eye on the foreground—the small hard things of the suburbs; but doing so represented a victory in a struggle against a romantic urge to remove it therefrom: the man who later repeats the axiom, "No ideas but in things," does so as a warning and a steeling of himself against the opposite temptation.[51] In *Paterson*, Williams had something tremendous to say; but, anxious to avoid an enthusiastic, romantic expression of it, he settled for what meaning could be transmitted by a network of multicolored details. He would rather fail in the manner of trying to pack more ideas into things than things can, in the normal run of matters, carry than in the manner of flying off, in Hulme's phrase, into the "circumambient gas"; just as Marianne Moore, as we saw earlier, would rather conceal her subject almost totally than parade the pageant of a bleeding heart at the Boston Arts Festival. Williams wants, in Hulme's sense again, to be classical; he is prepared to underplay his hand. In order to be decent and unromantic, he is prepared to lose something in intensity.

Does not the same motive—to guard himself toughly against the onslaught of romantic feeling—account for the half-articulate array of disjointed ideas and images in Dr. Evans' ruminations about Notre Dame in *Voyage to Pagany*? Evans is moved by cathedrals, but he will not let himself go:

> They looked at the famous cathedral: It is the lack of solution hardened into this form, twin towered, all the paraphernalia of the aisles. We should not be down-hearted if we can't solve it pronto, he said to himself. Of what else are all the great liturgies built?—the Egyptian, the tribal, the Greek—to hide the difficulty; the Christian today, to hide the difficulty; equal, colored glass before the blinding face of—this the me to you, impossible to communicate, impossible to put over anything important—the truth, as they call it familiarly, the heterosexual truth—just children trying to do it all at once. Blood in this street. The Church heads it all, the dead stops of life, every-

---

[51] "Tout classicisme," says Valéry, "suppose un romanticisme anterieur."

thing made static—stopped that is—made into a form beautiful.—It gave him a chill, that word.[52]

What can one do in the face of something "impossible to communicate" but fail in broad daylight with an insufficiency of
concrete imagery? This is better than to swoon.

In a letter to his elder son, Williams recalls that when the
boy burst into tears on being edged out of a victory in a canoe
race, he had laughed: "Why? Just to hide my own embarrass-
ment." [53] The concealment of feeling by the assumption of a
kind of mask is a tactic also in much of the poetry. The "essential poetry" in Williams, according to Wallace Stevens in his
preface, was "the result of the conjunction of the unreal and
the real, the sentimental and the antipoetic, the constant interaction of two opposites"; and this comment, though it angered
Williams, is just for a great deal of his verse. It is just, for example, in poems in which romantic memory is pitted against
present reality. In "Good Night," the former is sleazy, the latter
hard and clear. And yet there is a balance between them, only
if because the poet's protesting too much in defaming romantic
memory makes us recognize that it has some power over him:

> In brilliant gas light
> I turn the kitchen spigot
> and watch the water plash
> into the clean white sink.
> On the grooved drain-board
> to one side is
> a glass filled with parsley—
> crisped green.
>
> . . . .
>
> Waiting, with a glass in my hand
> —three girls in crimson satin

[52] William Carlos Williams, *A Voyage to Pagany* (New York: Macaulay,
1928), p. 50.
[53] *SL*, p. 202. The incident is recalled again in a later letter to the same
son, pp. 228–29.

pass close before me on
the murmurous background of
the crowded opera—
                                    it is

memory playing the clown—
three vague, meaningless girls
full of smells and
the rustling sounds of
cloth rubbing on cloth and
little slippers on carpet—
high-school French
spoken in a loud voice!
                    (CEP, p. 145)

Memory is a romantic thing throughout Williams' work. In the early poems he deals with it (or pretends to) summarily, as in "Good Night" or in the following passage from "Brilliant Sad Sun":

Look!
from a glass pitcher she serves
clear water to the white chickens.

What are your memories
beside that purity?
                    (CEP, p. 324)

"All the Fancy Things" (CEP, p. 321), which Stevens claimed to be romantic in the accepted sense, closes by suggesting the absurdity of thinking one can live on rarefied memories.

In such poems, even when the power the romantic has over him makes itself obliquely felt, Williams is manifestly resisting it. Later this resistance loses something of its sap: feeling, naked and unashamed, enters poems like "The Yellow Flower," "The Orchestra," and "To a Dog"; and memory receives increasing sanction. "To a Dog Injured in the Street" is largely informed by memories; in "The Descent" memory presents reality with deeper intensity—"no whiteness (lost) is so white as the memory / of whiteness";[54] and in "Shadows" there is the following:

> . . . we experience
> violently
> every day
> two worlds
> one of which we share with the
> rose in bloom
> and one,
> by far the greater,
> with the past,
> the world of memory,
> the silly world of history,
> the world
> of the imagination.
>
> (*PB*, p. 151)

Some of the severity against romantic memory seems to give way in the later poems.

Then in the last poems, another difference also shows a weakening of Williams' resistance against the romantic: except in *Paterson V* there is scarcely any prose; and, in the poems written in the three-part line, as many of the last poems are, no special formal provision is made for images, or bits of conversation, or statements which belong to the real world and exist beyond the poetry or are just coming over into it; for a regular rhythm dominates the whole. Only a little before he announced that he was going to use the three-part line for the rest of his career,[55] Williams had made much of his need, in the letter to Ralph Nash, to "fight his way to a world which breaks through to the actual," a need which is met by the prose passages in

---

[54] Memory actually suffuses the poetic line, that of Pound's "What whiteness can add to that whiteness, what candour?" from the *Pisan Cantos* and before that Pound's translation of *Confucian Analects* ([London: Peter Owen, 1933], p. 5).

[55] In a letter to John C. Thirlwall, June 13, 1955, *SL*, p. 334.

Paterson and the distinct passages of nonpoetry elsewhere. Now the presence in the poem of "the actual" is not so sharply marked as it was earlier. In the last poems, memories, old photographs, and other experience at second hand, and sometimes the ideal quality these suggest, are sanctioned, and the presence of the specifically nonpoetic is no longer thrown into relief. There seems to be an appreciable shift in the balance—not necessarily a stark change in Williams' attitude—of the reality-romantic ratio; it is as if the poet were becoming aware in age that the memories that play about a concrete percept become part of its reality or that one's own concept of ideality is itself, paradoxically, a kind of reality.

VIII

Some of these observations on the principles behind the poetic act in Williams may be summed up in a study of "The Desert Music" (*PB*, pp. 108-20), of which Williams said, "I feel that many of my culminating ideas as to form have entered into this poem," where "form" surely includes ideas and feelings.

In this poem, the context supplied by poetic invention is called music. By virtue of the poet's emotion the poem lifts the environment to expression and supplies context for certain members of humanity: the strip-tease dancer, the almost sub-human object huddled on the bridge, and the begging children. The poet sees the stripper in a context different from the one in which she literally appears:

                                  Andromeda of those rocks,
         the virgin of her mind   .   those unearthly
         greens and reds

                                  in her mockery of virtue
         she becomes unaccountably virtuous
                                  though she in no
             way pretends it   .

The fitness of the new description is accounted for as follows:

There is another music [other, that is, than the music of the
cabaret]. The bright-colored candy
of her nakedness lifts her unexpectedly
to partake of its tune   .

The music, the poetic context, also encompasses the object on
the bridge:

>   . . . The music
>   guards it, a mucus, a film that surrounds it,
>   a benumbing ink that stains the
>   sea of our minds—to hold us off—shed
>   of a shape close as it can get to no shape,
>   a music! a protecting music   .

These two persons are conceived in their unique forms by the
poetic context. One cannot say that they undergo metamorphosis,
because they remain what they were: the one "an old whore
in / a cheap Mexican joint" and the other an "it," a "shape
close as it can get to no shape."

Here is the invention in the poem, the new context—the
"music of survival"—given to parts of reality. But only a portion
of the poem is involved in this operation. A miscellany of perceptions frame these figures—the accidents of the trip to Juarez,
the tourist sights and sounds, which though they give an example of what Henry James called "saturation," "the air and
the very smell of packed actuality," are presented in negligible
rhythm and seem to be mustered by fanciful association with
pure arbitrariness. The first thing one must say of these perceptions that seem to have been by-passed by any poetic operation
is that they are the poet's acknowledgment of the real world
that lies always one step beyond his approaches, what we have
seen above in the symbols of the green rose and the virgin.
Then one may say that some of these apparently raw materials
from the world, like the words Williams speaks of in his review
of Rexroth, have caught ideas in their net.

Certain of these miscellaneous particulars are linked in an

"imaginative category"; the one-thousandth part that they have in common is the idea of protection and survival. Speaking of the whore, the poet mentions the "virgin of her mind," suggesting that it is protected from whatever compromise her body had endured; and for the shape on the bridge, he says there is a "protecting music." A few of the particulars which seem casually brought into the poem contribute to these ideas. But they do so with no cost to their actuality; indeed, the particular which is most nearly thematic is introduced by a remark which makes it seem the most arbitrary:

> —tell you what else we saw: about a million
> sparrows screaming their heads off
> in the trees of that small park where
> the buses stop, sanctuary,
> I suppose,
> from the wind driving the sand in that way
> about the city   .

Sanctuary: a number of the facts and objects represented in the poem illustrate protection, safety, and survival; because of the threat of the bomb and the poet's failing health, these themes pervade the whole volume of which "The Desert Music" is the title poem. There are other details one may adduce with decreasing conviction as to their thematic contribution. As an act of self-preservation:

> . . . I saw H. terribly
> beaten up in one of those joints. . . .
> · · · · · · · · · · · · ·
> . . . I do
> my drinking on the main drag   .

Self-protection as vigilance is instanced as follows:

> . . . a few Indians squatted in the
> booths, unnoticing (don't you think it)
> as though they slept there   .

With these Indians may be compared the four alligators in the
fountain, of which either the poet or Floss saw only two, though
"They were looking / right at you all the time." Then as protection there is the way the Indian woman carries her baby, and
the poet's anxiety at the sight of the candy, which is "aniline /
red and green" suggesting poison: "Do you suppose anyone
actually / buys—and eats the stuff?" Last, there is the cook,
with

> . . . an apron over
> the well-pressed pants of a street
>
> suit. . . .

There are also many images and pieces of incidental intelligence that do not illustrate at all ideas associated with protection. And, of course, the aniline red and green of the candy in
its association with the "bright-colored candy" of the nakedness of the stripper and "those unearthly / greens and reds"
makes an "imaginative category" that cuts across the one in
which protection is the thousandth part the elements have in
common. But if there were objection that an equal proportion
of facts illustrating protection could be adduced by picking at
random in, say, a guide to Juarez, or any travel book, or a
couple of Pound's *Cantos,* it could, I think, only be answered
by pointing to the theme of survival in the invented part of the
poem, to which certain of the sight-seeing details do seem to
provide a minor counterpoint. But this is not their only nor
perhaps their major achievement. What is more significant
about these particulars is that they provide an anchorage in
reality against a subjective romantic swell.

Poetry is described in "The Desert Music" as being "A matter of inspiration . . . / Of necessity"; by means of poetic invention certain conventionally ugly human figures are gathered
into the context of a higher plane of reality. One may say that,
given the "blessed mood," the poet is able to lift these odd peo-

ple into an expression of the "music of humanity." But then, if this way of putting it reminds us of "Tintern Abbey," the enormous difference between the two poems immediately strikes us: Wordsworth's comparable ecstasy was vouchsafed to him under conventional romantic circumstances when he was in nature, cloistered away from the busy world; Williams is at pains *not* to exclude the real world nor even to give it subordinate representation, but to keep it consistently before himself and the reader in hard particularity. It forms the solid classical ground from which, in good faith, the poet may take a controlled romantic flight. Or, to enlarge Marianne Moore's celebrated metaphor, he does not offer as a poem a flower in a cutglass vase but the whole uncultivated garden, toads and all.

At the same time, although he deliberately refrains from hiking off to the woods for the romantic experience, in the moments when such experience actually comes to him he is more or less detached from his environment; at least he is alone. He is, for instance, detached from the other customers in the cabaret, in which the girl

> knows her customers,
> has the same
> opinion of them as I
> have. . . .

Later, the ecstasy seems to come to him alone and seems to be unshareable:

> What's that?

Oh, come on.

> But what's THAT?

> the music! the
music! as when Casals struck
and held a deep cello tone
and I am speechless   . . . .

Then, "Now the music volleys through as in / a lonely moment I hear it."

The detachment is there. The large effect of the poem, however, is in strong contrast to that of "Tintern Abbey" simply by virtue of the weight of all the mustered realism, which states in its own way that the poet does his poetizing, like his drinking, on the main drag.

I spoke above of the classical objectivity serving as a ground for the romantic excursion, as if the poem were like some of Michelangelo's sculptures which still grow out of the uncarved stone.[56] But one may ask of "The Desert Music," as of other poems where the distinction shows in relief, whether the romantic feeling grows out of the antipoetic or whether the poet begins with the feeling and proceeds to seek a matter-of-fact context to ballast it. Williams' remark quoted above about fighting his way *to* "a world which breaks through to the actual" suggests the poetic straining toward the antipoetic, the "sentimental" (Stevens' word) toward the real. If this describes the way in which "The Desert Music" came about, then we may think of it as feeling trying to find pattern in sights and sounds objectively perceived rather than arising out of these.

But, we may ask, does the feeling actually find a pattern? If we turn back to Marianne Moore, it seems less questionable that the feeling grows out of the objective materials; or at least, not to probe the workings of poets' minds, our sense of pattern in Miss Moore is stronger than it is in Williams. One does not subscribe to the pejorative remark of Robert Frost that "everything is planned" in her poems when saying that it is the pattern the feelings engender rather than the naked feelings themselves that we immediately experience. In Williams, however, in "The Desert Music" at least, and in other late poems such as "The Yellow Flower" or "To a Dog Injured in the Street" or

[56] Cf. Barriss Mills, "The Method of *Paterson*," *Approach*, No. 38 (Winter, 1961), p. 24.

"Asphodel, That Greeny Flower," we sense the feeling itself—
I doubt that we get to know or share it—more strongly than and
separately from its context. We respond as Williams does to the
cello, not to the pattern of the music but to the isolated note:

> . . . when Casals struck
> and held a deep cello tone
> and I am speechless   . . . .

One might isolate this passage and say, *There* is the romantic! To take it out of context as if it were not part of a larger
thing would in a sense be unfair. But in another sense, it is *not*
part of its "context." Whether the antipoetic precedes and gives
rise to the poetic or whether the latter initiates a search for the
former, does one actually experience a satisfying poetic interaction between the two? Is there a relationship that enables
feeling to become articulate? Not really: there are the parts of
the poem informed by feeling and there are the other parts. The
unreal does not "fecundate the real" nor the sentimental, the
antipoetic, as Stevens found they did in the early poetry. They
seem rather to pull away from each other.

In "The Desert Music," as in other poems, we can see an
effort to encompass great disorder. Many miscellaneous perceptions are held in view, the poet's view; and, to his delight, among
some of them he has discovered the encompassing unity. It is a
matter of discovery: the stripper is lifted "unexpectedly" to partake of the music; the poet asks,

> What in the form of an old whore in
> a cheap Mexican joint . . .
> . . .   can be
> so refreshing to me, raise to my ear
> so sweet a tune, built of such slime?

He is searching in the poem itself for the unity that makes for
poetry. At the same time he throws the net wider than he can
draw it to, so that the fanciful perceptions remain miscellaneous.

But as we saw above, there is the possibility in poetry for what Hulme calls "the happy chance" and "the accidental discovery of effect." And Williams keeps his poem open to such happy accidents.

IX

Finally, a word about form, rhythm, and "the measure." We have seen above some of Williams' predilections about the over-all form of the poem.[57] We must look now to his ideas about and practices in form in the sense of the rhythms and pauses in the actual lines, the texture of the poems. He always showed a consuming interest in the line; most often it was a line yet to be discovered; it was a line that existed in the rhythms of American speech and one which in itself, not because of the meaning in it, would speak of our times. "I look," he says, "for a direct expression of the turmoils of today in the arts. Not *about* today in classical forms but in forms generated, invented, today direct from the turmoil itself—or the quietude or whatever it might be so long as it is generated in *form* directly from the form society itself takes in its struggles."[58] His interest in the line seems to have grown during the forties and fifties: he speaks of it frequently in the letters of that period, and in the *Autobiography* (1951) he reprints a large part of Charles Olson's essay on projective verse with its ruminations on head, ear, and syllable, heart, breath, and line. Then in 1955, after a career of experiment and discussion, he reports that he had discovered the line he had been looking for, in a passage in his own *Paterson* written years earlier, and he determines to use "no other form for the rest of [his] life" (*SL*, p. 334).

In this matter of form Williams needs, I believe, to be defended both from his critics and from certain of his own spon-

---

[57] Form in this sense, which in Williams is not a mold chosen beforehand but something discovered after, will be considered in the final chapter. See pp. 172–83.

[58] William Carlos Williams, "Letter to an Australian Editor," *Briarcliff Quarterly*, III (1946), 207.

taneous and compromising dicta. The critics have sometimes dealt with the difficult matter of form in Williams' poetry in the ready and easy way of stretching the poems out into blocks of prose to discover that they are not poetry at all! But in certain of Williams' pieces, this kind of manhandling obliterates the notification of the only formal element they contain—the rhythm which is perceptible by observing the end-line pauses. Such a rhythm, uninsistent though it may be, is the sole poetic agency that distinguishes some pieces from prose. One does not want to be "had" by poems which are only poems by virtue of their shape on the page, of which there has been, I believe, a good crop in recent years; and it must be admitted that Williams himself had an eye for the appearance of the printed poem on the page. On the other hand, only by the shape on the page can the way in which a poem is supposed to sound be communicated; and when this is mutilated, communication is corrupted. If even prose can be injured in its rhythms by printing,[59] how much more may poetry. According to Charles Olson, the typewriter gives the poet a chance to make a fairly exact score,[60] but it is of no advantage if editors ignore it or critics roll all its sweetness into a solid ball of prose. In an early letter, Williams complains to Harriet Monroe that her rearrangement of his poem makes it "physically impossible for anyone to guess how [he] intended it to be read" (*SL*, p. 39).

Then sometimes Williams himself played down the distinction between prose and poetry. But on the occasions that he did so, there were particular reasons or qualifications; and his belief in poetic form is not really compromised. In the Mike Wallace interview, for example, when he says, "Anything is

[59] Northrop Frye points out that prose rhythm may be injured when an emphatic word is printed at the end of a line instead of at the beginning of the next one (*Anatomy of Criticism* [Princeton, N.J.: Princeton University Press, 1957], p. 263).

[60] He observes that the typewriter can "indicate exactly the breath, the pauses, the suspensions even of syllables, the juxtapositions even of parts of phrases" ("Projective Verse vs. the Non-Projective," *Poetry New York*, No. 3 [1950], p. 19).

good material for poetry," implying not the familiar twentieth-century belief that there are no specifically proper or improper *subjects* but that written material simply is poetry, he requires that it be treated rhythmically. And rhythmic treatment, as we have seen, is the significant differential. Then, in another place, when he says, "I want to say that prose and verse are to me the same thing" (*SL*, p. 263), he is trying, as the context shows, to stamp out the idea that the prose passages in *Paterson* are "an antipoetic device." We have seen above that this is a fair description of them. But it bothered Williams all his life, and here he is overdoing his strong objection. In other remarks elsewhere he clearly recognizes a difference, in one place a complete cleavage, between poetry and prose.[61]

Williams is characteristically unwilling to gather his images or his snatches of American conversation and shift them about until they are molded into the regularly repeated rhythms of a prepared form. But it is equally clear from both his poetry and his frequently expressed concern in the prose that he is not satisfied to do without form altogether; he does not subscribe to what R. P. Blackmur calls the fallacy of faith in expressive form:[62] indeed, he feels the need for form so strongly that he even recommends that James Laughlin try using rhymed couplets to avoid bare statements.[63] In Williams' own best poetry the form is at work: the statement made by the rhetoric is not the total statement made by the poem, as is implied by those who reorganize the lines; form, in these poems, serves as an indissoluble part of the means of expression; and paraphrase is difficult.

It is, for example, the formal elements, the changing rhythms, that make "By the Road to the Contagious Hospital" a successful poem. Take away the variety of movement and there remains a prose statement, rather disordered, of images of winter

[61] *Spring and All*, p. 67. See also pp. 68 and 77–78.
[62] Blackmur, *Form and Value*, p. 256.
[63] Letter included in John C. Thirlwall, "William Carlos Williams as Correspondent," *Literary Review*, I (Autumn, 1957), 17.

and the brink of spring. Given the changing rhythms, the scene
is charged and elevated to express the feelings of the observer;
the form carries the feeling and makes it publicly available. The
stark images are in themselves delightful, if one likes this sort
of thing; but the poem goes far beyond imagism in the limited
sense of the word.

> By the road to the contagious hospital
> under the surge of the blue
> mottled clouds driven from the
> northeast—a cold wind. Beyond, the
> waste of broad, muddy fields   5
> brown with dried weeds, standing and fallen
>
> patches of standing water
> the scattering of tall trees
>
> All along the road the reddish
> purplish, forked, upstanding, twiggy   10
> stuff of bushes and small trees
> with dead, brown leaves under them
> leafless vines—
>
> Lifeless in appearance, sluggish
> dazed spring approaches—   15
>
> They enter the new world naked,
> cold, uncertain of all
> save that they enter. All about them
> the cold, familiar wind—
>
> Now the grass, tomorrow   20
> the stiff curl of wildcarrot leaf
> One by one objects are defined—
> It quickens: clarity, outline of leaf
>
> But now the stark dignity of
> entrance—Still, the profound change   25
> has come upon them: rooted, they
> grip down and begin to awaken

(CEP, p. 241)

The contribution of form is related to the play between poetry and antipoetry which makes the climax of the poem and to which I wish first to draw attention. The climactic phrase of the poem is "the stark dignity of / entrance." It is also the most poetic and least realistic phrase, implying as it does the actor, spring personified, entering upon a scene which is separate and different from itself, whereas scientifically speaking spring does not enter from elsewhere upon a scene. The word "entrance" is a metaphor expressing the poet's feeling. And this feeling is expressed earlier in the poem in rhythmic changes. After the climax of the poem, the fiction in the metaphor of entry is disposed of in the antithetical "still" (but still), which introduces a statement bearing an idea contrary to that of entry: spring is in fact deep in the scene, "rooted," gripping down, not entering upon it. In the metaphor and the withdrawal from it we have first the lifting of the environment to expression by means of the feelings and then the respect for the reality of the environment, which acknowledges that spring is a condition in the scene and not a spirit waltzing into it; we have poetry and the antipoetic.

Then to turn to the rhythmic changes, which are similarly making a fictive thing out of the scene. The first six lines of the poem present the wintry scene; and this description is crowned and summed up in the two-line section that follows. The inactivity of this scene, impressed by the use of "standing" twice, though with different denotations, and enhanced by the contrast of the surge of the clouds above it, is the strongest feature. The scene that follows in lines 9 to 13 is of the "twiggy stuff of bushes"; this scene also, as the rhetoric presents it, is inactive: literally, there is no image of movement here. But the rhythms modify our experience of it: the regular trochaic beat of the first two and a half lines invests the images with life and activity:

> All along the road the reddish
> purplish, forked, upstanding, twiggy
> stuff of bushes. . . .

The liveliness does not belong to the objective scene but is grafted on to it by the poet's excitement at the thought that spring, not yet manifest, is at hand. But the real situation, summed up in the following two-line section, is unexciting: "Lifeless in appearance, sluggish / dazed spring approaches—"; and the next four lines, 16 to 19, further deprive the bushes of the sense of upthrust and confidence with which the rhythm had endowed them. The sudden burst into regular trochaic rhythm thus works in counterpoint to the description of static scenery. Like the metaphor at the climax of the poem, the rhythm bestows upon the scene—here the "twiggy stuff of bushes"—a fictional quality and thereby expresses the poet's feeling. Needless to say, it gives the poem a complexity and an interest that the rhetoric itself would not give.

There are more off-the-cuff dicta of Williams' own against which he must be defended in this discussion of form. Remarks in letters, essays, and lectures cannot always be taken literally and accurately. His prose is, to a great extent, as hit-or-miss as his poetry. There are on the one hand the brilliant perceptions: no one, for instance, has said in so few words shrewder things about Marianne Moore; that she is like a "secret Niagara" (SE, p. 292) is only one example of the various exactly right things Williams says about her. Then, on the other hand, there is the kind of floundering around, the compulsive repetition with variations of a word that has a sort of numinous appeal to him, found for example in "The Poem as a Field of Action" (SE, pp. 280–91), where he does not rightly know what he is about. Much of the talk about the "new line" and "measure" comes into this latter category: it is excited talk, and one must look at it with no fundamentalist belief in the inspiration of every word. Sometimes the implications of the "line" as Williams suggests them are staggering: "If the measurement itself is confined," he writes, "every dimension of the verse and all implications touching it suffer confinement and generate pressures within our lives which will blow it and us apart" (SL, p. 332).

Or, "When Einstein promulgated the theory of relativity he could not have foreseen . . . its influence on the writing of poetry" (*SL,* pp. 335–36). Or "something has got to be done with the line," he says, "—it's got to be opened up . . . newly ordered. . . . When we do that we shall know why society is falling apart and how rebuilding itself. . . ."[64] These long-range reverberations, as imaginative as the ascription of the fall of Troy to a shudder in the loins, need not necessarily be gainsaid. But of course it is not logic but sympathetic magic that dictates that the line must be opened up on account of the relativity theory. One might equally well call for a firmer verse line to take its wages in the hour when the heavens were expanding. And incidentally, in light of the quotation above about the confinement of measure and its effects, the recommendation of rhymed couplets to James Laughlin looks rather like a booby trap.

In more immediate matters pertaining to measure, the dicta are not less confusing: "By measure I mean musical pace," Williams says in the most useful, analytical letter on the subject (*SL,* p. 326). But then in another letter he says, "The first thing you learn when you begin to learn anything about this earth is that you are eternally barred save for the report of your senses from knowing anything about it. Measure serves for us as the key: we can measure between objects; therefore, we know that they exist" (*SL,* p. 331). In this last sentence, what had been time measurement has become space measurement. It has been claimed that Williams is referring here to "meaningful word-groups (or phrases) as objects";[65] and if this is so, measure can be saved to mean pace. But we must remember Williams' delight in a kind of Donne-like play—the delight which comes up, for instance, with the observation that since "syphilis covers the body with salmon-red petals," one of the

[64] Williams, "Letter to an Australian Editor," p. 207.
[65] Mary Ellen Solt, "William Carlos Williams: Idiom and Structure," *Massachusetts Review,* III (Winter, 1962), 316.

"most delightful gestures" of "the philosophy of disease" is "bringing flowers to the sick." [66] It seems more likely that the remark about measure, unless it is simply a loose use of words, is an instance of Williams' characteristic play, with perhaps the hope that a piece of prosodic wisdom might emerge.

Then, again, much of the talk about the American idiom is unhelpful. In the letter to Kay Boyle in 1932, Williams says, "It is a contortion of speech to conform to a rigidity of line. It is in the newness of a live speech that the new line exists undiscovered" (*SL*, p. 134). The first sentence here speaks of Williams' consistent aim to do no violence to actuality, which is seen everywhere in his treatment of both speech and physical objects in poetry and in the novel. An object, of course, cannot but be distorted when it is brought into any art form (with the exception, if they be considered art, of Duchamp's "readymades"). Speech, on the other hand, can be incorporated into literature without modification—the popular misconception about Hemingway's dialogue (a misconception not shared by Williams, however) assumes that it has been. But, of course, art does modify reality and poetry does modify speech. Williams has much to say about American speech and about the fact that it is different from English—"a language which has not been taught to us in our schools, a language which has a rhythmical structure thoroughly separate from English" (*SL*, p. 335). And during his whole life he paid close attention to these rhythms as he heard them from day to day. But his best poetry, "By the Road to the Contagious Hospital," for one example, is not the speech of anybody in particular; it does not contain American rather than British rhythms. Poetry in general does not necessarily ring with a specific regional speech at all. Poetry in

---

[66] *Kora in Hell*, p. 76. The play on "measure" is carried on elsewhere: ". . . the only thing a man can do with his life is to measure it. If we can measure it, that becomes a truth, as in science, so in verse, so in life" (quoted by John C. Thirlwall, "The Lost Poems of William Carlos Williams: Or The Past Recaptured," *New Directions 16* [Norfolk, Conn., 1957], p. 26). What does measure mean here?

Williams may incorporate American speech by embedding a phrase of the real language of men that is not poetry within lines that are—the lines in *Paterson,* for instance, "Geeze, Doc, I guess it's all right / but what the hell does it mean?" (p. 138). Or it may be modified. If it were otherwise, we should have to conclude that the lower classes of Rutherford, New Jersey, *bourgeois gentilshommes* though they are not, have been speaking poetry all their lives! At length Williams discovered in his own work the line he had been searching for, and he cites the passage from *Paterson* beginning "The descent beckons" as representing "the culmination of all [his] striving after an escape from the restrictions of the verse of the past" (*SL,* p. 334) and, though he later modified the form, "[his] final conception of what [his] own poetry should be" (*I Wanted to Write a Poem,* p. 80). But this passage neither embodies nor reflects American as opposed to British speech rhythms. As one critic after another has observed, its rhythms are those of Eliot's *Four Quartets;* and this poem, insofar as it reflects any sectional speech at all, reflects that of the British upper classes. The important fact about the relation between Williams' poetry and speech is not that it embodies American, but simply that it is close to speech in general.

In most of the poetry he wrote during the last ten years of his life, Williams used a line of three parts. During the fifties he spoke often of the "variable foot," but in the letter to Richard Eberhart (*SL,* pp. 325–27) which gives the fullest consideration to the three-part line form, he does not mention the foot at all. (A variable foot is a strange term to use when speaking of measure: as Alan Stephens says, it is like speaking of an elastic inch.[67]) In this verse form, an equal measure of time is given to each of the three parts of the line. In the letter, Williams quotes a few lines from two poems, numbering the parts of the line, and says, "Count a single beat to each nu-

---

[67] Alan Stephens, "Dr. Williams and Tradition," *Poetry,* CI (February, 1963), 361.

meral." If each part of the line is equivalent to a beat, then the three parts are equal in length to each other and so are the full lines; to this extent the verse is regular. But since each part of the line and hence each full line may contain a widely variable number of syllables, the form is flexible.

One looks to Hopkins for comparison, as Williams himself did. Williams, however, found that Hopkins was "constipated" and "didn't go far enough" (SL, pp. 321, 335). Actually, the main difference is that Hopkins' theory and practice are based on the disposal of accented syllables, whereas Williams, except that he denies that the American idiom is based on the iamb which has dominated traditional prosody, speaks little of the accents in this new measure and bases his form on the time taken by the individual parts of the line. Speaking generally of all the poems in the form of the three-part line, one may say that each third part has one strongly accented syllable, one or more that receive secondary stress, and others that are unstressed; but there is rarely a repeated pattern of stressed and unstressed syllables. The significant feature of this form is the pause: since to each third of the line an equal measure of time is given and since some lines consist of only one or two syllables, pauses of varying length continually arrest the movement of the verse.

The typographical arrangement of the lines may not, once again, be considered arbitrary. In some cases it is demonstrable that Williams gains effects of emphasis by the disposition of words throughout the parts of a line. In the version of "Asphodel, That Greeny Flower" that appeared as "Work in Progress" in *Perspective*, Williams wrote that it was ridiculous

> what airs we put on
>   to seem profound
>   while our hearts gasp
> dying
>   for want of love.[68]

[68] *Perspective*, VI (Autumn–Winter, 1953), 175.

In *Journey to Love* the passage goes

while our hearts

gasp dying

for want of love.[69]

The ear can detect the difference, and the reason for it is clear enough: in the first version "hearts" shares a time unit with "gasp" and thus receives less emphasis than in the second version where it does not so share time, and where, in addition, it is immediately followed by the end-line pause. That "hearts" should get more emphasis is proper, since the lines are dealing with a minor antithesis between head and heart. Often in Williams' latest poems what may appear to sight as an arbitrary arrangement of words on the page is revealed to the ear as a beautiful, that is, a meaningful, disposition of pause and emphasis. Sometimes the form is not thus accountable; then it is like the nonorganic forms, in which most poetry in English is written, that may occasionally be shown to contribute to local meaning but most often may not. But with both Williams' form and the traditional ones, the possibility that they are functional must be admitted, even though we cannot articulate what that function is.[70]

The function of the form, however, is not only to be sought in the local emphasis; as we have seen, it is intimately bound up with Williams' total style, which embodies his concept of poetry. The relationship between the three-part lines and Williams' concept of poetry may be pointed up by studying it in an individual poem. The incompleteness of "The Mental Hospital Garden" (*PB*, pp. 97–100) consists in the failure of two or three extended metaphors to be perfectly asserted as such;

[69] William Carlos Williams, *Journey to Love* (New York: Random House, 1955), p. 69. This version also in *PB*, p. 170.

[70] For an example of a description of the function of measure, see Denis Donoghue's analysis of "To Daphne and Virginia" (*PB*, pp. 75–79), in "For a Redeeming Language," *Twentieth Century*, CLXIII (June, 1958), 540.

metaphoric equivalences remain on the brink of materialization, leaving a slight sense of mystery. This kind of incompleteness is familiar in Williams. Incompleteness is, in a way, the subject of "The Mental Hospital Garden" (as it is of some other poems), in which the early, incomplete spring, which Williams here and everywhere prefers to the fully burgeoning summer, almost becomes a metaphor for the disease of the patients. They and the season have in common a limitation, not shared by the bounty of sanity and summer. Early spring is the season when nesting birds must needs make use of old nests for materials

> against the advent of that bounty
>   from which
>   they will build anew. . . .

The limitation inflicted upon the patients, however, is a bounty of another kind: the young couples embrace because

> They are careless
>   under license of the disease
>   which has restricted them
> to these grounds.
> · · · · · · · · · · · · · · · ·
>   They are divided
>   from their fellows . . .

but they enjoy this liberating confinement as "a bounty / from a last year's bird's nest." Spring with its limitations almost stumbles into becoming a metaphor for mental disease. Later in the poem, summer similarly becomes or nearly becomes the equivalent of cure. The cured patients are baffled by the full bounty and unlimited summer of their freedom:

> Filled with terror
>   they seek
>   a familiar flower

at which to warm themselves,
but the whole field
accosts them. . . .

The argument I am trying to follow calls for some such crude statement as this about the poem; and the fact of its necessary crudeness is a part of that argument. It is because the metaphoric equivalences remain vague and inexplicit, like structures in a mist, that the poem is *not* the morbid-sounding statement above, but another thing which is not to be botanized in this way. And it is exactly the loose form that provides the permissive medium in which relationships need not be defined and argument need not come to a point. Unless one ignores the pauses between the parts of the lines and reads this poem as prose, the hesitance of the movement reflects the inconclusiveness of the evolution of the poem and the relationships in it. But the movement is more than a reflection (one needs to go beyond Pope's facile formula about the sound merely echoing the sense); it is the actual movement of the meditating mind, pursuing its disjunctive course among images as it looks with hesitation for the metaphoric relationships by means of which the outside world might be made into poetry. For the particular operation Williams wishes to perform, a tighter verse form would be inappropriate, indeed unthinkable. One need only imagine this tentative thinking process confined in the couplet or in the kind of blank verse that rides in triumph to Persepolis to realize that the form it has actually taken is the only form possible. Many other poems in *Pictures from Brueghel* are in the same form, and it is appropriate to them for the same or similar reasons.[71]

[71] Compare the observations made by Donald Davie upon Pound's typographical setting of "Donna mi prega" (*Ezra Pound: Poet as Sculptor* [New York: Oxford University Press, 1964], pp. 112–19). Davie concludes as follows: ". . . it is true that poetry of this kind, whether practiced by Pound himself or by others such as William Carlos Williams and Charles Olson and Robert Creeley, is a poetry that characteristically moves forward

Many of Williams' earlier poems are incomplete either in the manner of "The Mental Hospital Garden" or in another, and the verse form in which they are written is adequately loose. Thus, the reason for Williams' excitement over his new line is not quite clear. One of its functions, however, relates these last poems to modern painting and thus points back to the earlier work, which is likewise related, and to its ideals, specifically to Williams' loyalty to a world of discrete things and his nominalistic aim to use them exclusively to present ideas: ". . . no ideas but in things." An effect of the three-part line[72] is that by giving to each element in a sentence a separate and equal part of a line, Williams makes a particular of each element. It is not a brand new feature,[73] but its regularity is new. The effect is like that gained by printing Walter Pater in vers libre as Yeats does in *The Oxford Book of Modern Verse,* remarking that Pater was accustomed to give each sentence a separate page of manuscript. The mind lingers on each part as a separate sensation. In Williams, emphasis falls equally on each part of the line; thus, for example, a subordinate clause may receive as much formal emphasis as a main one; it becomes "another fact of the situation, instead of the familiar and consequently de-emphasized modifying clause." [74] The implications of this ob-

---

only hesitantly, gropingly, and slowly; which often seems to float across the page as much as it moves down it; in which, if the perceptions are cast in the form of sentences, the sentence is bracketed off and, as it were, folded in on itself so as to seem equal with a disjointed phrase; a poetry (we might almost say) of the noun rather than the verb."

[72] Bernard Engel, "The Verse Line of Dr. Williams: A Fact of the Thing Itself," *Papers of the Michigan Academy of Science, Arts, and Letters,* XLVI (1961), 665–70.

[73] Carl Rakosi, for example, observed early on the separation in Williams of key words from their modifiers ("William Carlos Williams," *Symposium,* IV [October, 1933], 444).

[74] Engel, "The Verse Line of Dr. Williams," p. 668. Compare again Pound's practice: "The breaking of the pentameter made possible, indeed it enforced, the breaking down of experience into related but distinct items. On the other hand, any submergence of the line by enjambement into larger units inevitably produced that blurring of edges that Pound and all the imagists, no less than Williams, would castigate as 'muzzy' " (Donald Davie, *Pound,* pp. 123–24).

servation are interesting. The syntactical relations between parts
of the sentence are weakened, and the poem is at liberty to move
according to association and fancy rather than according to logic:
in many instances a poem moves on from a clause that is syntactically subordinate, not the main one: in "Asphodel," Williams
is speaking of waste and attributing it to "the bomb." He asks

> What else was the fire
> at the Jockey Club in Buenos Aires
>
> . . . .
>
>   when with Perón's connivance
> the hoodlums destroyed
>   along with the books
>   the priceless Goyas. . . .
>   (*PB,* p. 168)

But he does not develop the idea of waste; he goes on:

> You know how we treasured
>   the few paintings
> we still cling to. . . .

He takes off from the pictures, which the rhythm has de-
subordinated as it were.

There is a similarity in this effect to that of the compound
sentence in Hemingway and his so-called "democracy of the
'and.'" But in view of Williams' own interests, the analogy
seems nearer in pictures. The three-part line tends to break
the rhetoric of the poem into its various parts, which we may
think of as the equivalents of pigments. The poet, or for that
matter the prose writer, who by pushing syntax to the margins
of our attention makes us dwell more on images or particulars
than on the relationships between them, brings the literary
form close to the condition of painting—at least to that of
modern painting, the kind to which Williams' taste ran. Williams may well have shared the taste of Marianne Moore, which
was, as we observed above, for pictures that do not have a design

on one and do not assert one thing at the cost of another. The traditional presentation in older pictures of a central subject in a subordinate environment gives way in modern painting to the general spreading of significant items over the whole canvas. The change may be seen as reflecting a change in men's minds. The "flattening out of climaxes" in art has been related to the "radical transformation of the Western spirit" which this century has witnessed:

> When mankind no longer lives spontaneously turned toward God or the supersensible world . . . the artist too must stand face to face with a flat and inexplicable world. This shows itself even in the formal structures of modern art. Where the movement of the spirit is no longer vertical but only horizontal, the climactic elements in art are in general leveled out, flat-tened.[75]

Williams' new line, then, playing down syntactical relationships and submitting details without subordinating them to a central idea, seems to be related, in its own small, refracting manner, to a feature of the modern mind. It is a remote relationship, perhaps; but as we have seen above, it is the kind of thing Williams himself used to assert without batting an eye.

On the other hand, there may be another reason for Williams' interest in this new line: in crying "Eureka" and clambering out of his bathtub over a matter of form, he may be disguising what in fact the exciting innovation really is. The passage in *Paterson* beginning "The descent beckons," which he later discovered to be in the form he had been seeking, is, as we have seen, among those later poems that deal in memory. And it seems possible that the attachment of his excitement to it is a case of displacement—the psychological trick by which an important feature of a situation is hidden by focusing upon another one. The measure of the passage from *Paterson* is new,

[75] William Barrett, *Irrational Man* (London: Heinemann, 1964), pp. 42, 43, 44.

but it is not so remarkably new as the departure the passage makes in its totality from the kind of poetry Williams had established as his own during the previous twenty-five years. It is conceivable that his real interest has been captured by the possibility of new subject matter.

CHAPTER V

LITERARY RELATIONSHIPS

THE RED WHEELBARROW and the paper nautilus, each in its respective poem, express the feelings of the poets. But in each case the object remains as in itself it actually is: the wheelbarrow shines in an actuality uncompromised by the context of rhythm in which it has been set; the paper nautilus is anatomized scrupulously. It is possible to be *exclusively* aware of each item in its own poem; it would be possible to miss the "point" that each item is making. These poems in this respect are characteristic of their authors' work: although the poets have something to say and, often, to say passionately, the saying of it is not allowed to blur the edge of their perception.

John Crowe Ransom uses a political metaphor to describe what a poem is:

A poem is, so to speak, a democratic state, whereas a prose discourse—mathematical, scientific, ethical, or practical and vernacular—is a totalitarian state. The intention of a democratic state is to perform the work of state as effectively as it can perform it, subject to one reservation of conscience: that it will not despoil its members, the citizens, of the free exercise of their own private and independent characters. But the totalitarian state is interested solely in being effective, and regards the citizens as no citizens at all; that is, regards them as functional members whose existence is totally defined by their allotted contributions to its ends; it has no use for their private characters, and therefore no provision for them.[1]

As we have seen, the poetry of Miss Moore and Williams is more "democratic" in this sense than that of poets who work in the mode of imagination. Fancy is an uncompelling faculty; and in poems where its machinery is largely at work, order is more of a by- than an end-product.

Their similarities should not obscure the differences between Williams and Miss Moore. In many of her poems, rhymes and repeated line lengths contribute to order and completeness. Such form is, after all, the index of her conviction; and conviction calls forth the ordered, finished statement, an expression of contentment that the truth has been ascertained and articulated. Although pattern in Miss Moore, when one exists, has often a minimal impact—there may be no literal impact at all, and we must look for the form, counting syllables and linking up eye-rhymes with a pencil—it works to this end: it sets a light seal of endorsement upon the point the poet is making with modesty and circumspection in the imagery.

Williams, on the other hand, is open: he eschews such endorsement as a closed order would supply, because as we have seen, the poem may be the process of discovery; or at any rate it consists of a miscellany of images and motifs the autonomy of which the poet is not prepared to distort by forcing them into a fixed design. There is the chance of his discovering something as he writes, so that he is unwilling and unable to iron out the roughnesses or harmonize the dissonances and carry the writing to formal completion. The first part of the first book

[1] John Crowe Ransom, "Criticism as Pure Speculation," *The Intent of the Critic,* ed. Donald A. Stauffer (Princeton, N.J.: Princeton University Press, 1941), p. 108.

of *Paterson*, for example, contains the descriptions of the Passaic Falls, a part of a letter, a further description of the water, a newspaper clipping, a quotation from *Historical Collections of the State of New Jersey*, a description of a picture in the *National Geographic Magazine*, and so forth. These are presented as if for themselves only; their autonomy is not infringed upon by the needs of design or form. That is to say, we are given the description of the falls or of a dwarf or of a photograph of the nine wives of an African chief as if the poet had nothing else in mind than that we should merely contemplate these things. No indication is given that each has a function to perform for the whole poem. Such indication would, of course, detract from our interest and absorption in the particular detail itself; it would diminish the emphasis that each item receives; but it is absent. Form in a poem of Williams, most noticeably in a long poem, does not shape and mold the parts according to the needs of the whole; it is imperfect: when we are in the middle, we may know neither how we got there nor where we are going next; when we are at the end, we have no sense of completion.

I propose to comment upon form in Williams by observing briefly how his departures from earlier norms are comparable with those of the baroque style in prose, which arose throughout Europe in the last quarter of the sixteenth century to challenge the Ciceronian period. Thanks to Morris Croll, on whose work on the baroque style I rely as have others before me, we can see in detail the changes wrought in the sentence structure; and these, writ large, are comparable with the changes made by Williams from the principles that have traditionally governed the creation of a long poem. The similarities are not, I believe, a matter of mere coincidence; and if we are not so imprudent as to claim for them more than a general equivalence, the causes of both sets of changes are worth comparing.

To the periodic sentence and the rotund Ciceronian style, the baroque writers "preferred the forms that express the energy and labor of minds seeking the truth . . . to the forms that ex-

press a contented sense of the enjoyment and possession of it." [2]
Some of the affinities Williams has with them will be observed
in the following description:

> They knew that an idea separated from the act of experienc-
> ing it is not the idea that was experienced. The ardor of its
> conception in the mind is a necessary part of its truth; and
> unless it can be conveyed to another mind in something of the
> form of its occurrence, either it has changed into some other
> idea or it has ceased to be an idea, to have any existence what-
> ever except a verbal one. It was the latter fate that happened
> to it, they believed, in the Ciceronian periods of sixteenth-
> century Latin rhetoricians. The successive processes of revision
> to which these periods had been submitted had removed them
> from reality by just so many steps. For themselves, they pre-
> ferred to present the truth of experience in a less concocted
> form, and deliberately chose as the moment of expression that
> in which the idea first clearly objectifies itself in the mind, in
> which, therefore, each of its parts still preserves its own pecul-
> iar emphasis and an independent vigor of its own—in brief,
> the moment in which truth is still *imagined*.[3]

Of parts of this program, Williams' work is strongly reminiscent: over and over again, for example, he is studious to avoid
arriving at the completed truth, "the sea," which "is NOT our
home." Then the "ardor of . . . conception" is sometimes obviously transmitted, as in "I *am* a poet! I / am. I am" (like the
sudden exclamation "That's it" in Stevens), but more often
obliquely in the very fact of the poem's existence. We have seen
also in Williams the inability of the poem to emerge (or his
unwillingness to permit it) from the approaches to it: often
the poem is a reflection of a thinking process rather than the
presentation of a thought-out conception and is comparable
with the work of the prose writers who aimed to convey truth

---

[2] Morris W. Croll, "The Baroque Style in Prose," *Studies in English
Philology in Honor of Frederick Klaeber,* ed. Kemp Malone and Martin B.
Ruud (Minneapolis: University of Minnesota Press, 1929), p. 428.
[3] *Ibid.,* pp. 430–31.

"in something of the form of its occurrence." [4] Again, their suspicion of the distorting effects of revision is like Williams' own distrust in the passage in *Paterson* where he advocates writing carelessly "so that nothing that is not green will survive." The most interesting similarity, however, is that between the prose writers' determination to retain for each particular part of the sentence its peculiar emphasis and the procedures of Miss Moore and Williams toward this end, which have received major attention throughout this essay.

We may also observe some miscellaneous similarities between Williams and individual writers in the baroque vein. Just as Williams' poems repeatedly give the impression of being not discoveries made but acts of discovering, so the anti-Ciceronian constructions of that other doctor, Sir Thomas Browne, constantly give his writing, accordingly to Croll, the "effect of being, not the result of a meditation, but an actual meditation in process. He writes like a philosophical scientist," Croll adds, "making notes of his observation as it occurs. We see his pen move and stop as he thinks." [5] Then, in Williams the poetic act often consists in arranging the world around the self; so, similarly but not identically, the world that Browne regarded was the self: ". . . it is the microcosm of my own frame that I cast mine eye on; for the other, I use it but like my Globe, and turn it round sometimes for my recreation." [6] Williams is

---

[4] "Beat" prose has shown the ultimate extent to which disruption of form can go in reflecting the process of thought or rumination: ". . . the long sentences, endlessly attempting to include the endless, the carelessness —even negligence—with the ordinary rules of grammatical function, so that noun, adjective, and verb interchange roles; after all, if the process is endlessly unpredictable and unfixed, grammatical categories are not relevant. It is a syntax of aimlessly continuing pleasure in which all elements are 'like.' Release, liberation from fixed categories, hilarity—it is an ongoing prose that cannot be concerned with its origins. There are no origins and no end . . ." (Thomas Parkinson, "Phenomenon or Generation," *A Casebook on the Beat*, ed. Thomas Parkinson [New York: Crowell, 1961], p. 288).

[5] Croll, "The Baroque Style," p. 448.

[6] Sir Thomas Browne, *Religio Medici and Other Writings,* ed. C. H. Herford (London: J. M. Dent, 1920), p. 83. Bacon thought this concept "fantastically strained."

reminiscent also of Montaigne, one of the major exemplars of the anti-Ciceronian style, in whose writings the self played a central role. But these two are even more similar in their respect for "things." The following remark of Erich Auerbach's about Montaigne and his *Essays* could be made about Williams and his poems: "They are based on no artfully contrived plan. . . . They follow chance. . . . Strictly speaking it is 'things' after all which direct him—he moves among them, he lives in them; it is in things that he can always be found, for, with his very open eyes and his very impressionable mind, he stands in the midst of the world." [7]

The style that avoids an arrival at formal truth avoids also any of the usual kinds of beauty as end products. Bacon diagnoses as "the first distemper of learning" the habit of hunting for "choiceness of the phrase, and the round and clean composition of the sentence, and the sweet falling of the clauses," rather than concentrating on matter.[8] Montaigne found that the "very beauty of Cicero's language, the faultlessness of his oratorical rhythm" was his defect; and, speaking of Cicero, he says, " 'Fie upon that eloquence that makes us in love with itself, and not with the thing.' " [9] How much of the modern temper speaks through that apostrophe! Bertolt Brecht, T. E. Hulme, Ezra Pound, Ford Madox Ford, Jean-Paul Sartre, Albert Camus, or Ignazio Silone might have made it; so might Bertrand Russell who believed, as Wallace Stevens tells us in "The Noble Rider and the Sound of Words," that it was of the utmost importance to citizens of a democracy to acquire an immunity to eloquence; so also might anyone else who honors the thing in its clear-cut existence and mistrusts the kind

[7] Erich Auerbach, *Mimesis: The Representation of Reality in Western Literature*, trans. Willard Trask (Garden City, N.Y.: Anchor Books, 1957), p. 258.

[8] Francis Bacon, *The Advancement of Learning*, I, 114, in *Essays Civil and Moral* (London: Ward Lock and Co., 1910).

[9] Morris W. Croll, "Attic Prose: Lipsius, Montaigne, Bacon," *Schelling Anniversary Papers by His Former Students* (New York: The Century Company, 1923), pp. 127–28.

of language that renders it down to an essence in satisfying cadences. Williams so successfully eschews eloquence that it never even appears to have been a temptation to him. Beauty is regularly an outworn object of quest, no longer to be desired; the word often occurs in his writing in close or loose connection with "staleness": in *Paterson*,

> . . .   Why have I not
> but for imagined beauty where there is none
> or none available, long since
> put myself deliberately in the way of death?
>
>   Stale as a whale's breath . . . ;[10]

or, speaking of the really "Beautiful thing," he calls it "a dark flame, / a wind, a flood—counter to all staleness" (p. 123); or, in the essay on Joyce, he says, "it would not be stretching the point to describe all modern styles in their grand limits as ways through a staleness of beauty to tell the truth anew." [11]

Williams' deprecation of the old effort toward beautiful writing coincides with the general acceptances of this century. In his own day it is reflected in the writers named above, any of whom might have said, "Prends l'éloquence et tords-lui son cou," if Verlaine had not already said it. In our own day one need not look far to see the same sentiments embodied in practice, while in precept the following remark of Louis Simpson's might speak for many, as it speaks for Karl Shapiro who quotes it:

A few years ago I was able to begin and finish a poem. I found that the poem was directed by certain external forces toward a certain end. But one day I found . . . that I no longer wished to please. . . . I found myself wanting to write

[10] William Carlos Williams, *Paterson* (Norfolk, Conn.: New Directions, 1963), pp. 30–31.

[11] *Selected Essays of William Carlos Williams* (New York: Random House, 1954), p. 75. Hereafter *SE*.

bad poems—poems that did not depend on stock responses. I wanted to write poems that would not please.[12]

A closer comparison between Williams' style and those of the baroque prose writers is facilitated by analyses Croll has made of passages from Bacon, Pascal, and Browne. He observes in these examples of the loose style the characteristic use of loose coordinating conjunctions that do not "refer back to any particular point in the preceding member; nor . . . commit the following member to a predetermined form."[13] He notices also the use of an absolute participle construction, "that commits itself least and lends itself best to the solution of difficulties that arise in the course of a spontaneous and unpremeditated progress." These procedures deliberately avoid giving to a "central or climactic member" that emphasis which it was exactly the aim of the round style to provide. Croll notes in the passage from Browne how he uses "which" to introduce "a new development of the idea, running to as much as five lines of print; yet syntactically it refers only to the last preceding word."[14]

This last feature is like one we have seen already in "Asphodel, That Greeny Flower," where the passage moves away from its main subject, the bomb, by taking off from one subordinate detail, the pictures. The other features mentioned are also familiar in Williams: his use of the absolute participle and other absolute constructions is very frequent, and he often goes beyond the looseness of Bacon or Browne in their use of conjunctions by omitting these altogether. The passage describing Madame Curie in Paris, quoted above, consists of a series of absolute constructions. There are no conjunctions until the "but" in the last line.

What is more significant, however, than syntactical similari-

---

[12] Quoted by Karl Shapiro in "A Defense of Bad Poetry," *Earlham Journal*, I (Spring, 1964), 3.
[13] Croll, "The Baroque Style," p. 443.
[14] *Ibid.*, p. 447.

ties is that the construction Croll finds in a sentence of one of the baroque prose writers is a small-scale model of the over-all construction in a long poem of Williams. In "Asphodel, That Greeny Flower," for instance, two pages of poetry are given to the description of a man seen in the subway, which has as slender a thread of connection to the preceding matter as Browne's five lines of print introduced by a "which." Nor does the description of the man have a firm and manifest relationship to the general topic of the whole poem. In *Paterson*, likewise, we have found large sections whose relationship to the whole is that of an absolute construction and other parts that are related in the way of loose coordination, referring back to no particular point in the preceding part and uncommitted to a predetermined form. As we try to think of the work as a whole—and it is not easy to do so—we do not see any one part as a climactic center, to which all other parts point forward or back and give emphasis in the fashion of a Ciceronian period; we see only linear interweavings of motifs. Form in Williams is not the product of a procedure in which all the details are subordinated to the over-all concept. One does not, first of all, identify the major statement of subject and then recognize other parts and details as subordinate thereto.

This kind of structure may be pictured on the analogy of the circle where details at the circumference are linked by radii to the center; and such a structure lends itself to summary—one may speak of the subject of the poem in terms of its central episode or statement and of the gathering there of themes and images. One may speak thus, for instance, of the subject of *Paradise Lost* as the fall of man, its cause, and Milton's writing about it all. Then one may find a central passage (in Book IX) and proceed to see how each other passage in the work by counterpoint, contrast, comparison, analogy, reflection, consequence, cause, or otherwise is related to the center. This is our habitual manner of approaching a literary work of any length; it is ingrained in us, and to make an approach of a different kind calls for unusual self-discipline and effort. The skill of the author of the traditional kind of poem is seen in his success at selecting from all the phenomena he might have presented those objects and incidents which bear upon his central episode and theme, at presenting such contributing details from the best angle, and at subordinating them in right proportions. In this relation of parts to center resides the form of the work. Such a form may, of course, be called a Procrustean bed or by any other pejorative name, because it controls the contents and to a facile view has no positive contribution: things as in themselves they actually are are forced to fit a given scheme; what did happen in the garden of Eden, if only we knew it, would be found to have given way to what Milton's preconceptions and general scheme require to have happened, and so forth. Content, then, becomes an extension of form—with modern prejudices one may say a *mere* extension of form—rather than the other way about, which, as we learn from the latest apologists, ought to be the case. What is true at the level of the main government is also true in the precincts: in *Paradise Lost*, again, the blank verse tends to dominate in the choice of words, and even where there are magnificent departures from its regularity, music is the controlling agency. Such a structure is analogous to the Ciceronian sentence which has, as Croll says, "a central or climactic member" to which the remainder of the sentence gives emphasis.

A long poem by Williams, however, may not be said to possess form of this type. It is immediately obvious that he is constrained neither by set rhythms and meters nor by the music of the verse (music here in the sense usually intended in referring to Milton). Furthermore, he is too anxious to protect the autonomy of the details of his poem to submit them to a shaping process. Each element in the poem exists for itself: either each item, image, or statement as in *Paterson*; or these and each phrase of a sentence as in the later longer poems. And it is not to be subordinated to a governing narrative or theme.

Form, if form there be, is to be discovered afterward, not imposed on the inviolate substances. The long poem is in this respect like the loose sentence, and an analogy for it would be not the circle but the skein: it is a linear construction, twisting this way and that, in which motifs like threads appear and reappear in varying contexts, emphases, and color formations.

We may now ask whether there is any meaning in the similarity between Williams' departure in his strategy with the long poem and that of the baroque writers with the sentence, or in the miscellaneous matters in which Williams is like Browne or Montaigne. Some of the similarities between the styles of the prose writers and those of modern poets must be fortuitous, because the styles are the men and the men are not the mere products of similar historical moments. And yet one similarity in the historical moments is worth mention. Anti-Ciceronianism was the literary expression of a great intellectual movement. "To distinguish rhetorical from intellectual process in the writings of professed naturalists," says Croll, "is to divide between the bark and the tree: whatever the motions of their minds, they will betray themselves in their style." [15] There is consonance between Bacon's pitch for an empirical, a posteriori study of nature, in which nature was to be observed in its own right without regard to previous principles and in which vulgar errors were to be dismissed, and a style that develops freely and is not bound to any dominating central part of a sentence or molded by requirements of external form. And, indeed, more generally one may consider the loose style to be associated with "the more skeptical phases of seventeenth-century thought." [16] It appears, Croll says, "in writers who are professed opponents of determined and rigorous philosophic attitudes."

There is no doubt that the comparable features in the style of Williams are associated as closely with *his* skepticism and with his opposition to long-standing attitudes, which appear

[15] Croll, "Attic Prose," p. 146.
[16] Croll, "The Baroque Style," p. 444.

most forcefully in Part II of *Paterson IV* where he celebrates Marie Curie. "Smash the world, wide!" he says; "it is a fetid womb," and so forth. In the same place, experience is a "drug" and the "key" is "antagonistic cooperation" (pp. 201–2, 208), which we may understand to mean the juxtaposition of discrete elements that cooperate but do not blend.

Many passages from Williams' various writings explicitly reveal his sense that the new philosophy of Einstein had called in doubt the old, accepted forms of poetry; and an air of defiance against old shibboleths breathes through letters, articles, and autobiography. It is, of course, partly a matter of disposition: if there had been no Einsteinian revolution, Williams would have found foes or windmills to tilt at. But one can go beyond all this; Williams abhors the given principles that have been handed down and seeks instead new ones that may be derived from the relationship of separate entities, as Marie Curie's discovery followed "a dissonance in the valence of uranium"; and one can view his style as a Baconian retreat from the previously accepted order of static truths into the very texture of the world. Newton remarked that he was merely picking up occasional shells on the beach while the whole ocean of truth lay undiscovered before him; and this was modesty, because he felt his business lay with the ocean. Williams might have made the same remark with different meanings: he is engaged in discovery but is shy of an ocean of truth; and therefore he picks up small, visible, encompassable facts and images, satisfied that his business is with them. Nor, similarly, is the sea the proper poetic ground to Marianne Moore, who derides the man in "A Grave" whose gaze is directed upon the whole great sea; nor, in "An Octopus," is her home the glacier which stands for truth, for although she finally approaches the thing itself, she devotes most of the poem to her fanciful periplum around its perimeter.

The kind of truth contemporary writers seek out and celebrate is small and local. Williams says that we "are eternally barred save for the report of [our] senses from knowing anything about" the world;[17] Brecht wrote on the rafter of the stable in Denmark where he set up in exile his temporary writing quarters, "Truth is a concrete." What we are certain of are the concrete details of the sensory world around us. But against any small local triumphs of certitude there stands in hostility the official truth in its official style and stale glory. It is surely worth observing the dramatization of the conflict between these two in *The Stranger*: Meursault is victimized for his unwillingness to accept as truth anything that he cannot himself know, and he knows only what his senses record. His life consists in a series of separate experiences which he evaluates individually: *café-au-lait* is good; so are swimming, cigarettes, and sleeping with Marie; the towel in the washroom at work which is always wet by lunch time is not good; and so forth. He does not add up the details of his life in order to evaluate the sum; he has no instinct to subordinate details to a larger structure. The Prosecutor, on the other hand, proceeds in a manner diametrically opposite: he musters whatever details he can of Meursault's life and evaluates them in sum; he is not interested in them as they actually are but only to the extent that they contribute to a meaning—a total picture to which each is subordinate.

The contrasting attitudes to details of Meursault and the Prosecutor are the same as those of the practitioners of the formless and the formed work respectively, and they may be compared also with the poets of fancy and imagination. Meursault, like a poet of the formless work and the fancy, appreciates particulars and holds them as disparate and autonomous; the other orders and uses them, dissolves and dissipates them in order to fuse them into a totality, and appreciates only the truth to which they contribute. The conclusion that Meursault is a killer because he did not weep at his mother's funeral is

<hr />

[17] *The Selected Letters of William Carlos Williams,* ed. John C. Thirlwall (New York: Random House, 1957), p. 331. Hereafter *SL.*

arrived at by the same mental operation as Lear's conclusion that because Edgar is destitute he must have had daughters.

There have been ages when the closed form and the round style have been prevalent and accepted. But our lot keeps an unepic, stumbling uncertainty about truth and takes some pride and feels some safety in it. For the periodic sentence, which Macaulay in his day wielded with such eloquence and inaccuracy, was the cause by which in their days "Italy went to rot . . . as the Roman Empire had been destroyed before her," according to Ezra Pound, exaggerating a little, probably.

II

Poetry that dwells on its texture, promoting, in Ransom's metaphor, the free exercise of the independent characters of its citizens at the expense of the effective statement of the total structure, is making no effort to be great. Texture, by definition, is the small stuff of existence—the shoes, sealing-wax, and cabbages, the bedroom slippers and wheelbarrows and broken bottles of our lives; and art that dwells upon it is accordingly unpretentious, "ungreat," or indeed trivial, depending on whether one wishes to favor or defame it. It is not entirely a matter of subject: the subject of a poem, says T. E. Hulme, may as well be a lady's shoe or a boy fishing as the siege of Troy. But could one in fact write the proper poem about the siege of Troy or man's first disobedience and still pay consistent attention to such details as *Paterson* embodies, which in the light of the majestic subject would seem pettifogging? A poet, one may say, with a great subject like the wrath of God in Lowell's "The Death of the Sheriff," does not spare time or rather emphasis for the texture of tiny details: he does not pause to consider the lovely coloration of the *Parmachenie Belle* because he is so preponderantly interested in what he can catch with it. And yet the question is loaded because it is asked from a traditional standpoint: in the twentieth-century perspective, any human subject is a great subject; Leopold Bloom is as great a man as

Odysseus; one man is as great a subject as many men; Paterson, New Jersey, is a cosmos.

Greatness may not be purely a matter of what subject the poet has chosen; but clearly if we are to speak of subject at all, one part of the work must be central and some subordination must have occurred, or at least indications must have been given to the reader so that he can perform the act of subordination himself. Without a manifest subject, no work of art is even eligible for consideration as great; works which do "not mean but be" need not apply. Marianne Moore is probably not trying to be great; and yet according to the criterion of magnitude and visibility of subject she is eligible to be considered so. She is more near to greatness in this sense than Williams is; her poems, though they revel in *dinglichkeit,* frequently proceed to what with more or less scrutiny may reveal itself as a moral truth and the subject. Although to justify the ways of the paper nautilus to a carefully screened, fit audience may not seem to be a procedure of great moment, the forthcoming subject, that love "is the only fortress / strong enough to trust to," is an important one. And so with the other poems, which dwell with "unconquerable gusto" upon the flora of Boston Common or Paradise Park, upon miscellaneous birds and beasts and fishes, and upon things one might get from Santa, but which prove to have subjects whose high seriousness even Matthew Arnold would hardly have denied.

Miss Moore is, of course, quite different from the nineteenth-century poet who adjusts his oratorical robe and delivers the uplifting moral truth in a ringing measure. She is very far indeed from such a performance. But having a serious subject, scrupulously inostensible as it is, she is different from Williams with his more characteristically modern style, which is without one.

Modern art avoids another kind of greatness. A modern poet, no less and perhaps more than his forebears, finds his *esse* in his art: his singleness in its pursuit is, I believe, generally demonstrable, even in Williams or in others with outside professions where "singleness" does not literally describe their commitment. Yet at the same time the poetry written does not propose itself as something that aftertimes will not willingly let die. "To the young generation," says Ortega y Gasset in his essay "The Dehumanization of Art," "art is a thing of no consequence." Although the artist does not make light of his work and profession, "they interest him precisely because they are of no transcendent importance." The idea of the arts as the salvation of mankind is abhorrent to him. "To his mind, the kingdom of art commences where the air feels lighter and things, free from formal fetters, begin to cut whimsical capers. . . . Were art to redeem man, it could do so only by saving him from the seriousness of life and restoring him to an unexpected boyishness." [18]

Modern art does not want to live forever—the point Williams makes in "Come On!" It wants to make an immediate impact. William Barrett records that it was something of a shock in reading Sartre's trilogy to find that he was "willing to aim so low."

> But all this now turns out to have been intentional: the deliberate aiming at the second-rate is part of Sartre's program for literature. The committed writer disdains the creation of masterpieces, and even the very concept of the masterpiece, with whatever silence, exile, or cunning it may exact, no longer seems to have any connection with that act of writing that aims essentially at making an impact, just as one might strike a blow or fire a pistol. [19]

[18] José Ortega y Gasset, *The Dehumanization of Art and Other Writings on Art and Culture* (Garden City, N.Y.: Anchor Books, 1956), pp. 45–46.

[19] "The End of Modern Literature," *Partisan Review*, XVI (September, 1949), 948. Compare the following remark of Robert Conquest: "When poets wish to give the most unalloyed praise, one hears such expressions as 'that was a bloody good poem of so-and-so's,'—(or even 'bloody good'). One does not find them—or at any rate not in its usual connotation—using the word 'great,' except possibly when discussing in some formal and stilted atmosphere the work of Aeschylus or Dante" ("Ezra Pound," *London Magazine*, III [April, 1963], 45).

Williams' poetry seems to fit such concepts as these: the apparent inconsequence of little pieces written between office visits of patients; the carelessness; "whimsical capers" like "Turkey in the Straw" ("I kissed her while she pissed"); the boyishness throughout. When Ortega says, "the new art consists almost exclusively of protests against the old," [20] we think of Williams on his own shore turning his back, like Whitman before him (though with less gratitude), on all that had been left wafted thither and of *Paterson* as a "reply to Greek and Latin with the bare hands." On the other hand, one remembers that his remarks about poetry, or the poem as he preferred to call it, not only do not make light of his profession but reflect a sense of the consequence of poetry more profound than Ortega observes: Williams explicitly voiced his belief in the power of poetry to redeem people. Wallace Stevens takes a similar stance: while his poetry is stocked with *jeux d'esprit* and incidental curiosities, he owned at the same time to a lofty ideal on behalf of poetry—a wish "to formulate a theory of poetry that would make poetry a significant humanity of such a nature and scope that it could be established as a normal, vital field of study for all comers." [21]

III

The poetry of William Carlos Williams is art of our time: avoiding greatness, beauty, and truth as traditionally conceived, it is our very own. And its most important single feature is the permissiveness given to the life and movement of its texture that a firmly fixed pattern would preclude. The work of later poets who acknowledge Williams as their father is similarly characterized: form does not contain or constrain the particulars of the work but is discovered, so it is said, at each moment as the writing proceeds.

[20] Ortega, *The Dehumanization of Art,* p. 41.
[21] Letter to Archibald MacLeish, quoted in *Opus Posthumous,* ed. Samuel French Morse (New York: Alfred A. Knopf, 1957), p. xvi.

The poetry of one of the young men in whom, says Williams, the old man lives on does not entirely fit the broad stereotype submitted here. In some of the poems of Allen Ginsberg, a species of Victorian greatness differentiates him from the contemporaries with whom he is usually associated. He is, on the other hand, explicitly a "son" of Williams. He was born in Paterson, New Jersey, and educated through high school there. A long letter originally over the initials A.P., which have been taken to stand for Allen Paterson, appears in the second part of Book IV of *Paterson,* which presents a good paternal relationship to contrast the bad one between Phyllis and her father in the first part. The letter is a self-introduction written to accompany nine poems. The younger poet speaks of his determination to be original and at the same time acknowledges the influence of or at least an affinity with the older one:

> I envision for myself some kind of new speech—different at least from what I have been writing down—in that it has to be clear statement of fact about misery (and not misery itself), and splendor if there is any out of the subjective wanderings through Paterson. . . . [A]t least one actual citizen of your community has inherited your experience in his struggle to love and know his own world-city, through your work, which is an accomplishment you almost cannot have hoped to achieve. . . . I may need a new measure myself, but though I have a flair for your style I seldom dig exactly what you are doing with cadences, line length, sometimes syntax, etc., and cannot handle your work as a solid object—which properties I assume you rightly claim. I don't understand the measure. I haven't worked with it much either, though, which must make the difference [p. 205].

In March, 1952, writing to Robert Lowell, Williams describes Ginsberg as "coming to personify the place [Paterson] for me" (*SL,* p. 312). A letter above the initials A.G. in Book V of *Paterson* thanks Williams for an introduction he had contributed, the one to *Howl,* presumably.

In his notes to the recording of this poem, Ginsberg says he began his poetic career by writing poems "adapted from prose seeds, journals, scratchings, arranged by phrasing or breath groups into little short-line patterns according to ideas of measure of American speech [he'd] picked up from W. C. Williams' imagist preoccupations." [22] But *Howl* is not of this kind at all and indeed, except for its introduction, owes Williams almost nothing. The measure of the poem, each line as a single breath unit, Ginsberg says is a natural consequence of Williams; but there is no line in Williams quite so taxing.

Those characteristics of Williams' poetry that have been thought of as significant throughout this essay are absent from *Howl*;[23] and other characteristics that *Howl* does possess betray attitudes quite foreign to Williams. In certain poems written before and after he wrote *Howl,* Ginsberg, like Williams, musters chunky details of realism: "Sunflower Sutra" (*Howl,* pp. 28–30), for instance, contains packed descriptions of the flower and its sordid industrial environment. But the details in this poem are not fancifully adduced: the sunflower and its ecology are the subject. Elsewhere Ginsberg, more like Williams, enlarges realistically upon details that are not immediately manifestly relevant to whatever unemphasized subject there may be: in "Sather Gate Illumination," for example:

Those white stripes down your chocolate cupcake, Lady (held in
    front of your nose finishing sentence preparatory to chomp),
they were painted there to delight you by some Spanish industrial
    artistic hand in bakery factory faraway,
expert hand in simple-minded messages of white stripes on
    millions of message cupcakes.

(*NAP,* p. 192)

In general, such presentation of objects is the aim of the Beat

---

[22] *The New American Poetry: 1945–1960,* ed. Donald M. Allen (New York: Grove Press, 1960), pp. 414–15. Hereafter *NAP.*

[23] Allen Ginsberg, *Howl and Other Poems* (San Francisco, Calif.: City Lights Books, 1959), pp. 9–22.

poets. Commenting upon what these inherited from Williams, Lawrence Lipton writes, "The object mirrored in the poetic image, that comes first. The poet comes clean; he tells only what he *knows*, what his vision has shown him, and he tells it starkly, but with energy, energy from the mysterious source of all artistic energy, says it—and stops." [24]

Howl rarely deals in images in this way. Ginsberg calls the first section "a huge sad comedy of wild phrasing, meaningless images . . ." but, except for occasional powerful and undistorted glimpses of real things like the "yellow paper rose twisted on a wire hanger in the closet," the texture of this poem does not consist of real images: "unshaven rooms," "paint hotels," "backyard green tree cemetery dawns," "ashcan rantings," "stale beer afternoon"—these do not describe concrete objects or tell starkly what the poet's vision has shown him.

This kind of verse obviously owes nothing to Williams and his "things"; it may owe something to Hart Crane and his disrupture of logical language or to Rimbaud; though it is Part II of *Howl*, with its visions induced by peyote that is more reminiscent of Rimbaud, who accustomed himself to hallucinations: "je voyais très franchement une mosquée à la place d'une usine, une école de tambours faite par les anges," he says in "Alchimie du Verbe" from *Une Saison en Enfer*, and he concludes by finding "le désordre de mon esprit" sacred. We saw above that objects become blurred or even distorted when images of them are used by the imagination for conveying meaning and feeling; in most of the images in *Howl* the objective world suffers complete distortion so that no mental picture of it is deducible from the words. The images have lost their contours on account of the pressure of feeling and meaning they are being made to bear. The meanings are much less precise than those we have observed hanging to the images of other poetry of the imagination; but all vaguely contribute to the vague ideas of ecstasy and

[24] Lawrence Lipton, *The Holy Barbarians* (New York: Messner, 1959), pp. 235–36.

destruction. Though Ginsberg calls them "meaningless images" they are not really images and not entirely meaningless. The process employed is not far removed from that of *The Bridge,* although the deliberateness of Crane is not matched by Ginsberg, and the kind of careful subtlety that provides such techniques as "cross-hatching" [25] in Crane is absent in *Howl.* But the following line, dominated as it is by sound—the alliteration of *b, br,* and *dr*—by feeling, and by general vague idea, shows some of the characteristics of the kind of verse that Crane wrote:

> who chained themselves to subways for the endless ride from Battery
> to holy Bronx on benzedrine until the noise of wheels and
> children brought them down shuddering mouth-wracked
> and battered bleak of brain all drained of brilliance in the
> drear light of Zoo. . . .

> (*Howl,* p. 10)

Crane habitually does better than this, but not essentially differently. Here, for example, is a passage where description of objects has indisputably lost on points to the sound, feeling, and idea:

> And you, aloft there—Jason! hesting Shout!
> Still wrapping harness to the swarming air!
> Silvery the rushing wake, surpassing call,
> Beams yelling Aeolus! splintered in the straits!

Crane does better than Ginsberg. But Ginsberg, considering that the speed of composition allowed little time for polishing and shopping around for consonants and vowels, shows that he is not without an ear. Sometimes a line will expire with a whimper, a banal throwing away of whatever sound effects had been built up; but often the strength is kept up to the end:

> with dreams, with drugs, with waking nightmares, alcohol and
> cock and endless balls

> (*Howl,* p. 9)

[25] Barbara Herman, "The Language of Hart Crane," *Sewanee Review,* LXIII (Winter, 1950), 62.

or

> who crashed through their minds in jail waiting for
>   impossible criminals with golden heads and the charm
>   of reality in their hearts who sang sweet blues to
>   Alcatraz.

(Howl, p. 15)

The first part of *Howl* enjoys form only to the extent that the line length is ordained according to the length of breath—the length of breath, be it said, of an athlete or of Allen Ginsberg only when in good form. The word "who" opens almost every line, after the poem gets rolling: "I depended on the word 'who,'" says Ginsberg, "to keep the beat, a base to keep measure, return to and take off from again onto another streak of invention . . ." (*NAP*, p. 415).

In the second part a number of disagreeable objects and facts of life and surrealist projections from them are gathered up into the image, or rather the *word*, "Moloch." There are many apostrophes, each presenting a new and squalid aspect of modern civilization: "Moloch! Solitude! Filth! Ugliness! Ashcans and unobtainable dollars! Children screaming under the stairways! Boys sobbing in armies! Old men weeping in the parks!" or

> Moloch! Moloch! Robot apartments! invisible suburbs! skeleton
>   treasuries! blind capitals! demonic industries! spectral
>   nations! invincible madhouses! granite cocks! monstrous
>   bombs!

In the body of this part of the poem each line opens with "Moloch" as in the earlier part each line had opened with "Who." The poem "names the monster of mental consciousness that preys on the Lamb"—the "Lamb in America" whose suffering is lamented in Part I. The visions of Moloch are due to peyote; in part they are visible visions; in part they are meaningful nonimages. In Part III, the words "I'm with you in Rockland" open each unit and are followed first by short and then by increasingly longer passages as the poem progresses. This procedure gives the sense of a build-up, a rise to climax in the penultimate stanza (or line), and a quiet close with all passion spent in the last one.

There is not a great deal of Williams in all this, which is admittedly experimental work. If the word "who" is used to "keep the beat," one may question whether it is worth keeping: it can hardly be said to provide a pattern against which expression can strive to produce those significant tensions that make the best conventional verse splendid; nor on the other hand is there variety of form in the line which might contribute, as an organic form, to the varying meanings. Form is not an extension of content. On the other hand, the repeated "who" is a "figure of grammar" that brings cohesion to this part of the poem; and there are precedents in both Whitman and the Litany.[26] Ginsberg is justified in claiming that he has used Whitman's line "in the light of early XX Century organization of new speech-rhythm prosody to *build up* large organic structures" (*NAP*, p. 416). Then in Part III the formal crescendo mentioned above makes an appreciable and easily recognizable contribution to the rise and final decline of the intensity of feeling for which there is parallel notification in the rhetoric.

[26] The similarities between *Howl* and parts of the Prayer Book are immediately apparent:

We beseech thee to hear us, good Lord.

That it may please thee so to rule the heart of thy servant, The President of the United States, that he may above all things seek thy honour and glory;

We beseech, etc.

That it may please thee to bless and preserve all Christian Rulers and Magistrates, giving them grace to execute justice, and to maintain truth;

We beseech, etc.

That it may please thee to illuminate all Bishops, Priests, and Deacons, *etc.*

We beseech, etc.

The sense of cohesion given here by the identical opening phrases to groups of words is also obtained in *Howl*.

Speaking of the measure of *Howl,* Ginsberg says it is a nat-ural consequence of Williams, though it "probably bugs [him] now"; and one wonders whether here or elsewhere among those who acknowledge his paternity an aging Williams may not have looked at the strange blossoming of his poetics with an amazement like Goethe's at the prospect of the young Lord Byron acting out the half-baked ideas of his own youth. *Howl* has little in common with any poems of Williams'. The destruc-tion of the "best minds" of a generation, the avowed subject, is a "great" one. In all his poetry, Williams did not say anything as "great" as the first line of *Howl.* In his introduction to the poem, he observes the traffic in horrors and commends Ginsberg for a detachment from them which does not, I believe, exist. Williams does not deal in horror; nor in face of a society which is an anathema to him also does he assert the self in the way Ginsberg does. He is, in his later poems, terribly conscious of the existence of the bomb, as who is not; and his efforts are directed to placing himself in context for the sake of security: "It is ourselves we organize in this way . . . for integrity of understanding to insure persistence, to give the mind its stay." But it is not a Promethean self he is thus organizing: in "As-phodel, That Greeny Flower," for instance, the context he is seeking to order himself into consists of some pictures, some friends—men, women, and children—and presumably a kind of love, which is not the kind that served in an earlier age to assert the ego.

> With your smiles
> and other trivia of the sort
> my secret life
> has been made up. . . .[27]

"We have lived," says Wylie Sypher, "through gigantic disas-ters, but they do not seem to be ours. To write about them would

---

[27] William Carlos Williams, *Pictures from Brueghel and Other Poems* (Norfolk, Conn.: New Directions, 1962), pp. 168–69. Hereafter *PB.*

be a romantic luxury; we are struck dumb before such catastrophe. Our need is not to seek a self—much less to assert a self
—but to get out from under a self, to escape from a heavy
burden of freedom." [28] This is not the aim or manner of Ginsberg's rebellious poem, which does assert self and does celebrate
the fact that social disasters have overcome the friends of "Holy
Allen."

The subject of *Howl* is roughly the same as that of the poem
"Thou Shalt Not Kill" by Kenneth Rexroth; and in reviewing
Ginsberg's poem Rexroth praises it mostly for its truth to life,
though in passing he offers a eulogy to its technique. "Listen
you," says Rexroth,

> do you *really* think your kids act like the bobby soxers in those
> wholesome Coca-Cola ads? Don't you know that across the
> table from you at dinner sits somebody who looks on you as
> an enemy who is planning to kill him in the immediate future
> in an extremely disagreeable way? Don't you know that if you
> were to say to your English class, "It is raining," they would
> take it for granted you were a liar?

If you don't know these and similar truths, "you're headed for
a terrible awakening. *Howl* is the confession of faith of the
generation that is going to be running the world in 1965 and
1975. . . ." [29]

All this may or may not be. But the assumption that the people seen doing and suffering in *Howl* are real people is wrong,
because the poem is not an image of young people in general or
particular (in one line the poet pauses to add parenthetically,
"this actually happened") but only an intense subjective pro-
jection of the mood of one of them. One of the more famous
instances in which life and times are portrayed in terms of a
prevailing mood is "Locksley Hall"; but here the speaker knows

[28] Wylie Sypher, *Loss of the Self in Modern Literature and Art* (New
York: Alfred A. Knopf, 1964), p. 70.
[29] Kenneth Rexroth, "San Francisco Letter," *Evergreen Review,* I (1957),
11.

his eye is "jaundiced" and knows its condition accounts for his conception of the world; and the poet, Tennyson, is of course outside the whole situation. But there is the same humorless luxuriance in evil situations in both these poems, in *Howl* all the way through, in "Locksley Hall" in lines like these: "Then a hand shall pass before thee, pointing to his drunken sleep, / To thy widow'd marriage-pillows, to the tears that thou wilt weep"; or "But the jingling of the guinea helps the hurt that Honor feels, / And the nations do but murmur, snarling at each other's heels"; or "Slowly comes a hungry people, as a lion, creeping nigher, / Glares at one that nods and winks behind a slowly-dying fire."

Howl resembles "Locksley Hall" also in the implied notion that life *ought* to be better than it is. Tennyson's speaker explains that his concept of the world is a bitter one partly because he had earlier entertained optimistic visionary expectations of it: he had "dipt into the future" and seen "the Vision of the world, and all the wonder that would be." The very intensity of Ginsberg's protest at the disasters that have overcome "the best minds" and indeed America itself implies a romantic belief that life *ought* to be glorious. F. R. Leavis draws attention to this same characteristic in the poetry of Thomas Hardy and labels him a Victorian on account of it. When one passionately exclaims against evil days, one reveals belief that they should and could be better; when one asks, "Where are the eagles and the trumpets?" one implies belief in the possibility of glory. Considering how much Victorianism there is in official America— the respect for wealth, the concept of the "great man," the synonymity of quality and quantity, the fear of sex, and the wholesale resort to cliché in writing, speaking, and indeed living —when one considers these similarities and others, it does not seem entirely inappropriate that Ginsberg's protest against his times should take the same form as that of the Victorian Tennyson.

Ginsberg's world owes him not only a living but an ecstasy.

"Sunflower Sutra" reveals the same expectations of the world through its passionate indignation at the degradation suffered by the sunflower, which is a symbol for the human soul, as it grows in the squalor of the shunting yard:

—We're not our skin of grime, we're not our dread bleak dusty imageless locomotive, we're all beautiful golden sunflowers inside, we're blessed by our own seed & golden hairy naked accomplishment-bodies growing into mad black formal sunflowers in the sunset, spied on by our eyes under the shadow of the mad locomotive riverbank sunset Frisco hilly tincan evening sitdown vision.

(*Howl*, p. 30)

The passage is Lawrentian and belongs, as Lawrence does, to the past. It does not speak in the voice we have come to recognize as that of our own day. Our world is absurd; precluded as we are from believing in the possibility of the solution of our problems, people who wait for Godot seem to us ridiculous; precluded too from the view that we are entirely other than what we seem, we accept that we *are* our "skin of grime," among other things perhaps. It is the human condition to be growing like the sunflower in the filthy yard; and although it may be a Sisyphus-like existence, it is better to endure it than to be plucked by Allen Ginsberg.

IV

The vision of mankind as bearing "beautiful golden sunflowers inside," a religious idea which for centuries has enabled some men to maintain a respect for human nature in its most ragged state, is not modern; and we may set against it at once the concept of "objectism," a word coined by Charles Olson, who defines it as

the getting rid of the lyrical interference of the individual as ego, of the 'subject' and his soul, that peculiar presumption by which western man has interposed himself between what he is as a creature of nature (with certain instructions to carry out) and those other creations of nature which we may, with no derogation, call objects. For a man is himself an object . . . [*NAP*, p. 395].

Turning from Ginsberg to Olson, we find more clear indication that we are in the orbit of William Carlos Williams' influence. Olson is both "son" to Williams and "father" to a number of contemporary poets a little younger than he, such as Denise Levertov, Robert Duncan, and Robert Creeley, among others; and "Charles Olson," says Creeley, "is central to any description of literary 'climate' dated 1960." [30] Olson has earned his prominence both by his poetry and by a manifesto, "Projective Verse vs. the Non-Projective." [31] Here we have a long statement governing some of the significant departures of the verse of the fifties and sixties. In parts it bears clearly the marks of the influence of Williams, and some of the principles used above in presenting his poetry are reaffirmed. If only it were all more clearly expressed, this document might be of inestimable use in coming at our most recent poetry.

Certain of the aphorisms in the manifesto are old and have been taken for granted for so long that it seems now almost as if Lord Acton first mouthed them along with "all power corrupts." Others, however, are relatively new and singular: poetry is expected to do things that have never previously been thought to be in its power, and some of its familiar traditional accomplishments are ignored, depreciated, or faulted. Projective verse is, first, distinguished from traditional verse, which was based on the "inherited line, stanza, over-all form"; then three charac-

[30] Robert Creeley, "Olson & Others: Some Orts for the Sports," *Big Table*, I, No. 4 (1960), 119.

[31] Published first in *Poetry New York*, No. 3 (1950), pp. 13–22; reprinted in part in Williams' autobiography (pp. 329–32); reprinted as a volume on its own (New York: Totem Press, 1959); reprinted in Allen (ed.), *New American Poetry* (1960); and again in Olson's *Human Universe and Other Essays*, ed. Donald Allen (San Francisco, Calif.: Auerhahn Society, 1965), pp. 51–61.

teristics are outlined. The *"kinetics"*: ". . . a poem is energy transferred from where the poet got it . . . by way of the poem itself to . . . the reader." Second, the *"principle"* that "FORM IS NEVER MORE THAN AN EXTENSION OF CONTENT." Third, the *"process"* by which "the principle can be made so to shape the energies that the form is accomplished": "ONE PERCEPTION MUST IMMEDIATELY AND DIRECTLY LEAD TO A FURTHER PERCEPTION." The first characteristic is interesting in that the poem is a means of conveying not meaning but energy:

> It is a matter, finally [says Olson], of OBJECTS . . . every element in an open poem (the syllable, the line, as well as the image, the sound, the sense) must be taken up as participants in the kinetic of the poem just as solidly as we are accustomed to take what we call the objects of reality; and that these elements are to be seen as creating the tensions of a poem just as totally as do those other objects create what we know as the world.

This idea is in part familiar, since we have seen in Williams the concept, illustrated for example by the anecdote about Alanson Hartpence, that words are not merely the medium for transmission of meaning but are themselves parts of the poem. Olson says that "objectism" is "to be taken to stand for the kind of relation of man to experience which a poet might state as the necessity of a line or a work to be as wood is, to be as clean as wood is as it issues from the hand of nature, to be as shaped as wood can be when a man has had his hand to it." The notion that a poem of this kind transmits energy, not simply meaning, is difficult to grasp, and we must return to it. Nor is it clear why the elements of the poem, if they are to be considered analogous to objects of the world, should of themselves create the "tensions" of the poem: tensions are the product of the sophisticated contrivance of the poet, without which they do not exist in a poem any more than they do in nature, between, say, the tobacco jar, the coffee cup, and the ashtray on my desk. Tension is a quality that poets have driven out of projective verse by their strong efforts to make it spontaneous. Olson proceeds: "The objects which occur at every given moment of composition (or recognition, we can call it) are, can be, must be treated exactly as they do occur therein and not by any ideas or preconceptions from outside the poem. . . ." Again familiar after Williams, this precept outlaws once more the activity of the Coleridgean imagination, which dissolves and diffuses sheer perceptions for the sake of the ineffable reality, and it also outlaws the practice in poems like *Howl,* where objects are indeed subject to "preconceptions from outside the poem" and bent toward an ulterior end.

The second characteristic of projective verse, the principle that form is never more than an extension of content, is not new. For although there are brilliant poems, in Auden for example, in which form is no more an extension of content than the beer bottle is an extension of the beer, the concept of organic form is by now thoroughly familiar. Only the air of discovery that accompanies it here is surprising: "There it is, brothers, sitting there, for USE."

The third feature is that one perception must lead to a further one: "Keep it moving as fast as you can, citizen." This instruction is apparently intimately related to the kinetic nature of poetry: the energy must not be permitted to leak out, so to say, by any loose coupling. In a later passage Olson says, "The descriptive functions generally have to be watched, every second, in projective verse, because of their easiness, and thus their drain on the energy which composition by field allows into a poem. *Any* slackness takes off attention, that crucial thing, from the job in hand, from the *push* of the line under hand at the moment, under the reader's eye, in his moment." Robert Creeley says that "what he is getting at is the too-frequent habit among certain writers where the man is just talking round and round, without having taken his particular insight to any terms of possibility, without transmission of energy." [32] The main burden of this precept in Olson is not that he would deny the lovers of poetry the space to wander in that Keats wanted to provide for them or that he mistrusts the kind of elaboration of description characteristic of Marianne Moore, but that he wants, as we shall see below, to concentrate attention *within* the poem. We have seen something of this aim in brief in Williams when he forces us to consider a red wheelbarrow not out there in the chicken run but right here in the poem.

The essay proceeds to speak of the roles of the ear and the breath: the head shows by way of the ear in the syllable; the heart, by way of the breath in the line. "I take it," says Olson, "that PROJECTIVE VERSE teaches, is, this lesson, that that verse will only do in which a poet manages to register both the acquisitions of his ear *and* the pressures of his breath"; then: "It is by their syllables that words juxtapose in beauty, by these particles of sound as clearly as by the sense of the words which they compose. In any given instance, because there is a choice of words, the choice, if a man is in there, will be, spontaneously, the obedience of his ear to the syllables"; and "the line comes (I swear it) from the breath, from the breathing of the man who writes, at the moment that he writes. . . ."

It would not be hard to misconceive parts of this essay, and it would not be culpable. The two major peculiarities of the ground rules may, I think, be drawn out and attended to by comparing them with positions with which we have grown familiar and also by summoning some of Robert Creeley's comments upon them. First, let us consider the way in which feeling gets into a poem: we have seen that there is in general a difference between the uses of imagery of Eliot on the one hand and Pound, Williams, and Miss Moore on the other, inasmuch as Eliot uses imagery of the world outside to express feelings

---

[32] "Robert Creeley in Conversation with Charles Tomlinson," *the Review,* No. 10 (January, 1964), p. 34.

within, the process of the celebrated objective correlative, whereas the others tend to look at the world for itself. But the images of Pound and company are bound to have feelings attached to them: resigned pathos, say, in "Old Ez folded his blankets"; a feeling not to be summarily designated in Miss Moore's images of Hubert, "tense with restraint"; and boyish gaiety in Williams, naked, waving his shirt in "Danse Russe." Nevertheless, in Miss Moore feeling is typically resisted, and the resistance is made by proliferation of images. In Williams, similarly, imagery is used to counter feeling, or at least to ballast and balance it. But in Williams rhythm is another notification of feeling: feeling frequently brings objects of the world into a rhythmical context; the rhythm of "The Red Wheelbarrow" denotes an "unquenchable exaltation." In all poetry, rhythmic variations traditionally accompany the expression of feeling; but the expression is more sophisticated—more artistic, in fact— where the rhythm is less imitative. Olson's rules prescribe rhythm for the expression of feeling: ". . . the HEART, by way of the BREATH, to the LINE," he says. Creeley adds the following:

> . . . the heart . . . has to do with the senses of emotion. When one is excited the heart beats fast; this, in effect, creates a quicker rhythm and the breath comes short. Now, the head, the intelligence by way of the ear to the syllable— which he calls also "the king and pin"—is the unit upon which all builds. The heart, then, stands, as the primary feeling term.[33]

The length of line, then, which is a feature of the rhythm, is controlled apparently by feeling. But this process is merely imitative: excitement makes the heart beat fast. Believing as he does that the human is a mere undistinguished creation of nature, Olson consistently devaluates all the self-conscious, sophisticated, and stylized methods of expressing feeling in art;

[33] *Ibid.*, pp. 30–31.

and the kind of expression his rules provide for belongs to the same genre as swearing or howling or the muttering of jungle drums: blood calling to blood.

The point can be illustrated by comparing a passage from Frost with one from Robert Creeley, whose aims for poetry are apparently similar to Olson's. These two passages have been put together for a slightly different purpose by a critic in *The Times Literary Supplement,* who remarks that "the subject matter in both cases *might be* in the same area—an extreme fatigue." [34] The feeling in "After Apple-Picking" is expressed by the familiar means of images and rhythms:

> One can see what will trouble
> This sleep of mine, whatever sleep it is.
> Were he not gone,
> The woodchuck could say whether it's like his
> Long sleep, as I describe its coming on,
> Or just some human sleep.

Creeley's lines are as follows:

> After, what
> is it—as if
> the sun had
>
> been wrong to return,
> again. It was
> another life, a
>
> day, some
> time gone, it
> was done.
>
> But also
> the pleasure, the
> opening

[34] "Songs Around the Mountain," *Times Literary Supplement* (Nov. 25, 1965), p. 1070.

relief
even in what
was so hated.[35]

Here the imagery, with Creeley's characteristic reticence, is drastically attenuated; and the rhythm conveys the feeling, although it cannot be abstracted from the meanings of the words. These lines are the cry of their occasion: the feeling is right there, raw, unmediated, and not recollected in tranquillity, as Frost's may be said to have been.

The second significant characteristic of Olson's essay is that it is not concerned with meaning. The emphasis on prosody, Creeley says, accounts for the fact that some deny the relevance of what Olson is saying:

> They argue the poem as a means to recognition, a signboard as it were, not in itself a structure of "recognition" or—better —cognition itself. Some, then, would not only not hear what Olson was saying, but would even deny, I think, the relevance of his concerns. The great preoccupation with symbology and levels of image in poetry insisted upon by contemporary criticism has also meant a further bias for this not-hearing, since Olson's emphasis is put upon prosody, not interpretation.[36]

Elsewhere Creeley says, "The poem is not a sign-board, pointing to a content ultimately to be regarded; but is, on the contrary, a form inhabited by intelligence and feeling. It is the way a poem speaks, not the matter, that proves its effect." [37]

Again the relegation of the meaning of the poem to a back seat is familiar after Williams. For him, in one description of the process of making a poem, words come to the poem on account of properties other than their denotations; then, once in the poem, they may ensnare meanings—a procedure we have

[35] *A Controversy of Poets,* ed. Paris Leary and Robert Kelly (Garden City, N.Y.: Anchor Books, 1965), p. 57.
[36] Creeley, "Olson & Others," p. 121.
[37] Robert Creeley, "The New World," *Yugen,* No. 7 (1961), p. 13.

seen in one form in the appearance, first, and subsequently the meaning of Sam Patch in *Paterson*. Our traditional response to poetry is to receive consciously the meaning of the words, letting their sounds, including rhythm, affect us at a level beneath that at which our intellect is engaging the meaning. Olson, it seems, wishes us to invert this response:[38] we are to listen to the sounds and let the meaning work upon us as it will, just as we direct our attention to the movement in a ballet, while the changes in lighting provide nuances; at least this, as a rule of thumb in reading Olson's poems, will serve provisionally as a corrective against our more usual and indeed more natural responses.

By receiving the poetry thus, it will be the energy that is transmitted, the process Olson seems to think to be the proper one for a poem. When we speak of the energy in a painting of Van Gogh, it is the transmission of a visual sensation which the mind interprets as energy; if we record energy as being transmitted by lines of Shakespeare, it is something received by the mind through the meanings of the words and, in addition, our response to the rhythms: via such a complex of media, for instance, Shakespeare provides us with the idea-feeling of energy in Hotspur's speeches. But according to Olson's precepts all verse, not just certain passages, conveys energy; and that energy is contained in all the features of the poem, the objects as he calls them—syllable, line, image, sound, and sense. And our response to the poem is not an intellectual one, modified by feelings, but what we must think of as felt energy, in the transmittal of which meaning plays a part but not an overbearing one. Or, to put the same matter another way, we must try to "see" the images of the poem as if by way of the touch of our hands, as a child may say, "Let me *see*," as he puts forward his *hand*.

---

[38] Denise Levertov says that readers ought to go beyond their characteristic concentration on those elements of a poem that reason can grasp. She quotes a poem and says, "Hearing the poem as a sound-structure is the way into its world" ("An Approach to Public Poetry Listenings," *Virginia Quarterly Review*, XLI [Summer, 1965], 427–28).

Let us test this proposition first on a poem of Williams' to which attention has been drawn by criticism:

> As the cat
> climbed over
> the top of
>
> the jamcloset
> first the right
> forefoot
>
> carefully
> then the hind
> stepped down
>
> into the pit of
> the empty
> flowerpot.[39]

"The poem lives in its trajectory," says Hugh Kenner, "not in its statements." [40] Yes; but the statement, the meanings of the words, is of course necessary to it. If our experience of the poem is in the felt energy provided by the rhythms, we still need the image of the cat—we have to *know* it is a cat and not an alligator, however little our total response owes to intellect.

Some lines in *The Maximus Poems* have the same quality as Williams' poem: our experience is in the felt energy in the transmittal of which meaning has played its part:

> The others beneath him . . .
> The others beneath him to looard
> So that when the sea struck he was
>   thrown out the farthest
> We watched him go, & nothing we could do, no way to
> lower a dory in the sea, & no line to throw that
> far[41]

[39] William Carlos Williams, *Collected Earlier Poems* (Norfolk, Conn.: New Directions, 1951), p. 340. Hereafter *CEP.*

[40] Hugh Kenner, "The Drama of Utterance," *Massachusetts Review*, III (Winter, 1962), 329.

[41] Charles Olson, *The Maximus Poems* (New York: Jargon/Corinth, 1960), p. 141.

The longest line gives us, supposedly, the feel of being thrown out farthest; the end-line pause in "no way to / lower a dory," the feel of the querulous hesitation that belonged to the situation (I am assuming, perhaps wrongly, that "So" to "farthest" is one line and that "lower a dory" is the beginning of a new line). Presumably John Keats also transmits "kinetics" when we feel his personification of autumn stepping across the brook (the end-line pause) without moving her head: "And sometimes like a gleaner thou dost keep / Steady thy laden head across a brook. . . ." [42]

We must look further, however, in considering this matter of the suppression of meaning in Olson. Keats's "Ode to Autumn," like thousands of other poems, is evocative: it takes us outside the poem to the world in which we have experienced autumn, and thus it leaves attention outside the poem, an effect that has been traditionally expected and discovered in literature. Olson would say, therefore, that energy leaks out. He is anxious to prevent the sense of words, their descriptive meanings, from taking attention away from the poem in such a manner. Creeley says, "A poetry denies its end in any *descriptive* act, I mean any act which leaves the attention outside the poem" (*NAP*, p. 408). In a long poem of Olson's, words tend to be related not descriptively to the world outside but literally to other words in the poem. The procedure, though it denies our traditional assumptions, is not absolutely foreign to our ideas of poetry; but it exaggerates the distinction between the assertive, descriptive everyday use of language and its inward literal use in poetry. [43] To the extent that the meaning is in relationships within the poem, Olson's poetry is ultraliteral. It is to this extent and for this cause that meaning is played down: the poem is intended to *be*. Interpretation, it was recently declaimed, is the revenge of the intellect upon the world: "To interpret is

---

[42] See F. R. Leavis, *Revaluation* (New York: George Stewart, 1947), pp. 263–64.

[43] See Northrop Frye, *Anatomy of Criticism* (Princeton, N.J.: Princeton University Press, 1957), pp. 73–82.

to impoverish, to deplete the world—in order to set up a shadow world of 'meanings.' " [44]

The reader may feel that he is barred from the private world of the poem and is merely looking on generously, as if he were politely enduring an evening of someone else's Kodachromes. This is not quite the situation: allusions and references to the world outside are not so stringently outlawed. Denise Levertov has pointed out that one does not leave the attention outside the work when it is *"led to awareness* of things that though not named, not visible, exist within the universe of the work." [45] Through their literal meanings the items of a poem gradually gather descriptive meanings and become public. As we read *The Maximus Poems* we learn a vocabulary of symbolism for birds, sailors, and ships,[46] although our attention is strongly pre-empted not by what these *are* in other contexts but by what they *do* in their own.

In this matter of meaning, how does Olson differ from Pound? Pound does not believe that ideas exist only in things, for ideas endure apart from their particular manifestations. He does believe, however, that only through their existence in things can they be known; and hence throughout the *Cantos* he associates concrete objects, expecting the reader to derive the latent meaning from them. The kind of activity the reader is to perform is by now well known, since criticism has often enough performed it in public for him: he puts together these images or those descriptions of actions, or indeed he puts together one canto with another or one block of cantos with another block; and then meaning will appear, as it appears in a mosaic as one backs away from it. This kind of activity, however, only makes sense if there is some degree of form in the work. The *Cantos* hardly measures up to the useful rule of thumb, which Marianne Moore

[44] Susan Sontag, "Against Interpretation," *Evergreen Review*, VIII (December, 1964), 78.
[45] Denise Levertov, "An Admonition," *Things*, I (Fall, 1964), 5.
[46] See Maxine Gauthier, "Suggestions Towards a Reading of *The Maximus Poems*," *Northwest Review*, VIII (Summer, 1966), 24–38.

quotes from Kenneth Burke's *Counter-Statement*, that "a work may be said to have form in so far as one part leads a reader to anticipate another part and be gratified by the result." [47] And yet in various ways order or at least vestigial signs of it have been remarked: Canto XLV, for instance, has been called the core of the poem; significance has been found in the position of the *ching ming* ideograph at the end of LI, the center of the poem (this before Pound went over the hundred); and the whole poem has been assimilated to the scheme of *The Divine Comedy, Inferno, Purgatorio,* and *Paradiso.* That it gives some sense of order, however unimpressive, must be due to a relationship between parts and whole which constitutes a kind of form.

In Williams' *Paterson,* on the other hand, meaning is not to be extracted, and form is not to be adumbrated in this manner. Nor do we find when we turn to Olson's work that things are to be put together: meaning is not to be *derived* from the things that in their accumulation make up the poem, which present only themselves; it is rather to be left in them. This is, I believe, the point being made in the following passage from "The Kingfishers":

. . . The message is
a discrete or continuous sequence of measurable events distributed
   in time

is the birth of air, is
the birth of water, is
a state between
the origin and
the end, between
birth and the beginning of
another fetid nest

is change, presents
no more than itself

[47] Quoted in *A Marianne Moore Reader* (New York: Viking Press, 1961), p. 242.

And the too strong grasping of it,
when it is pressed together and condensed,
loses it. . . .[48]

"The Kingfishers" moves forward continuously, not looking back and not relating its separate parts to one central part that is to receive emphasis, the traditional procedure of a sizable work of literature. There is no dominant part to which other parts variously contribute reflections, echoes, causes, effects, or whatever; like *Paterson,* though a good deal shorter, it does not thrust upon us a manifest subject. On the other hand, like *Paterson* again, there are images that, relating to each other, create motifs that interweave the poem. These motifs and images the reader must receive differently from the images and larger sections of the *Cantos*: if the latter are like a mosaic in which a pattern can be distinguished, the parts of Olson's poem are rather like the related parts of a musical piece whose "meaning" is only that complex of sensations rendered up as the piece proceeds and the internal relation of motifs to one another.

The images of "The Kingfishers" relate to each other rather than to the outside world and, like the images in *The Maximus Poems,* gather the connotations they come to own—action, creation, decline, destruction, and, dominant over all these, change. The motifs these images supply interweave through the poem: for instance, the east of creation and the west of decline in the following antiphonal passage:

> la lumiere"
> > but the kingfisher
> de l'aurore"
> > but the kingfisher flew west
> est devant nous!
> > he got the color of his breast
> > from the heat of the setting sun!

[48] Charles Olson, "The Kingfishers," *The Distances and Other Poems* (New York: Grove Press, 1960), p. 9.

There are motifs of birth and decay in the description of the kingfisher's nest: the young are born and fed and they grow in a nest of "excrement and decayed fish." In the following the same motifs appear:

> They buried their dead in a sitting posture
> serpent   cane   razor   ray of the sun

> And she sprinkled water on the head of the child, crying
> "Cioa-coatl! Cioa-coatl!"
> with her face to the west

> Where the bones are found, in each personal heap
> with what each enjoyed, there is always
> the Mongolian louse.

It might serve to think of this poem as conveying a message (Olson's word) by presenting its motifs with variations through different images as orchestral music repeats its melodies in different instruments. The restatements of melody differ in intensity and rise from the matter-of-fact, third-person narrative beginning to the lyrical splendor in the middle part of the last section, with its echoes of the rhythms of "Ash Wednesday" and of the line from the *Pisan Cantos,* "what whiteness will you add to this whiteness, / what candour?" that we have already seen echoed in Williams' "The Descent," a poem with similar implications to those here:

The light is in the east. Yes. And we must rise, act. Yet
in the west, despite the apparent darkness (the whiteness
which covers all), if you look, if you can bear, if you can, long
    enough

        as long as it was necessary for him, my guide
        to look into the yellow of that longest-lasting rose

so you must, and, in that whiteness, into that face, with what candor, look

and, considering the dryness of the place
      the long absence of an adequate race

   · · · · · · · · · · · · · · ·

hear
hear, where the dry blood talks
      where the old appetite walks. . . .

The poetic ground rules which produce such lines as these are well worth our attention.

v

The influence of Williams upon contemporary poets is not usually heard in local echoes but is for the most part pervasive and general. His influence is greater than that of Miss Moore, and it is different: she is not felt as a mentor, showing the way in open poetry; but certain of her local techniques are copied, and often her rhythms and her tone are heard in younger poets.

The impulses which have gone into a poem may not be mapped with any certainty: one seems to hear the voice of an earlier poet, often, without being able to assert its presence with any confidence. Miss Moore's voice seems audible, for instance, in the following from Auden,

     . . . an age when
        Courtesy would think: 'From your voice
   And the back of your neck I know we shall get on
        But cannot tell from your thumbs
   Who is to give the orders. . . .' [49]

Her voice is heard even clearer in certain passages throughout Richard Wilbur's work. Here, for example, are the opening lines of "Grace":

     So active they seem passive, little sheep
     Please, and Nijinsky's out-the-window leap

---

[49] W. H. Auden, "On Installing an American Kitchen in Lower Austria," *Homage to Clio* (London: Random House, 1960), p. 24.

> And marvelous midair pause please too
> A taste for blithe brute reflex. . . .[50]

Again, in Charles Tomlinson, one registers Miss Moore's influence: it is hard to imagine that he would have written

> . . .   a bridge
> Does not exist for its own sake.
> It commands vacancy,[51]

if she had not written

> Nor was he insincere in saying, 'Make my house your inn.'
> Inns are not residences.[52]

Miss Moore's voice is heard equally clearly, as will appear below, in the poems of Robert Duncan.

In Denise Levertov the influences of Williams and Miss Moore are both audible. That of the former is pervasive: as she says, he among others has "given // the language into our hands";[53] but it is the voice of Miss Moore that one hears more often, especially in the later poems.[54] In "Art (*After Gautier*)," from *With Eyes at the Back of Our Heads*, quotations from Cezanne, Jean Hélion, and Ruskin are copied precisely, acknowledged, and built rather than blended into the texture of the poem exactly in the manner of Marianne Moore. The penultimate stanza of the poem, however, is a pure echo of the

[50] Richard Wilbur, *The Poems of Richard Wilbur* (New York: Harcourt, Brace and World, 1963), p. 219.

[51] Charles Tomlinson, "More Foreign Cities," *Seeing Is Believing* (New York: McDowell Obolensky, 1958), p. 22.

[52] Marianne Moore, "Silence," *Collected Poems* (New York: Macmillan, 1959), p. 95.

[53] Denise Levertov, "September 1961," *O Taste and See* (Norfolk, Conn.: New Directions, 1964), pp. 9–11. Hereafter OTS.

[54] Miss Levertov says, "I feel the stylistic influence of William Carlos Williams, while perhaps too evident in my work of a few years ago, was a very necessary and healthful one, without which I could not have developed from a British Romantic with almost Victorian background to an American poet of any vitality." "Biographical Notes," *NAP*, p. 441.

rhythmic voice of Williams, and it is his sentiment that is expressed:

> The gods die every day
> but sovereign poems go on breathing
> in a counter-rhythm that mocks
> the frenzy of weapons, their impudent power.[55]

The general statement of the poem is that

> The best work is made
> from hard, strong materials,
> obstinately precise—
> the line of the poem, onyx, steel.

Such a statement might have come from Williams, though it might also have come from Pound, or for that matter Gaudier-Brzeska or Wyndham Lewis. In "Beyond the End," from *Here and Now*, there is, for one example of the influence of Miss Moore, the definition with its careful discrimination that is so characteristic of her: "It's energy: a spider's thread: not to / 'go on living' but to quicken, to activate: extend." [56] But in *The Jacob's Ladder* (1961), the echoes of Miss Moore's voice sound from many poems: sometimes in the use of quotations, as, for example, in "A Common Ground";[57] sometimes in rhythm:

> Those who were sacred have remained so,
> holiness does not dissolve, it is a presence
> of bronze, only the sight that saw it
> faltered and turned from it . . .
>
> (p. 21)

from a poem titled "Come into Animal Presence"; and once in the sudden illumination followed by definition:

[55] Denise Levertov, *With Eyes at the Back of Our Heads* (Norfolk, Conn.: New Directions, 1959), p. 73. Compare especially Williams' voice in "Asphodel, That Greeny Flower."

[56] Denise Levertov, *Here and Now* (San Francisco, Calif.: City Lights Books, 1957), p. 6.

[57] Denise Levertov, *The Jacob's Ladder* (Norfolk, Conn.: New Directions, 1961), pp. 1–2. Hereafter *JL*.

The authentic, I said
breaking the handle of my hairbrush as I
brushed my hair in
rhythmic strokes: That's it,
that's joy, it's always
a recognition, the known
appearing fully itself, and
more itself than one knew.

(p. 57)

Her aims in poetry are not the same as those of Miss Moore
or those of Williams: unlike Miss Moore she is not out among
animals, plants, and baseball players to find the solid grounds
for moral truth; nor is she anxious like Williams to refashion
the world with herself in it. Neither of these aims is necessarily
incompatible with hers, but she seems mostly concerned to
bring to articulate expression by means of poetry the half-felt
sensation or to focus and explore the situation of which she is
half aware. Something, as she says in "The Thread,"

. . . is very gently,
invisibly, silently,
pulling
(*JL*, p. 48)

at her; or her subject is things seen "a step / beyond the world"
(*OTS*, p. 60), or it is

. . . something
not quite caught, but filtered
through some outpost of dreaming sense
the gist, the drift. . . .
(*JL*, p. 33)

She is very conscious too of the speaking power of objects:

All trivial parts of
world-about-us speak in their forms
of themselves and their counterparts!

she says, in "A Straw Swan Under the Christmas Tree" (*With Eyes*, p. 32), and she illustrates. Or in "Our Bodies," in lines which recall Marianne Moore again:

> I have
>
> a line or groove I love
> runs down
> my body from breastbone
> to waist. It speaks of
> eagerness, of
> distance . . .

while "Your long back" and other features

> say
>
> what sky after sunset
> almost white
> over a deep woods to which
>
> rooks are homing, says.
> (*OTS*, pp. 72–73)

In her latest book, *O Taste and See* (1964), Miss Levertov is pre-eminently a love poet and, at that, a pre-eminent one. The heights she wants to climb in this mode are sometimes giddy, but, as we shall see, she is well-shod and roped. At other times, she dwells upon the body with what one must recognize as decorum.

She works mostly in the mode of fancy, and in this respect she is like Miss Moore, and Williams and his literary descendants. Many of these scions are published in Donald M. Allen's anthology, *The New American Poetry,* to which much reference has already been made here; and the poets of this volume are anxious on the whole to present objects unmodified by literary needs, in the manner Olson prescribes or Jack Spicer when he wishes that the lemon of the poem could be such as the reader could cut or squeeze or taste. Denise Levertov is also published in *The New American Poetry*, and her treatment of objects is to some extent in accord with that of her colleagues in this volume. Unlike any of the others, however, she is also published in the Meridian anthology,[58] in which are collected a less homogeneous group of young poets whose techniques vary more widely than those of the poets Donald Allen has anthologized; and the fancy for her is only one way of proceeding. There are other ways which set her far apart from Miss Moore and Williams.

One use to which she puts fancy is as a means of discovery: "The Dead Butterfly" illustrates how discovery is made when the image produced by fanciful likeness is permitted to develop without constraint.

I

Now I see its whiteness
is not white but green, traced with green,
and resembles the stones
of which the city is built,
quarried high in the mountains.

II

Everywhere among the marigolds
the rainblown roses and the hedges
of tamarisk are white
butterflies this morning, in constant
tremulous movement, only those
that lie dead revealing
their rockgreen color and the bold
cut of the wings.

(*With Eyes*, p. 14)

The resemblance of the butterfly's wings to the "stones / of which the city is built" is a limited one, which extends only as far as their common coloring, "green, traced with green." This

---

[58] *New Poets of England and America: Second Selection*, ed. Donald Hall and Robert Pack (New York: World Publishing Company, 1962).

is the one point of likeness; the bringing together of the two objects is an operation of the fancy. The fancy, however, characteristically permissive, has developed the image of the stones beyond mere usefulness, adding the inoperative detail—"quarried high in the mountains"—that T. E. Hulme would have condemned as excess. This line, in its sounds and rhythms and especially in its connotations, gives a sense of mystery and majesty which, belonging primarily to the stones, spills over and endows the dead butterfly. Thus the work of the fancy has discovered some glory in the butterflies.

It is interesting to conjecture why the two stanzas of this poem should have been presented in the order in which we have them, solidly numbered. More naturally, the familiar view of the butterflies would have preceded the special impression that the exercise of fancy has provided. One effect of the inversion is that the aura of the last line of the first stanza is now carried forward to counterpoint the "tremulous" and even trivial movements of the live insects in stanza II. It supplies a background, one may say, against which these movements may be considered. And the use of a background in this fashion is interesting to observe, since it is a technique Miss Levertov repeats and which we shall see again below.

Discovery is made, or at least it is prepared for, in the fanciful association of the dead butterfly with the stones. Later, in "Clouds" (*JL*, pp. 46–47), there is a more explicit raid into fanciful relationships for the discovery of qualities in experience. The poem opens with a somber image of roseate clouds rising in the evening. Then the poet senses that her lover's flesh is cold "as if death had lit a pale light / in your flesh," or, to be discriminating,

> . . .   not cold
> but cool, cooling, as if the last traces
> of warmth were still fading in you . . .

as it is fading from the evening clouds. The poet therefore forces into her mind a vision of "a sky of gray mist" only to discover, by looking intently at it, that

> its gray was not gray but a milky white
> in which radiant traces of opal greens,
> fiery blues, gleamed, faded, gleamed again . . .

and then that

> a field sprang into sight . . .
> a field of freshest deep spiring grass
> starred with dandelions
> green and gold. . . .[59]

The induced vision of the sky with its cold, damp, gray mist has an arbitrary, fanciful similarity with the touch of death in the bed; and it is a means of probing the touch of death to discover something about it. The poem proceeds to ask explicitly whether the simile does in fact provide a valid insight:

> Is death's chill that visited our bed
> other than what it seemed, is it
> a gray to be watched keenly?

We assume that it is: that the poetic process has lightened the burden of the prospect of the lover's death by discovering in it qualities that offset the conventional bleakness. The poem turns back at the end to the image with which it had opened—the clouds of the evening. But these are not now "somber," and the scene is not "grim"; they are now "in pomp advancing, pursuing / the fallen sun."

Finally, the heuristic operation of the fancy may be seen, clearly and explicitly, in "About Marriage" (*OTS*, pp. 68–69): "Don't lock me in wedlock," it begins; and then in a long parenthesis it describes an encounter the poet had had with birds in

---

[59] Miss Levertov's use of color and color contrasts here and in "The Dead Butterfly" and indeed frequently throughout her work is similar to W. C. Williams', though it need not be the result of influence, of course.

a park in the "green light of / May." One cannot see in each of
the images in the parenthesis a reflection of one or another
aspect of marriage; rather the poet has associated her encounter
in the park with her marriage and has adduced many details of
that encounter on the off chance, as it were, that certain of them
would reveal things to her about her marriage. After the parenthesis, explicitly justifying the array of fanciful images she has
proffered, she says,

> It's not
> irrelevant:
> I would be
> met
>
> and meet you
> so,
> in a green
>
> airy space, not
> locked in.

The description of the encounter is relevant because of the possibilities it contains for a marriage:

> . . . long
> shadows and cool
>
> air . . . ;

"blossom on the threshold of / abundance";

> the birds saw me and
>
> let me be
> near them.

The imagination would have withheld the details, and made a
metaphor, perhaps, as this: ". . . marriage is an encounter with
birds in a cool park," which is fraught with potential "links of
relevance." When details are spelled out, however, the imagination is forestalled, indeed, crippled. But then such a metaphor

would suggest little or nothing about marriage that was not already contained in our existing concept of it.

"Clouds," cited above, consists of one long central section, in which the gray fog is discovered to be opalescent, and other smaller sections grouped before and after it in rough symmetry. The poem closes with the image of the roseate clouds with which it had opened. Such a pattern, as unobtrusive as the patterns of many of Marianne Moore's poems, is not rare in Denise Levertov's poetry. But equally frequent is the poem that moves from one concept or situation or both on to another without turning back to the opening imagery. The following early poem is quoted entire because it shows a number of characteristic features; I withhold the title for the moment.

> 'The will is given us that
>   we may know the
> delights of surrender.' Blake with
> tense mouth, crouched small (great forehead,
> somber eye) amid a crowd's tallness in a narrow room.
>   The same night
> a bird caught in my room, battered
> from wall to wall, missing the window over & over
>   (till it gave up and
>   huddled half-dead on a shelf, and I
>   put up the sash against the cold)
> and waking at dawn I again
> pushed the window violently down, open
>   and the bird gathered itself and flew
>   straight out
>   quick and calm (over the radiant chimneys—
>   (*Here and Now*, p. 11)

The use of a quotation is reminiscent of Marianne Moore, and what it says is exactly what she might say. The two major images, Blake "crouched small" and the sparrow, are fancifully related, both man and bird being confined. There is a certain amount of symmetry in the poem: Blake and the sparrow; the cold night and the warmth in the morning, notified by "radiant chimneys"; the bird surrendering at night and the bird flying off in the morning. But these few symmetrical elements do not serve to reinforce meaning. "Clouds" opens with an image of clouds and, when the wheel has come full circle, closes with an image of clouds. The two images are different, and their difference is marked, since they are two visions of the same scene. This difference in similarity is thus a notification of what the poem has achieved, a notification that the pattern of the poem—the fundamental similarity between beginning and end —has facilitated. No such pattern, however, serves to express or reinforce the meaning in the poem about Blake and the bird: it is, for instance, an *open* poem and breaks off without an ending in the middle of a parenthesis—a practice reminiscent of Williams and Olson. Furthermore the discernible elements of pattern serve mainly as foils to each other: the idea of the "delights of surrender," for example, recurs ironically in the middle of the poem as an image of a bird "huddled half-dead on a shelf"; and of course the ending of the poem does not by difference in similarity register what has occurred since the opening; on the contrary, the exaltation at the end in the freedom of flight—freedom broadened, even, by the open end—completely upstages the so-called "delights of surrender" of the opening and moves away. The poem's title is "The Flight," which is a reference not to the totality of the poem but to the end, the point to which it has led and where it breaks off. For the poem is not *rounded* off, it simply *leaves* off because the words stop.

"The Flight," like certain other poems, sets up one postulate only to depart from it at the end with action that contradicts it. The breach of pattern marks a difference from the practice of Miss Moore in many of her poems; but we are reminded still of the way she sets up, as a foil, a literal or metaphorical view which is wrong or crude and proceeds to substitute a more perceptive one. Miss Moore, however, usually pays more courtesy to pattern: in "The Steeple-Jack," for example, although the initial pretty picture is severely qualified by the realistic view, the conclusion to the poem—"It scarcely could be dangerous . . ."—owes something to both pictures and creates a sense of pattern. Similar respect is paid to the pattern of "In the Public Garden," in which the last stanza concerning the general admiration of art repeats the motif of the public festival announced in the first stanza and formally concludes the official poem. Denise Levertov's "Clouds" shows a comparable adherence to pattern when the clouds reappear, although revealing a different aspect.

Such a violation of pattern as seen in "The Flight," on the other hand, is also characteristic of this poet. To put the matter simply and barely, she often wants to move on from where she started without looking back to where she was; and it is worth examining a few poems which variously implement this urge and studying their implications. For one thing, she wants to get on in a poem into what, for her, is the very essence of poetry— the remote sensation, the perception just out of range of vision. This is where the poem is, and she wishes she could begin at that place where "the quick of mystery" actually exists. "At the Edge" begins,

> How much I should like to begin
> a poem with And—presupposing
> the hardest said—
> the moss cleared off the stone,
> the letters plain.
>
> (*With Eyes*, p. 49)

But she knows she cannot, because there is groundwork that must be done: "What use to pretend the stone discovered . . . ?" Indeed, the poem may not be there but elsewhere, "in animal eyes gazing / from the thicket."

One is often conscious that the opening of one of her poems

is groundwork: an image, a situation, or a postulate submitted merely to be departed from; or, more exactly perhaps, a scene upon which the major action or statement of the poem is to be staged. The two stanzas of a poem called "Lonely Man" are respectively scene and statement. Naturally, the statement of "your" loneliness in the second stanza draws from the scene in the first as action draws from scene in the drama.[60] The scene, like the imagery in Marianne Moore, is developed beyond strict requirements, however:

> trees on the plain lifting
>   their heads, fine strokes
>   of grass stretching themselves to breathe
> the last of the light.
>
>   (*JL*, p. 79)

Then, even granted that it contributes to the sense of loneliness, it is the great breadth of the scene upon which the poet bases her statement that is striking; the poem begins a long way back from its essential statement: it opens, "An open world / within its mountain rim." The volume, indeed, in which this poem occurs opens by reminding the reader of the cosmic dimensions in space and time which provide the background for the poems that follow.

> As you read, a white bear leisurely
> pees, dyeing the snow
> saffron. . . .

And as you read too,

> . . . many gods
> lie among lianas: eyes of obsidian
> are watching the generations of leaves . . .

and "the sea is turning its dark pages." It is as if Denise Levertov

---

[60] Kenneth Burke elaborates and illustrates the matter in *A Grammar of Motives*.

feels that before zeroing in on the pure poem itself, she must pan the whole circumference.

In drawing attention to the procedure in which this poet moves from scene to poem, I do not want to overemphasize the distinction between them. If this distinction certainly exists in her consciousness, so too does the conviction, which is declared in "At the Edge," that without the scene the poem cannot exist. In "The Desert Music," of William Carlos Williams, there are, as we have seen, prosaic perceptions, contributing uncertainly to the theme of protection, that back the poetic operation; and we have found that in Williams generally the pure poem cannot exist except somewhere in the approaches to it; indeed, is it not true, have we not heard and been told from the beginning, that the pure dance itself cannot be distilled and distinguished from the dancer?

In "Five Poems from Mexico" (*JL*, pp. 26–28) interesting variations are played by each short component poem on the relationship of the pure product to its own impure context. In each there is scenic background of a kind and against it, or following it, action or the essence of the poem. The process is most clear in the fifth poem, "Sierra," which presents first the golden ridge of the back of the "bull-mountain" and then,

> . . . Shadows
> of zopilotes cross and slowly
> cross again
> thy flanks, lord of herds.

Zopilotes are black Mexican vultures. This concluding poem of the series presents simply a backdrop with moving figures in the foreground. The first, second, and fourth poems present a drab scene and then, superimposed upon it, some vivid colors: "The cowdung-colored mud" in the first poem, "The Weave,"

> . . . bears the silken
> lips and lashes of erotic

> flowers towards a sky of
> noble clouds. . . .

The poem closes:

> . . . fling
> magenta shawls delicately
> about your brown shoulders laughing.

In the second, "Corazón," white clouds are the background for the personification of Mexico with "a blanket of geranium pink drawn up / over his silent mouth." In the fourth, "Canticle,"

> . . . from the altar
> of excrement arises
> an incense
>
> of orange and purple
> petals. . . .

The third poem of this series, "The Rose," suggests that the background, or what is the equivalent, performs another function, which after Williams and Miss Moore is again familiar. The drab opening image in this poem and a comment of calculated banality that closes it serve to ballast the intense sensuous experience in the central statement—a tactic we found executed in their various ways by these two earlier poets. In "The Rose," what in the other poems was more strictly scene has been replaced by the figure of a shabby old man: following him as he "shuffles from rose to rose" the poet enjoys sensations of unalloyed luster: she discovers

> the golden rose, color of bees' fur, odor of honey,
> red rose, contralto, roses
> of dawn-cloud-color, of snow-in-moonlight,
> of colors only roses know,
> but no rose
> like the rose I saw in your garden.

It is like one of those lovely lyrical passages in Henry Green of a memory edited into an ecstasy; or it is like Keats among his luxuries. But the poet is manifestly anxious not to fade far away and quite forget the weary world and indeed insists on coming back to earth in her friend's garden, presumably wanting, in Williams' words, to fight her way back to the real world in spite of the lure of the romantic garden.

There used to be an old cliché in literary history, which it was sometimes possible to believe, that so-and-so "prepared the way" for so-and-so. Miss Levertov's acknowledgment of Williams' influence quoted above is well taken: it is possible to believe that he prepared her way, and it seems evident also that she has already gone beyond the path he cleared. The disciplines he imposed upon himself after his juvenile flirtation with Keatsian poetry deprived Williams, as we have seen, of some of the effects which poetry may with perfect propriety be expected to deliver. Like winter, he cleared the ground; but then he suffered only the buds of early spring to flourish. In Denise Levertov's imagery, on the other hand, the high midsummer pomps are permitted to come on. But the blossoms do not by any means make the plants stoop with oppression of their prodigal weight: she is rich where Williams and some others among his followers are spare, but she is in perfect control of the *enargia* she produces. Her imagery is not merely a place for the lovers of poetry to wander in; on the contrary, her "things" turn very often into "ideas." A poem rests far less often than one of Williams' on a straight, though rhythmical, presentation of one corner of the world: Williams, whose love of the world is all-embracing, picks up and poetizes scores of unnoticed things that the dull swain treads on daily with his clouted shoon, and he builds himself with energetic joy into the world he discovers. But Williams does not habitually use his perceptions to reflect or create the nuances of feelings and slight emotions in the way Denise Levertov does.

Images in her work sometimes serve as objective correlatives, and they are sometimes coinages of the imagination. In her imagery generally much more respect is paid to the thusness of things themselves than we found, for instance, in *Lord Weary's Castle*; and occasionally with a sense of shock we recognize that though these things appear autonomous they are in fact serving the poet's ulterior purposes in the manner made famous by T. S. Eliot or in the way we have seen them used by Robert Lowell.

To illustrate the employment of an objective correlative let us consider, finally, "A Sequence" (*JL*, pp. 8–10), a poem that shows something of the power of this poet, which lies not at all in majesty of language or rhythms but in what, prior to detailing it, we may call tact or rightness. The five parts of the poem record the arising of a quarrel, its crisis, and subsequent resolution. There are a few dramatic details, including the setting of the scene and an occasional line or two of dialogue; but in the main the poem records the parabola of feeling in its imagery and its rhythms. The first two sections are as follows:

i

A changing skyline.
A slice of window filled in
by a middle-distance oblong
topped by little
moving figures.
You are speaking
flatly, 'as one drinks a glass of

milk' (for calcium).
            Suddenly the milk
spills, a torrent of black milk hurtles
through the room, bubbling and
seething into the corners.

ii

'But then I was another person!'
The building veiled

in scaffolding. When the builders leave,
tenants will move in, pervading
cubic space with breath and dreams.
Odor of newmade memories
will loiter in the hallways,
noticed by helpless dogs and young children.
That will be other, another
building.

We see here that the anger of the other party appears in his speech, which is described in terms of milk: the simile between the kind of flat speech that precedes the onset of anger and a person drinking a glass of milk for its calcium is one of the imagination. There are the obvious links of relevance in that both activities are cold, unexciting, reasonable, and even a little burdensome. The milk then becomes black lava as the cool speech becomes angry. Here the links are even stronger: there is fear associated with both, there is the suddenness of the eruption, and both come from hearts of fire.

The poet's answer to this angry speech is to plead, "But then I was another person." Then, in order to embody this concept and feeling of being another person, she abstracts from the immediate scene, which had been briefly outlined in the first five lines, the objective correlative of the building under construction. She chooses, somewhat as L'Allegro and Il Penseroso choose, such objects as will suit her mood; and by means of these objects the mood is defined, as they are for Milton's men. Unlike the simile of the milk and the lava, the image of the building is one of the fancy, with its due accretion of circumstantiality. And yet the image is not developed purely for its own sake and the details are not purely gratuitous; for the entry into the building of its complement of tenants and abstractions —breath, dreams, and memories observed by dogs and children —is part of the objective correlative and thus part of the formula for the particular mood. (The mood is roughly opposite— if moods may be allowed to have opposites—to that of Keats in the penultimate stanza of "Ode on a Grecian Urn," which is objectified in the little town "emptied of its folk, this pious morn.") One may think of the poet, uncertain as to what would be the exactly right notification of the nuance of her mood (and Keats is equally uncertain; his image is framed as a question: "What little town . . .."), mustering whatever details are fancifully associated with the main image chosen as a formula, but not actively selecting and forcing into regiment only what can be made to contribute to idea.

In the resolution of the quarrel in the fifth part of the poem, we find that the image of the building has taken on the appearance of allegory. When the quarrel is over and the new personality, which the new building represents, has become established, "the absurd angel of happiness walks in"; later, the same angel,

> dressed for laughs as a plasterer,
> puts a match to whatever's
> lying in the grate: broken scaffolds,
> empty cocoons, the paraphernalia
> of unseen change. . . .

But the allegory is tenuous; and the plasterer, as will appear, is an image of the imagination, not part of a closely knit allegorical scheme. "How irrelevantly," the poet says, "he walks in"; but the irrelevance is only apparent, like that of the apparent heterogeneity of the images in "The Death of the Sheriff." Upon inspection, the introduction of the plasterer reveals itself as an apt and perfect stroke.

Another detail in the fifth part purveyed by the imagination is apparently irrelevant but really apt: the poet reminds the other party of the scene against which the quarrel had erupted:

> '. . . you were
> preparing to leave for
> three weeks—**Here's the check. And**
> **perhaps in a week or so**

I'll be able to send you a
pound of tomatoes.' Then
you laugh too, and we clasp
in naked laughter. . . .

The rightness of these details is made clear when we read the short essay, "A Note on the Work of the Imagination," that followed this poem when it appeared in *New Directions*,[61] in which Miss Levertov speaks of the fidelity of the imagination. In a dream, the kind where one is conscious that one is dreaming, "the idea came to me of looking in the mirror as a test of how far in fidelity the dream would go." In spite of the fear that the mirror would show a blank or strange face, she dared to approach it, only to see a "misty whiteness" glimmering round the top of her head. This, however, transpired to be a mist of dew in her hair. Her profound and beautiful comment is worth quoting at length:

> The creative unconscious—the imagination—had *provided,* instead of a fright, this exquisitely realistic detail. For hadn't I been walking in the misty fields in the dewfall hour? Just so, then, would my damp hair look. I awoke in delight, reminded forcibly of just what it is we love in the greatest writers— what quality above all others, surely, makes us open ourselves freely to Homer, Shakespeare, Tolstoi, Hardy—that *following through,* that *permeation* of detail—relevant, illuminating detail—which marks the total imagination, distinct from intellect, at work. . . . The feared Hoffmanesque blank—the possible monster or stranger—would have illustrated the work of Fancy, that *"by invisible wires puts marionettes in motion, and pins butterflies to blotting-paper, and plays Little-Go among the Fairies"* (Landor, in *Imaginary Conversations*).

The distinction made here between fancy and imagination is in line with that which we have seen earlier: the details provided by the imagination are faithful and contribute to the

---

[61] *New Directions* 17 (Norfolk, Conn., 1961), pp. 45–47, 49–50.

whole; those provided by fancy, though they fit at one point or another, may be wayward and grotesque.

In the light of these considerations, we may see the so designated "irrelevancies" discussed above as the work of the imagination. They fit. But we have to look to a level deeper than the texture of the poem to discover their context. The angel of happiness, "dressed for laughs as a plasterer," the *seeming* irrelevance of whose entry is remarked because of its actual relevance, is an instance of the fool who puts things right. How perennially the fool in his occupational clothing (the village policeman, the plumber, the char, the gardener) is an object of laughter *because* in the end it is he whose insensitive performance of absolutely essential mundane duties resolves a crisis that has developed at a more ethereal level of life. The detail of the pound of tomatoes is similarly a coinage of the imagination. The image has no links of relevance with other images in the preceding part of the poem, but it certainly has links with those other manifold petty-housekeeping details of existence, which routines by their very boredom give life stability. The detail is right, like the halo of dew, because it is exactly such a detail as *would* have returned the antagonists from the spirited level of their quarrel.

The receptiveness of her poetry to whatever signals emerge from those deep levels of the mind where imagination operates distinguishes Miss Levertov somewhat from her fellows, whose interests are crowded upon techniques. But she is not by any means backward in recognizing the importance of these (and indeed in implementing that recognition). A brief poem from *Here and Now* shows her appealing to technique as a means of resisting the surge of romantic feeling; the hearer of the piano music is bidden to open his eyes and watch the pianist's hands:

> Don't forget the crablike
> hands, slithering
>   among the keys.
>   Eyes shut, the downstream

> play of sound lifts away from
> the present, drifts you
>   off your feet: too easily let off.
>
>   So look: that almost painful
>   movement restores the pull, incites
>   the head with the heart: a tension, as of
>   actors at rehearsal, who move
>   this way, that way, on a bare stage, testing
>   their diagonals, in common clothes.
>   ("The Hands," p. 15)

The last image speaks of Miss Levertov herself, who having paid attention to techniques can permit the entry on stage of profound resonances.

VI

A much stronger consciousness of technique is manifest in the poems of Robert Duncan, who is the last of the sons of Williams to whom I wish to give brief consideration for the sake of the light their work may throw on that of the parent. A brief study of *The Opening of the Field*,[62] will reveal techniques and attitudes that we have seen in Williams but which Duncan has carried further than he did. These attitudes, which are described below, are used by this poet to maintain the detachment of a scholar-gypsy in poetry: his most manifest intention throughout the volume seems to be to create a place in poetry where intuition may flourish and to prevent the encroachment upon it of fixed, formal, unmagical knowledge and old orders, as the legendary scholar took to the hills and fled the contagion of Oxford. The title page of the volume, designed for the author by his friend Jess Collins, shows a group of children playing ring a ring o' roses in a playground. It is to the state of childhood that Duncan would return us; by means of poetry he proposes to bring us as receptive children

---

[62] Robert Duncan, *The Opening of the Field* (New York: Grove Press, 1960). Hereafter *OF*.

to an open field where, by the magic of childhood, intuitions are available. The genius of a child is given some attention by Duncan in "Pages from a Notebook," which appears among the "Statements on Poetics" in *The New American Poetry* (pp. 400–407). He speaks first of the crippling of the imagination by parents. Then, what seems most relevant to a study of *The Opening of the Field,* he says, "It is the key to our own inner being that the child offers us in his self-absorption." He adds: "Every moment of life is an attempt to come to life. Poetry is a 'participation,' a oneness. Can the ambitious artist who seeks success, perfection, mastery, ever get nearer to the universe, can he ever know 'more' or feel 'more' than a child may?" In his *Art and Reality* lectures, Joyce Cary tells of a child who, untutored by convention, drew a swan as a powerful, swimming animal, all feet. An older child, looking on, disdainfully "improved" on the picture by doing a conventional, graceful Christmas-card swan. The spontaneous intuitive perception of an individual thing had been replaced in the older child by the intellectual apprehension of a concept: the individual thing had become a representative of a general category. It is the earlier kind of response that Duncan associates with childhood and wishes to elicit in the reader and in himself by his poetry. "A man that looks on glass," says George Herbert,

> On it may stay his eye,
> Or, if he pleaseth, through it pass,
> And then the heav'n espy.

But Duncan would wish a man's eye to remain on the glass and to derive the poetry from the patterns thereon.

At least to some extent: while the gypsy part of this poet seeks a place where he may undo his corded bales undisturbed by the encroachment of formal knowledge, the scholar part recognizes and indeed reveres wisdom. "Writing is compounded," he says, "of wisdom and intuition"; although it seems that wisdom must be brought low and reinstructed by the

other. Thus in "A Poem Beginning with a Line by Pindar,"
Psyche, who is a figure of wisdom—"Scientia / holding the
lamp"—must be brought low in the sorting of the seeds:

> . . . Psyche
> must despair, be brought to her
> > insect instructor. . . .

And similarly, Ezra Pound, the "father of many notions," must
turn to the insect world:

> . . . The old man at Pisa
> mixd in whose mind
> (to draw the sorts) are all seeds
> > *as a lone ant from a broken ant-hill*
> had part restored by an insect, was
> upheld by a lizard. . . .
> > > (*OF*, p. 65)

Old wisdom, however, may be used for new poetry: ". . .
though I contrive the mind's measure / and wrest doctrine from
old lore," says the poet, "it's to win particular hearts, / to stir
an abiding affection for this music . . ." (p. 61).

I take it that the recurring image in *The Opening of the Field*
of crossed or double vision refers to the duality which looks to
both wisdom and intuition: one eye focused on the surface
and the other beyond it, with a result that recalls the two kinds
of vision in Marianne Moore; but I do not pretend that from
lines such as the following or indeed from any of Duncan's
lines meaning springs fully formed: once again, the reader
must not key his mind to the reception of meaning by itself,
which is the merest susurrus at the edge of one's sensations.
The image occurs first in "A Poem Slow Beginning":

> but that's not the way I saw.
> Crossd
> the sinister eye sees the near

as clear fact,
           the far
blurs; the right eye
    fuses all that is
immediate to sight. . . .
             (p. 14)

It appears again, suitably enough, in "Crosses of Harmony and Disharmony":

. . . the lines of the verse do not meet,
imitating that void between
    two images of a single rose near at hand, the one
slightly above and to the right . . .

      "the double vision
due to maladjustment of the eyes" like
"visual delusions arising from some delirium
illustrates surrounding spatial regions",

"pure mode of presentational immediacy".
             (p. 45)

Other instances of the double vision will appear later. Meanwhile, we may observe that the duality is extended in a special way to hearing: puns and etymologies abound in the poetry—the surface sensation of the word playing against its usual, expected meaning. The poem quoted from immediately above, for example, opens with the misheard line of a Christian hymn which should read "Gladly, the cross I'd bear" but is heard as "Gladly, the cross-eyed bear." The pun gives the poet the opportunity for fanciful play between images of bear and Christ, such as "Old Stinker sweaty with beastly nails" and "the Sun crownd on His tree / with beastly nails."

There are, then, two kinds of sensation, one receiving wisdom, the other intuitions. The poet favors the latter and fears the encroachment of wisdom when it is manifested as old law.

He has spoken, for instance, in "Pages from a Notebook," of our obligation to honor Christ and at the same time of his hostility to the impositions of Christianity. In the poem about crosses, he says,

> There was no law of Jesus then.
> There was
> only a desire of savior,
> man-gate of God,
> a roar of the Holy Sea seeking
> lion's mouth
> to take the place of placid potencies,
> old orders.

The old orders in Duncan are to be used for the sake of new intuitions. His attitude toward them is like that of Jack Spicer toward the sun and the sea:

> One can only worship
> These cold eternals for their support of
> What is absolutely temporary. . . .
> (*NAP*, p. 142)

The echoes of Marianne Moore in *The Opening of the Field* are most audible when Duncan makes use of quotations in exactly her manner: he holds them up, that is, as something to be looked at—looked at with the "sinister eye"—before their autonomous *dinglichkeit* is dissolved into meaning. Enough instances of this practice have already been quoted in passages above adduced for other purposes. The double vision is by no means strikingly similar to this phenomenon in Miss Moore, but the effect is comparable: her view of concrete detail is a corrective to the broad sentimental view and leads to accurate expression of feeling and moral judgment; his short view is a corrective to the traditional, old, formal knowledge and gives rise to intuitive knowledge. One poem in this volume, "The

Maiden," two lines of which we have seen earlier, acknowledges its debt to Miss Moore: the last paragraph, subtitled *The Close,* goes as follows:

> Close to her construct I pace the line,
> the containd homage arranged, reflections
> on Marianne Moore's natural style, an artifice
> where sense may abound. As in a photograph of her
> I found the photographer with his camera had caught
> artfully a look where this flame took my mind
> of beauty in which a maiden's
> unlikely hardihood may be retaind.
>
> (p. 29)

As we shall see shortly, Duncan pays tribute to Miss Moore as one model for what is fundamental to his style. Meanwhile, we may notice that his similarities with Williams are more obvious. There is, first, throughout *The Opening of the Field,* a recurring motif of destruction, and related in one way or another to that destruction is the flourishing of the new. Such a motif we have seen in Charles Olson's "The Kingfishers"; and before that we have seen it in Williams: sometimes, as in the Marie Curie passage of *Paterson,* it is accompanied by strong contempt for the old order, the swamp as he calls it; sometimes it appears as an unimpassioned observation of the fluctuation in the nature of life, like the alternation (celebrated all the time in Wallace Stevens) between the ascent of creation and the descent of destruction in the passage beginning "The descent beckons. . . ."

The close interrelation of decay and beauty, again reminiscent of "The Kingfishers," is seen in the following passage, which is one of a series of prose poems entitled "The Structure of Rime" that appear irregularly throughout the volume:

> . . . the Fish that sends from the stench of Its decay iridescences of green, lavender, pink, cerulean of Its living scales.

And from the white bars of Its skeleton washd by the sea, bleachd by the sun, everlasting tones resound in the everlasting image of the Fish, fins and forkd tails of the radiant.

(p. 71)

The capitalization here suggests that the fish is a symbol for Christ, after the old mnemonic ἰχθυς; and Christ in His death is, of course, a prime instance of creation growing out of destruction. It may in addition be a phallic symbol; it may be a symbol for poetry which, as will appear below, is like a salmon that dies in its ascent of the stream in the process of reproducing its kind.

In another poem, "Atlantis," old destruction and revival come together in a more or less direct statement:

> Thought flies out from the old scars of the sea
>   as if to land. Flocks that are longings
> come in to shake over the deep water.
>
> It's prodigies held in time's amber
> old destructions
> and the theme of revival the heart asks for.

(p. 75)

The subject of "This Place Rumord to Have Been Sodom" is destruction; but out of destruction (in a manner admittedly obscure) comes salvation: in the last two lines, Sodom, which had been cursed and destroyed, is redeemed: "This place rumord to have been Sodom is blessed / in the Lord's eyes" (p. 23).

The last poem in *The Opening of the Field*, "Food for Fire, Food for Thought," illustrates, perhaps best of all, Duncan's belief in the creativity of destruction. The poem, first, makes much of the ephemerality of the intuitions the poet creates:

> We trace faces in clouds: they drift apart,
> palaces of air—the sun dying down
>   sets them on fire;

descry shadows on the flood from its dazzling mood,
or at its shores read runes upon the sand
    from sea-spume.

But it is exactly such evanescent visions and not fixed, formal knowledge that the poet wants: "This is what I wanted for the last poem, / a loosening of conventions and return to open form." Then, out of the fire fed by language which is addressed in the poem as "you," the flames of intuition come.

You have carried a branch of tomorrow into the room.
Its fragrance has awakend me—no,

    it was the sound of a fire on the hearth

    leapd up where you bankd it, sparks of delight.

Finally, the motif of destruction appears in the word "purged": because by a kind of destruction we can be returned to the flexibility and informality of childhood, we are eligible to receive intuitions:

We are close enough to childhood, so easily purged
of whatever we thought we were to be,

    flamey threads of firstness go out from your touch.

    Flickers of unlikely heat
    at the edge of our belief bud forth.

It is frequently at the "edge" of the known or the formal that intuition flourishes.

The poem also contains a remark that links Duncan with Williams and Miss Moore in the common use of fancy. We do not have in Duncan such sharp concrete images, linked together by association, as we have in the other two. But it is clear that by their very nature intuitions, like discoveries, are to be derived not from the work of the imagination but from that of the fancy, which gives space for small, unplanned thoughts to develop. We have already seen the fancy in operation in the poem "Crosses of Harmony and Disharmony," where the poet's fancy, liberated by the mishearing of the hymn, is allowed to play over the associations between Christ and the bear. Earlier in this book, Coleridge's description of Luther's vision was adduced as an example of imagination; but in Duncan's last poem a similar figure is used to illustrate the play of the fancy. After speaking of the return to open form, the poem goes on:

> Leonardo saw figures that were stains upon a wall.
> Let the apparitions contain in the ground
>   play as they will.

Throughout the volume there is more than a trace of the kind of permissiveness that lets fancy play in these lines. Often, in fact, the poet, like D. H. Lawrence, shows a feminine receptivity to experience and plays a feminine role opposite it for the sake of receiving intuitions that appear at the edge of knowledge. Thus "the counsels of the Wood," in "The Structure of Rime VII," are

> *Lie down, Man, under Love. The streams of the Earth seek passage thru you, tree that you are, toward a foliage that breaks at the boundaries of known things.*
>
>   (p. 20)

In "The Structure of Rime III" he is swung by the language—"Swung in your arms, I grow old" (p. 16). In "The Ballad of the Enamord Mage" we find the poet *"waiting for the rime, / that know not the meaning of my name"* (p. 23). Or in "The Structure of Rime IX" he complains that his "spirit is like a reservoir that cannot draw up its knees" (p. 71).

The most significant point at which Duncan is reminiscent of Williams, however, is not in the intertwining motifs of destruction and revival which are more dominant in Duncan than Williams, nor in the common play of fancy, but in the concept they share of words as things and the poem as a thing.

For Duncan as to Williams, words come first; and the dance they engage in is observed by the sinister eye before the other eye searches out meaning. Thus they work their magic. The poem called "The Dance," coming at the beginning of the volume as if a statement of a general procedure, might in its entirety illustrate the point. I quote one brief passage:

> Lovely their feet pound the green solid meadow.
> The dancers
> mimic flowers—root stem stamen and petal
> our words are,
> our articulations, our
> measures.
>
> (p. 8)

The dancers here move into expression with the naturalness of the growth of plants, from root to petal; and in turn "our words" are as the feet of the dancers. That is the statement. But the words are dancing themselves: the absence of punctuation after "petal" permits the phrase of which it is part to stand in apposition to "flowers" and also to move as the inverted complement to "our words are." Standing by itself, however, this clause says also that words *are* as opposed to words *mean*. We must notice too the symmetry of this dance: "our . . . are"; "our . . . our"; and we must notice the pauses, enforced by the breaking up of syntax by line endings, which permit the dance to speak through its silences. In a prose passage incorporated in parentheses near the end of the poem, the poet remembers how he worked in a dance hall: "I'd dance until three, then up to get the hall swept before nine—beer bottles, cigarette butts, paper mementos of the night before. Writing it down now, it is the aftermath, the silence, I remember, part of the dance too, an articulation of the time of dancing. . . ."

In such a manner as the above, Duncan has come to make poetry which seems to go beyond Pound's practices in *logopoeia* —"the dance of the intellect among words." Duncan says,

The reality of what is witnessed disciplines the speech, and it is only by poetry, by the making-up of the real through language . . . that one can witness. ["Without invention," said Williams, "nothing lies under the witch-hazel / bush."] Meanings and functions are intimately related, if not merely different aspects of the same event. Now: Mr. Pound's *logopoeia* seems to be not only a verbal manifestation by a physiological manifestation. . . . [I]t is the action of the language, the muscular correlation of the now differentiated parts of the poem, that so expresses itself.[63]

In this style, called "locomotor writing," Joyce's *Ulysses* "remains, like the 'Cantos', Marianne Moore's or William Carlos Williams' opera, a masterpiece of this mode. If we are seriously involved, we must go to school to these."

Duncan tends, then, as does Olson, to look away from the meaning of the word in order to concentrate, with the sinister eye, upon its other properties; and this process is perhaps what he means when he says, "one may lose sight of the target in order to gain insight of the target."[64] But "meanings and functions are intimately related" so that the performance of words as physical entities in the dance is only artificially separable from their performance as meanings. As meanings, they point to things; and it is from the presentation of things—the presentation of things to be felt as contacts, one must add—that intuitive ideas arise. Duncan speaks of the "potencies in common things" and of " 'princely manipulations of the real.' "

But he is not imagistically rich: rather seldom do we run into the vivid image with sharp edges. Sometimes a shadowy image such as Wallace Stevens might have written—"The lamps strung among / shadowy foliage are there"; occasionally cosmic, Shelleyan imagery, like "the rubble of the world," appears. As a whole, the poetry is far from imagistic.

[63] Robert Duncan, "Notes on Poetics, Regarding Olson's 'Maximus,' " *the Review*, No. 10 (January, 1964), p. 39.
[64] *Ibid.*, p. 38.

Not only are words thought of as physical entities, but the poem itself is such an entity. We can do no better than conclude this brief description of his poetry with an image of it that Duncan himself provides, in which it is seen as the title suggests: "Poetry, A Natural Thing" (p. 50). I quote the poem entire, drawing attention first to the Moore-like use of quotations, the motif of destruction followed by new life in both the salmon and the antlers of the moose, the poem as a "muscular" thing speaking its meaning through felt energy, the lack of interest in conventional beauty, and the sense that the poem speaks some primitive truth.

> Neither our vices nor our virtues
> further the poem. "They came up
>   and died
> just like they do every year
>   on the rocks."
>
> The poem
> feeds upon thought, feeling, impulse,
>   to breed itself,
> a spiritual urgency at the dark ladders leaping.
>
> This beauty is an inner persistence
>   toward the source
> striving against (within) down-rushet of the river,
>   a call we heard and answer
> in the lateness of the world
>   primordial bellowings
> from which the youngest world might spring,
>
> salmon not in the well where the
>   hazelnut falls
> but at the falls battling, inarticulate,
>   blindly making it.
>
> This is one picture apt for the mind.
>
> A second: a moose painted by Stubbs,
> where last year's extravagant antlers

lie on the ground.
The forlorn moosey-faced poem wears
   new antler-buds,
   the same,

"a little heavy, a little contrived",

his only beauty to be
   all moose.

VII

Duncan's poem must mark the end of this essay: we have moved deviously from the idea of the poem with things in it which are not to be shaped by structure to the idea of the poem as a thing itself. We see it here feeding "upon thought, feeling, impulse, / to breed itself," its only beauty to be itself— "all moose," autotelic beyond previous expectations of poetry.

May one safely make general comments after this study, without being glib, without being too succinct? Although one has scrutinized a pool among the rocks, Marianne Moore might have said, one is aware of one's ignorance of the Pacific Ocean. All the same, it would take more than Roman fortitude not to entertain some tentative speculations, far from exhaustive, about the relationship of this kind of poetry to our own age of "campings" and "happenings," beards and disobedience; and though they may hardly be called conclusions, these may perhaps be permitted.

The first step mentioned above, the submitting of disparate items, each apparently existing for itself in the poem, reflects a latter-day nominalism due, however mediately, to the breakdown of the old systems. The world is fragmented; and the war accelerated the fragmentation, physically and metaphysically:

> . . . five or six fractured steps had withstood the explosion and formed a projecting island of masonry on the summit of which rose the door. Walls on both sides were shrunk away, but along the lintel, in niggling copybook handwriting, could

still be distinguished the word *Ladies*. . . . A floorless angle
of the wall to which a few lumps of plaster and strips of em-
bossed paper still adhered was all that remained of the alcove
where we had sat, a recess which also enclosed the mechanical piano. . . .[65]

Once again, the world is all in pieces "all coherence gone; /
All just supply, and all Relation."

Poetry need not, of course, imitate formlessness with formlessness. But the poet has lost faith in the large structures and
abstractions and, moving in an opposite direction from that
taken by "Newspeak" in *1984,* has gone back to the small solid
details with respect to which he is absolutely certain where he
stands; and his loyalty to these in their own right would account
for his cavalier disregard for form in the old sense. Furthermore,
confining himself to a world of such small hard facts, a man
could be honest.

The second development noticed, the poem as not being
about anything but being itself a thing, may owe part of its
origin to the same cause in the spirit of the age. If the world
has disintegrated into its parts, society in general has failed to
admit the disintegration, and it still abjectly appeals to the old
abstractions and structures as if they were still valid; and thus,
whether in the mouths of committee chairmen seeking the
wrong kind of glory or in those of gingerbread citizens seeking
the wrong kind of comfort, its language is phoney. The poet's
response then has been, first, distrust and contempt, which we
see clearly enough, for instances, in Lawrence Ferlinghetti's
poem about Christmas trees and Olson's about the Melville
occasion at Williams College, in Duncan's return to the incor-
rupt simplicities of the child, in Ginsberg everywhere, and in
Creeley's horror at the poisonous misuse of language in *Real-
politik*. The poet's response has also been to withdraw into his
own world—to withdraw, in fact, into his own poem, enclosed

[65] Anthony Powell, *Casanova's Chinese Restaurant* (Boston: Little Brown,
1960), pp. 1–2.

off from the world of bad language, where horrid voices "extol the doughnut" or lie in the highest places. And so the poem's language, referring only to the limited occasion and world of the poem, is not tainted by association with contemporary rot. The charge of the general that this caviar is meaningless and yet, somehow, sordid too, the poets might well not only repudiate but fix to the language used by the accusers.

Poets and poetry need not have reacted in this way, and all poets have not. There are those of certainly no less seriousness, sincerity, and integrity who do not write in this fashion. In the words (pejorative) of an editor of the kind of poetry we have been discussing, these others use "outworn instruments": ". . . the so-called academic poet, whatever the urgency of his own convictions, chooses to write in time-worn, pre-existent patterns, and often enough in outworn language, as if he himself did not take himself or the poem seriously enough to want to make it heard *now* by all those beings in the midst of whom he must spend his life." This editor desiderates a kind of poem "that means something because it is no longer *about* something but *is* something. . . ." Traditional methods are anathema, for unripeness is all; and poetry which accepts limitations is suspect in sincerity. But, of course, even avoiding "pre-existent patterns" one cannot avoid all limitations: all poetry and all human actions are performed within, in spite of, and sometimes because of limitations ("Because it is there"), which in the end, because freedom consists in overcoming them and because "means bless," are the author's opportunity to be effective or heroic.

INDEX